BEYOND WORDS

Beyond Words

Sobs, Hums, Stutters and other Vocalizations

Steven Connor

REAKTION BOOKS

Published by Reaktion Books Ltd
33 Great Sutton Street
London EC1V 0DX, UK

www.reaktionbooks.co.uk

First published 2014

Printed and bound in Great Britain
by TJ International, Padstow, Cornwall

A catalogue record for this book is available from the British Library

ISBN 978 1 78023 258 4

Contents

ONE

Ahem

Aristotle's Cough

'I see a voice' says Bottom, absurdly, peering as Pyramus through a crack in an imaginary wall at the speaking lips of his lover, Thisbe, in *A Midsummer Night's Dream* (V.i.190). Absurd as they are, his words can help us grasp the similarity between hearing a voice and seeing a face. For seeing and hearing may both be understood, not as a passive registration of visual or auditory stimulus, but as an active and interrogative scanning of the visual and auditory fields, in search of particular kinds of form. Present somebody with a complex or unintelligible arrangement of dots or stripes, and they are likely to begin by trying to resolve it into a face. Presented with a similarly confused set of sounds, human beings seem equivalently impelled to wonder at the outset if there is a voice to be made out in them. The face and the voice are the two most important forms that stand out from William James's 'great blooming, buzzing confusion' of sense impressions.[1] We may say that, for this reason, face and voice come to represent the emergence or figuring out (*figura* = face) of form itself.

In this sense, voice may be imagined as the antonym of noise, and noise as the matrix or ground of voice. Noise is anonymous, mechanical and meaningless; voice is personal, animate and expressive. Noise is accident, voice is intent. Noise has no importance, voice is full of portent. Though we can train ourselves to listen away from voices, or can under certain circumstances start to hear them as 'mere' noise, the effort this requires indicates the very strong predisposition that we have to pick out voices from noise, and to identify foreground auditory phenomena as voice. It makes obvious sense for us to be attuned to voices as we are attuned to faces. It also makes sense for us to identify voices with animation, agency and intent ('Is there anybody out there?'). Animism and paranoia have more survival value than equanimity. Of the two creatures who might have wondered whether that low rumbling they just heard was really the growl of a tiger or just distant thunder, the one disposed to hear the noise as an animal voice is more likely still to be among us than the one displaying a more relaxed and philosophical attitude.

This book has grown out of some prolonged reflections on two remarks. The first snagged my eye when I was reading Aristotle's discussion of the voice in Book 2.8 of his *De Anima* for a book I had thought of writing about the history of ventriloquism, and has niggled at me ever since.[2] Aristotle defines voice as 'a particular sound made by something with a soul; for nothing which does not have a soul has a voice'.[3] But quickly, and as though in the same breath, Aristotle enters an important qualification: 'not every sound made by an animal is voice (for it is possible to make a sound also with the tongue or as in coughing).'[4] For something to be voice, 'that which does the striking must have a soul and there must be a certain imagination (for voice is a particular sound that has meaning, and not one merely of the inbreathed air, as a cough is).'[5] So only sounds made by animals, that is, beings with souls, can count as voices, but not every sound that an ensouled being might make will necessarily itself have soul in it. Aristotle does not use the word 'soul' (*anima*) in our contemporary sense. He clearly seems to mean, at this point in *De Anima* at least, something like the capacity or intent to mean, which he associates with an act of imagination (*phantasia*). So ensouled sound is sound under the pressure of a kind of picturing intent. Soul seems to try to bend sound into image. Unensouled sound – mere *psophos* – is sound as such, bare of imagination or semantic purpose. It is accident rather than intent. It is therefore characteristic of animal sound ('animal' now in our modern sense, not in Aristotle's sense of an ensouled being), or certainly the sound of certain animals. In fact, the Greek word *psophos* is found in English almost exclusively in the biological names of certain creatures, such as *Psophia crepitans*, the grey-winged trumpeter bird, though it also provides the word *psophometer*, an instrument which gives a reading of the subjective aural effect of noise in a communication circuit.

Not all ancient commentators assumed that coughing is necessarily the opposite of soul or meaningfulness. A ninth-century Arabic translation by Thābit ibn Qurra of the Aristotelian compendium known as *Problemata physica* reflects on the fact that the cough is not universal in the animal world, and indeed might almost be thought to be in some respects characteristic of humans rather than animals:

> *Why is it that some animals cough, while others do not, for example a man coughs, but an ox does not?* Because the animals the temperament of whose brain is very cold and liquid collect in their brain excretions which are not concocted. And when the head contains these putrid excretions they flow down to the lungs and this results in coughing. Now the brain of man is colder and more liquid than that of other animals. This suits man's nature, because it helps him to think and to form sound judgments, a function that is fulfilled particularly by cold brains. As to the reason for its liquidity, this helps man to form images in his mind and to get a picture of the things that he has thought out. Because of the coldness and liquidity of man's brain, a lot flows down to his breast, and that is why most of them cough from time to time.[6]

The physical constitution of the ox is completely different. Its brain is very hot and dry, compared with that of other animals. That is why only few excretions collect in its brain, and why the thin fluid that does not belong anywhere is not formed in it, meaning that oxen do not cough (though they surely do, don't they?).

So the voice, like Caliban's isle, is also full of noises, not least, of course, when the mouth from which the voice issues is itself full, whether of mucus or marmalade. The voice is supposed to be suffused with spirit, and itself often to have such an insufflating action. But the voice is not always quite itself, for there is much in the voice that is not altogether voice. The voice is not all Geist, it is full of poltergeists, noisy, paltering parasites and hangers-on, mouth-friends, vapours and minute-jacks. We need to be on the alert against the encrustations and adulterations of this infinite interior malady.

At this point, a rather obvious objection ought to arise. Aren't all the sounds of the voice in fact just noises? And aren't all the significant sounds of language just accidents of the breath that have been given significance? Or one could ask the question the other way round: surely nothing that forms part of the repertoire of speech can really be said to be just noise, or to be truly meaningless? What then is the difference between the kinds of noise that we call sounds, and other noises? Is it as simple as the difference between sounds that soul means to make, and sounds made accidentally or by mistake? Linguists nowadays are perhaps more likely to define articulate sounds, not as ones made with signifying intent, but as sounds that form part of a language, in the sense of a regular structure of similarities and differences, which alone makes them able to embody meaning. Outside such a system, any and every vocal sound would simply be a noise, or accident of sound (*psophos*). On this view, too, it would seem to make no sense to mark off certain features of speech as noise from other features of speech that are taken to be meaningful, sense-making sound. All phonemes, or distinguishable elements of speech, are at once noises and sounds.

This objection can be allowed without mortal damage to my purpose and process in this book. For my concern is with those features of speech that seem to reach outside its enchanted phonemic domain, to open language up momentarily to the world of sound events beyond articulate speech. In this respect, though I have organized this book around certain groups or families of sound, I am really interested in the forms of attention that such sound-groups elicit, forms of attention that, as it seems to me, focus on what I have called their noisiness, here distinguished, not as a phonetic feature, but as a semantic one. Noisy sounds will not be viewed as unintended or accidental sounds, but sounds intended to signify the unintended or accidental, as in the waiter's 'ahem', which is not intended to clear his throat, or will be misunderstood if it is. The noises of the voice are therefore sounds that express or enact the *idea* of noisiness. I focus attention on the crossovers that result between the meaningless and the meaningful in vocal noise, and the particular kinds of meaning-making work done by the noises of the voice. This means that I will be attempting to pick out not so much noisy sounds as noise-effects or noise-events in speech – points at which there seems to be a significant suspension, or at least complication, of signifying intent. Such events are not rents in the fabric of language so much as remissions of our assumption that what we are hearing is voice, purely and simply. So this could be said to be a book less about the noises than the 'noisance' of the voice, the useful nuisance of the voice's noisings.

I said there were two remarks which had incubated this book. The second, alongside that of Aristotle about the cough, was an observation occasionally made by my mother, though also by many people of her generation, that German was a 'guttural' language. When I first heard her say this, I had never learned any German, and hardly ever heard any spoken outside war films, in which it was represented by shrieks of '*Schnell!*' '*Heraus!*' and the harshly expectorant '*Achtung!*' When I began to learn it, around the age of thirteen or fourteen, I was pleased but puzzled by how soft and lispingly mellifluous it felt and sounded in my mouth. The fact that when I speak German I nevertheless sound, as one of my students once publicly remarked with admirable lack of inhibition, like 'a tank commander', suggests that the old prejudice about the kind of thing I thought ought to be audible in German may not be entirely extinct in me. For a generation brought up during the years of the Second World War, and inheriting prejudices about German militarism from the recently concluded First World War, especially if they had been exposed to newsreel broadcasts of Hitler's bawling rhetoric at Nazi rallies, it may have seemed natural to find the sound of German as bestial and barbaric as the enemy from whose barking mouths it issued. I will suggest below that this prejudice has roots that reach much further back, having to do with the growing inhospitability of English to sounds produced in the back of the mouth. In fact, we will see that the values of particular sounds, and the vocal methods used to employ them, often have this phonopolitical force and function.

Sound Pictures

For Aristotle, noise is the deficit of imagination, the picturing intent of ensouled speech. But there is another, and opposite sense in which vocal noise may itself be thought of as a kind of picturing, namely in what is known as 'iconicity', the idea that language works by various forms of mimicry, particularly, but not exclusively, in sound.

There are two principal forms of iconicity, known as phonomemes and phenomemes.[7] The first mimic the sounds of objects in the world, whether mewing cats or pattering raindrops, most familiarly in the form of onomatopoeia. Where phonomemes of this kind are sound-pictures, phenomemes are 'diagrams' in the sense defined by C. S. Peirce (also the originator of the term 'icon' in this linguistic sense of a mimetic sign), which represent 'the relations, mainly dyadic, or so regarded, of the parts of one thing by analogous relations in their own parts'.[8] The phenomemic diagrams on which I will concentrate in this book suggest the mirroring in the physical disposition of the vocal organs or in the physics of sound production of the actions or forms in the world which they may represent, sometimes combined with the visual forms of written letters, as when, for example, the mouth mimics the letter *o* in making the sound associated with it, and may therefore seem to be mimicking the shape or vacancy of a h*o*le or b*o*wl. Attempts to find systematic correspondences between the physics or physiology of vocal sounds and their meanings are unlikely to produce satisfying results in the long term, and this book does not offer any serious support for such a venture. However, it seems as though there is a strong predisposition among those thinking about vocal sound to pick out or emphasize such rhymings of sound, shape and meaning when they can be picked out. Perhaps word formation itself, which is a sort of unconscious thinking with sound, is also always a kind of thinking about sound, even if it is not clear who or what is doing the thinking. Iconicity is the name for a desire, the longing for words and things to rhyme with each other, rather than any fact of the matter; but it also measures the sedimented effects of this desire for sound-sense convergence in patterns of sound clustering.

We can suggest a tendency towards positive bias-confirmation in thinking about language. That is to say, when there seems to be a pattern that can be picked out in language, it will be operative. The absence of pattern, no matter how much more statistically likely it is, seems to have little weight. This makes the easy refutation of what many speakers of English feel to be the natural association between the letter *i* and littleness – the existence of the words *big*, *immense* and *infinite* – beside the point, for such patterns of sonic seeming are self-performing and self-confirming. If a pattern can be made out, and it is, then there it is. What is more, the very activity of picking out the pattern, perhaps especially in the face of long odds that make the pattern highly unlikely, may reinforce it. This is why it is inadequate to say that sound assists or amplifies sense. In fact, under certain, not entirely predictable circumstances, sense assists and amplifies the process of looking for sound patterns that, once found, then retroactively seem to assist and amplify the sense. And perhaps so on, in self-prolonging feedback loops.

Indeed the tendency to overestimate the frequency and force of sound-sense convergences may also exert an influence on the ways in which the physics or physiology of speech production may be described and imagined. The mouth that is at work in vocal iconicity is not just the producer of sounds, it is also itself produced by them. This is not to say that none of the features of the imaginary mouth have any relation to the physiology of the mouth and throat. But it is to say that the conceptions of height, lowness, frontality, backwardness, softness, hardness, tension, lassitude, et cetera, in it are idealizations of this physical organ. We might propose an imaginary mouth that bears the same relation to the actual physiological mouth as the sensory homunculus does to the physical body; a mouth, that is, whose shape is the proportionate profile of its usages. When I change usage – when I speak another language, for example – this mouth changes, the hardware remaining the same but being transformed by the software. This software mouth cohabits but is never coextensive with the physiological mouth, the one I use to ingest food and eject wind and vomit, and in which flies and tiny annoying threads make entry. A particular kind of mouth is needed to speak a particular language, or dialect – otherwise, we would not speak of 'getting your tongue' round difficult words. But languages produce different mouths – or what, adapting the term 'voice-body' that I used in my book *Dumbstruck*, might be called mouth-bodies.[9] For the mouth is more than just the part of the body specialized for the production of speech. It is the way in which, the place in which, the whole body may be taken up in vocality.

Aristotle does not consider the consequences of the mixture within the voice of meaningful utterances and meaningless noises. The aim of this book is to try to make some sense of these noises, to listen more systematically to the sense they might make. The study of iconicity is still a minority area within linguistics, with a strong prejudice against it. But this book is not really a work either of linguistics or phonetics. This is because it is concerned less with what language actually is or how it actually works is than with popular conceptions of what it is. I draw deeply on Gérard Genette's history of this linguistic tradition in his remarkable *Mimologics* (1995),[10] but *Beyond Words* differs from his work firstly in that I am less concerned with charting linguistic traditions than with what might be called a popular poetics of language, and because my concern is in any case not so much with language as with how folk apprehensions of the workings of language help to form an imaginary or even magical conception of the voice.

In this, I will be required to work with what might be called a logic of abjured avowal, which constrains me simultaneously to make clear my disbelief in the things so many people seem to want to think about language and how it works, while affirming the tenacity and persistence of those ways of thinking. I mean in particular beliefs about the particular indwelling powers or qualities of certain features of language, or of language as such. My belief in the inexistence of what is believed about language would fain be as obdurate and unyielding as my belief in the existence of the beliefs themselves. In what follows, no credence is to be taken to attach to beliefs in the magical power of language, or to particular components of it, or to the belief that certain sounds are naturally tied to or expressive of certain forms or ideas. Yet I do not believe that entirely consistent incredulity about these things is entirely advisable either, or even possible. The problem is that asserting the existence of the belief starts to confirm belief in the existence of what is believed. It is not that there might be something in such ideas after all, so much as that the effect of so many people listening and speaking and writing and reading as though there were something in them is so very far from being negligible.

It would seem sensible, for example, to acknowledge, that, depite the assurances of many bored or desperate English teachers over generations, there is nothing absolutely or intrinsically mazy or meandering about the sound of Coleridge's 'Five miles meandering with a mazy motion'.[11] If there were, the same woozy waviness would have to attach to every sequence of iterated *m*s we ever encountered – in the title of Shakespeare's play *Measure for Measure*, for example, or a phrase like 'Smithfield Meat Market'. I have thought almost every day in the writing of this book of the story of the reader of Eliot's *The Waste Land* who spoke of being moved to tears by the power of the poem's final repeated Sanskrit word 'Shantih. Shantih. Shantih', to meet the brusque, buck-yourself-up enquiry whether he got the same numinous charge from the phrase 'sea-shanty'. Yet it seems undeniable that that are plenty of prompts in place to provoke the willed illusion of such an effect, prompts that we ignore only through wilful inattention.

So, alas, much of this book is going to have to consist of nonsense. It concerns the kind of magical phonetics involved in fantasies like that of my mother's generation about the guttural Germans. It is a book about the phantasmal life, of excitements, identifications and recoils associated with particular vocal sound-families, such as the guttural, the fricative, the sibilant, the dental. It maps out and manipulates what may be called a dream theatre of the mouth, that crucible in which sounds are not merely sounded, but also shaped and palpated. Accordingly, it operates, not in the realm of phonetics proper but in what might be called phonophenomenology. The phonetics it will offer must often be a folk, fake or funny-farm phonetics – in the daft, disreputable, yet deeply rooted ideas that many people, many of them literary writers, have about the specific powers of certain sounds. These beliefs about the power of sounds and the letters that encode are spread across mystical traditions like that of the Kabbala and ordinary instincts and prejudices. This book is a meditation on the kinds of magical thinking attached to the sounds of the voice and the imaginary mechanics of their production. The reason why we might want to take such magical thinking seriously is that language is made, not by linguists, but by its inexpert but often stubbornly opinionated users, which suggests that their (our) fantasies and prejudices may exercise a significantly formative pressure on the ways in which language comes about and functions. It may well be a misapprehension to think that language is formed and governed by a set of fixed and universal sound-meanings, but this is a misapprehension that itself governs and gives rise to much of language. For there is no theatre of the mind or body that so teems with magical thinking than that which relates to the forms and powers of the voice. The *vox et praeterea nihil*[12] – the voice and nothing more – is not easily to be distilled out from the busy delusions, fantasies and fixations to which it gives rise, for these fantasies are formative and performative, conditioning our comprehension and experience of the voice.

TWO

St . . . st . . . st

Viva Voce

What is the voice? The voice is always a dream voice, and we can never speak about the experience of the voice except in the register of fantasy, desire, phantom, myth. Even, and perhaps especially when we may speak of the materiality of the voice, we evoke imaginary substance and mythical powers.

The voice goes out from the body as the body's twin – as a body double. It took me six years of writing *Dumbstruck*, a book I got into the habit of calling a 'history of the disembodied voice', to let on at last to myself and others that there is no disembodied voice – no voice that does not have somebody, something of somebody's body, in it.[1] Yet, all too often, the voice is experienced as the more-than-body, as the body projected, perfected. We live in an age of amplification, transmission, of voices that are larger-than-life, that are life itself enlarged. But the voice is also imagined as superlative in other ways – as the body refined, for example, or made more subtly sensitive, or more fluent. The voice is the body's second life, something between a substance and a force – a fluency that is yet a form. The voice is lived and imagined as the life of its subject. Indeed, we may say that the very idea of life is derived in part from such magic fantasies of vigour and virility. The voice is so saturated by the anxious dream of our 'life', because it is itself one of the most important components of that will-to-life. The phantasm of the 'living voice' is the principal carrier of our hallucination of life. It is subject to a paradoxical vital economy. While drawing on the body for its force, and therefore subject to the vicissitudes of the body, it is nevertheless imagined to have the power to radiate new life back to the body from which it emanates. But, as a surrogate or supplement, the voice is also itself in need of supplementation – hence the anxious regimes of voice cultivation, nurture, hygiene and healing which have multiplied since the end of the eighteenth century.[2]

In this chapter, I want to focus on one particular form of vocal impediment, stammering or stuttering. For most of its history, stammering has been regarded as the result of some material or physical, rather than spiritual cause. At the same time, it has been the repository or occasion for the most extraordinary material fantasies, or phantasmal materialisms. The Hippocratic school of Kos held that stammering came from excessive dryness of the tongue. Galen, the principal authority for humoral theory in medieval Europe, blamed excessive moisture. His views are preserved in the influential *De proprietatibus rerum* of Bartholomaeus Anglicus, here in the translation of 1582 by Stephen Batman:

> *Galen* sayth, that sometime it happeneth, that the tongue stutteth and stamereth by too much moisture when the stringes of the tongue may not stretch and spread into the utter parts thereof for too much moysture, as it fareth in dronken men, that stamer when they bee soe much in moisture in the braine. Therefore *Galen* sayth, that kindlye stamering men stamer through too much moisture of the braine, or else through too much moisting of the tongue, or for both.[3]

The fifteenth-century Italian physiognomist Bartolomeo della Rocca, known as Cocles, attributed stammering to engorgement of the tongue through alcoholic vapours: 'The tounge that lispeth or stamereth: declareth that persone to feare, to drynke wyne . . . the drounke do stammer, stut, or lyspe, because the vapoures of the wine dronke in, into that parte of the tounge named the sponge, enlarge the same, and change it fro hys natural state and forme.'[4] Francis Bacon also saw stammering as a physical impediment, but identifed coldness, or dryness, rather than swelling, as the cause:

> The *Cause* may be, (in most,) the *Refrigeration* of the *Tongue*; Whereby it is lesse apt to moue. And therfore we see, that *Naturalls* doe generally *Stut*: And we see that in those that *Stut*, if they drinke Wine moderately, they *Stut* lesse, because it heateth: And so we see, that they that *Stut*, doe *Stut* more in the first Offer to speake, than in Continuance; Because the *Tongue* is, by Motion, somewhat heated. In some also, it may be, (though rarely,) the *Drinesse* of the *Tongue*; which likewise maketh it lesse apt to moue, as well as *Cold*; For it is an Affect that commeth to some *Wise* and *Great Men*; As it did vnto Moses, who was *Linguae prapedita*; And many *Stutters* (we finde) are very *Cholericke Men*; *Choler* Enducing a Drinesse in the Tongue.[5]

Alexander Ross, who was as querulous as he was credulous, and made a career out of defending improbable traditions against the new ideas of writers like Bacon, Wilkins, Browne and Harvey, took issue with Bacon's arguments. The stutterer's speech is not, he thought, congealed, but rather overheated:

> He makes *Refrigeration of the tongues the cause of stuttering*. If this were so, then old men should stutter more then young men; for old men are colder. But we know the contrary, that not the coldnesse, but rather the over-heating of the tongue causeth stuttering, and this he acknowledgeth in the same Section, that *many stutterers are very cholerick men*. But choler is hot, then it seemes that both heat and cold is the cause of stuttering. But indeed the true cause in some is a bad habit or custom contracted from their infancy, in others eagernesse of disposition; for hasty and eager natures usually stutter, and whilst they make the more haste, they use the lesse speed; in others again stuttering proceeds from some infirmity or impedim[en]t in the tendon, muscles, or nerves of the tongue. As for drinking of wine moderatly, which he saith, *will cause men stut lesse*, is a thing I could never yet observe in those stutterers I have bin acquainted with.[6]

The replacement of humoral theory by more mechanical theories of the body's functioning encouraged efforts to account for stammering in terms of physiological failures, through the adoption of incorrect or inadequate methods of speech production. But some old ideas clung on gamely. William Abbotts's *Impediments of Speech*, first published in 1879, was reprinted into the 1890s, despite the fact that, or perhaps because, it attributed stammer to breathing through the mouth rather than the nose, and proposed that the severity of stammer was related to the weather – 'the majority of stammerers being worse during wet, cold weather than when the air is more dry and bracing'.[7]

Charles Kingsley, one of the nineteenth century's many stammerers, wrote emphatically of the need for the stammerer to build up the fabric of his body in order to hold the diabolic voice at bay: 'whosoever can afford an enervated body and an abject character, the stammerer cannot. With him it is a question of life and death. He must make a man of himself, or be liable to his tormentor to the last.'[8] Kingsley believes stammering is the effect of egotism, of allowing too much of self into the voice, which ironically deprives the self of authority over its voice, delivering it up to the devilish vocality of the stammer:

> Let him, therefore, eschew all base perturbations of mind; all cowardice, servility, meanness, vanity, and hankering after admiration; for these all will make many a man, by a just judgement, stammer on the spot. Let him, for the same reason, eschew all anger, peevishness, haste, even pardonable eagerness. In a word , let him eschew the root of all evil, selfishness and self-seeking; for he will surely find that whensoever he begins thinking about himself, then is the dumb devil of stammering close at his elbow.[9]

For Kingsley, the debility and diabolical mutilation of the voice that are the stammer can only be combated by a remorseless regime of bodily conservation and reinforcement, endlessly vigilant to any threat of collapse or weakening:

> Let him betake himself to all manly exercises, which will put him into wind, and keep him in it . . . Let him play rackets, and fives, row, and box; for all these amusements strengthen those muscles of the chest and abdomen which are certain to be in his case weak . . . And let him, now in these very days, join a rifle-club, and learn in it to carry himself with the erect and noble port which is all but peculiar to the soldier, but ought to be the common habit of every man; let him learn to march; and more, to trot under arms without losing breath; and by such means make himself an active, healthy, and valiant man.[10]

Most of the many forms of therapy that were developed in the nineteenth century depended on and encouraged the conviction that the gap between the self and its voice could be healed by repairing speech from the outside in – through the regularization of rhythm, encouraging attention to verbal patterns, focussing and channelling force, construing speaking as a kind of singing, and so on. The very fact that such methods often seemed to meet with success encouraged a concern that speech might not be a mere external accessory; its suggestion that the voice could indeed be rebuilt from the outside itself cast doubt upon the innerness of the voice, the belief in the innate bond between the speaker and his speech.

Mechanical theories of stammer may have persisted for so long, and tend to recur so frequently, because they seem to accord so reassuringly to a dualistic fantasy in which the voice, somehow fully formed in the mind or the soul, is imagined simply as being projected through the more or less imperfect instrument of the body, suggesting that problems of articulation must come from forms of mechanical impediment, rather than from the possibility of noisiness or self-impediment in the voice itself. Freud's development of psychoanalytic theory encouraged a turn to psychogenic theories of the functioning of the stammer. Stammering seemed to be the perfect example of a physical disturbance that enacts contrary impulses – the impulse to speak, and the impulse to withhold speech. Different psychoanalytic theories emphasize different forms of anxious ambivalence. The psychoanalyst Otto Fenichel thought that the stammerer was in the grip of an anal-sadistic impulse to utter obscenities: 'It is well known that for stutterers words may have the significance of faeces', he airily began one article on the subject.[11] Because speaking means 'utterance of obscene, especially anal, words; and secondly, an aggressive act, ultimately to kill', the stutter is both the repression of this impulse and the autoerotic pleasure gained from holding back words 'as faeces were held back in infancy', such that 'one may indeed speak of a displacement upward of the functions of the anal sphincter in stuttering.'[12] Stammering has been seen as the unsuccessful account to manage oral anxieties relating to nursing.[13] It has also been seen as the result of a struggle between the stammerer's huge investment in the magical power of words and the countermanding need to repress his own desire for verbal power. Stammering is therefore to be understood as the enactment of castration anxiety: 'to speak, or to speak well, means to be potent; to be unable to speak – to be castrated.'[14]

Psychoanalysis sometimes comes close to analysing the fantasies invested in the magical omnipotence and, we might add, the fearful failure, of the voice. But its own mythical apparatus of entities and energies participates in and prolongs that delusional apparatus rather than dissipating it, making psychoanalysis itself part of the cultural dreamwork which forms and deforms the voice.

Phonophobia

There is a strong association between vocal and other kinds of impediment, especially of the gait. Roger Ascham complained in 1545 that

> yf a man nowe a dayes have two sonnes, the one impotent, weke, sickly, lispynge, stuttynge, and stamerynge, or havnge any misshape in his bodye: what doth the father of suche one commonlye saye? This boy is fit for nothynge els, but to set to lernyng and make a prest of, as who would say, ye outcastes of the worlde, havyng neyther countenaunce tounge nor wit (for of a perverse body cumeth commonly a perverse

> mind) be good ynough to make those men of, whiche shall be appoynted to preache Goddes holye woorde.[15]

The odd idea that stammering might be a preacher's impediment has a long history. Marc Shell observes that Moses had difficulty walking as well as talking.[16] Limping is a kind of tipsy lisping of the legs. 'Stamerynge, yn speche' and 'Stamerynge, in goyng' are associated in the *Promptorium parvulorum*, an Anglo-Latin lexicon of 1440.[17] Up to the middle of the nineteenth century, for a horse to 'stammer' was for it to stagger. Titubation, meaning toppling or reeling progress, was a common synonym for stammering. For the Freud of *Beyond the Pleasure Principle*, the limp is the expression of the strange syncopations of the life-instinct, which wishes always to go forward, to keep on keeping on, and the death instinct, which wishes to tarry, procrastinate, or return to a less exacting earlier state of things. The painful syncopations of the stammerer, in which anxious pause and spilling profusion alternate, seem to be governed by this rhythm. Freud in fact ends his text with the words '*Es ist keine Sünde zu verhinken*' – 'it is no sin to limp.'[18] Though Freud makes no strong association between speaking and limping, he might from time to time have recalled the odd facility demonstrated by his first master Charcot in imitating the irregular gaits characteristic of different kinds of neurological lesion; Charcot taught his students the accents of their damaged cadence, schooling them to listen for his patients' signature lurches and shuffles.[19]

So much of our fantasy of being the privileged beneficiaries of life is invested in the voice that the deficit of the voice can often seem like a mortal injury, a gash in the soul itself. The speech of the stammerer or the lisper is the aural enactment of the wound borne by the castrato. And yet castration has also been linked to a release or enhancement of vocal power. The voices of castrati exhibited not just the capacity to inhabit the higher registers denied to the broken male voice, but also an amazing, preternatural strength or 'body', as though the robustness of the sexual life had been channeled into the voice. As the minor or symbolic form of castration, circumcision is also associated with the unloosing rather than the inhibition of speech. Moses protests to the Lord God in Exodus 4:10 'I am slow of speech, and of a slow tongue.' A little later he says '*Ani aral s'fatayim*' – 'I am of uncircumcised lips' (Exodus 6:12, 6:30). A legend of the childhood of Moses explains that as a child he was subjected to a test which involved a hot coal being applied to his lips, hence his subsequent vocal disability. This story reappears in Isaiah's account of how his 'unclean lips' are made clean by a seraph who touches them with a hot coal (Isaiah 6:5–7). The circumcision that Freud and others have thought of as a sacrificial wounding is also conceived in Judaism as an opening, and can thus be applied to the heart (Leviticus 26:41) or ears as well as to the mouth or the penis: 'Their ear is uncircumcised, and they cannot hearken', the Lord complains in Jeremiah 6:10, and his words are repeated in the New Testament: 'You stiff-necked people, uncircumcised in heart and ears, you always resist the Holy Spirit.' (Acts 7:51).

It is not just the tongue that is twisted for the stammerer. The voice of the stammerer is imagined as twisted, tangled, contorted, a body closed in or folded over on itself. During the nineteenth century, the fantasy of the knotted voice led to efforts literally to excise the stammerer's vocal clot. A German physician called J. F. Dieffenbach, encouraged by the success of a procedure to rectify Strabismus or squint by cutting through recessed or over-taut eye tendons, extended the principle to stammerers. (Along with limping, squinting is one of the forms of suspicious bodily wryness upon which history has regularly looked askance, and they have sometimes been associated.[20]) Dieffenbach makes clear the extent of his horror at the predicament his procedure is designed to remedy. His account of the sufferings of the stammering boy for whom he developed his operation offers a term which might be used to characterize one's own and others' revulsion at the imperfect voice – *phonophobia*:

> The presence of a stranger invariably affected him in a manner most painful to behold. His face became distorted; the alae of the nose worked convulsively; his lips moved quiveringly up and down; his eyelids were expanded into a wild and eager stare; the tongue was now stiff, now played convulsively within the mouth; and the muscles of the throat, larynx and trachea were sympathetically affected.

> Thus, after terrible efforts, the boy gave utterance to a mangled and imperfect word; – now for a time was his speech free, and words chased one another with incredible velocity, till confusion ensued amidst the thronging sounds; and the same painful scene was thus again and again renewed. The peculiar physical horror which constitutes a stutterer, and which is excited by the effort to speak, is very similar to that which gives rise to the excitement and spasm of the hydrophobic patient at the sight of water. This internal movement might, on that account, be called phonophobia.[21]

The boy's struggles at speech are represented as a painful, repeated parturition in which speech is the agency of death rather than the witness of life. The boy is taken up into his paralysed voice, and the 'mangled and imperfect speech' that is its product is a doubling of the grotesquely maimed voice-body that he has become. He is at once alienated from his own speech and imprisoned in it. Dieffenbach was not the only writer to suspect the tongue of getting in the way of clear speech. William Abbotts advised that 'The tongue is not so necessary to speech as is commonly supposed. In the case of stammerers, indeed, it is apt to become a cause of impediment, through getting into a wrong position for pronouncing various sounds.'[22] The point here seems to be that the voice is itself the agency of its own blockage: it is not just a constricted voice, but a *vox constrictor* in whose toils the boy struggles.

Dieffenbach's operation consisted in excising a deep wedge three-quarters of an inch wide from the root of the boy's tongue. He coolly warned amateur surgeons of the sanguinary consequences: 'That the hemorrhage was considerable, may be imagined from the nature of the operation, which should not be attempted by all persons indiscriminately.'[23] Nevertheless, he claimed complete success:

> At the present time, not the slightest trace of stuttering remains, not the slightest vibration of the muscles of the face, not the most inconsiderable play of the lips. His speech is throughout clear, well-toned, even, and flowing. Neither inward emotions, nor unexpected external impressions,

> produce the slightest hesitation; he can speak, read, and entertain himself, indifferently with friends or strangers.[24]

He looks forward with hilariously grisly relish to more of this kind of procedure:

> Amidst the prevailing rage for modifying operations, I foresee that my having described the three principal available methods, cannot fail to open to Surgeons a vast field for the discovery of modifications, and the creation of instruments. We shall have conical and oblique incisions, from the surface and under the skin! Actual and potential cautery! We shall have knives and scissars [sic] with improved curves, and a thousand variously fashioned forceps and hooks. They will set the blades at angles with the handles to allow of a better light falling into the mouth. Opportunity is likewise afforded to professional antiquarians to hunt after a name for this operation. To them I freely make over the right of baptism.[25]

There is a hint of religious revelation here. Baptism (which in a sense replaces circumcision in the New Testament), suggests the coming of new life in the conferring of a voice, and here seems to be an answer to the hydrophobia to which Dieffenbach has earlier compared the patient's phonophobic predicament. In Isaiah, revelation is explicitly and influentially characterized as vocal as well as optical clouding; with the promise that 'the eyes of them that see shall not be dim, and the ears of them that hear shall hearken . . . and the tongue of the stammerers shall be ready to speak plainly' (Isaiah 32:3–4) Dwight N. Hopkins's and George C. L. Cummings' book on the theology of Black American slave narratives takes its title from an anonymous slave conversion narrative in which the angel Gabriel appears to a slave in a field, promising him 'lo! I have cut loose your stammering tongue and unstopped your deaf ears. A witness shalt thou be, and thou shalt speak to multitudes, and they shall hear.'[26]

Marshall McLuhan remarked during a conversation with John Lennon in 1969 that 'language is a form of organised stutter.'[27] It may indeed be that the phenomenon of voice is best thought of as a kind of stutter in the order of things – an obstacle, a black hole, a convulsive interval – in which life holds back from itself and curdles into voice. It is against this apprehension that we should understand efforts to shore up and indemnify the voice against the death, or the myriad *petits morts*, which it comprises. The history of stammer and efforts to rectify it are an attempt to bind up a wound in the idea of voice itself, and thus an attempt to quarantine the freedom and life of the voice from the baseness and deathliness that can invade it.

But if stuttering is an impediment, it is also oddly generative. Stutterers tend to become skilful synonymizers, trick-recyclists, unbelievers in the church of the *mot juste*. For the stutterer, there are always too many words, and yet never quite enough. As a stutterer, Charles Dodgson was well-equipped to appreciate the sentiments he articulated during the Mad Hatter's Tea-Party:

> 'You should say what you mean,' the March Hare went on. 'I do,' Alice hastily replied; 'at least – at least I mean what I say – that's the same thing, you know.' 'Not the same thing a bit!' said the Hatter.[28]

Indeed, though stuttering is usually an affliction, it can also be a temptation, a tipsy sin of the tongue to complement what Augustine defined as 'voluptates aurium', the 'ravishings of the ear'.[29] Plutarch offers a similar warning in the course of an essay on how to hear poetry. Somebody with properly instructed judgement can 'both heare and read any Poemes without hurt and danger', as it is put in Philémon Holland's rendering.[30] But one must beware of a less judicious kind of listening, which makes one liable to being infected by ugliness and deformity. Such listeners are 'like unto those disciples who counterfeited to be crump shouldred and buncht backe like their master Plato, or woulds needs stut, stammer and maffle as Aristotle did: surely such a one will take no great heed, but soone apprehend and interteine many evill things'.[31] (Perhaps this passage is the origin of the rumour that the Stagyrite himself was a stammerer.) The nineteenth-century physiologist John Good advised that 'Children . . . ought never to be intrusted in the company of a stutterer, till their speech has become steady and confirmed.'[32] An adorable stammerer in my class at school caused an epidemic of libidinous mimicry among her would-be consorts. There is a paradoxical polyphiloprogenitiveness in the ways in which stutter can multiply and transmit itself.

I'm Getting Mixed

But the voice is more than the body's adventure or excursus, its way of going out from itself. For the voice can also sicken, thicken, ail, age, go awry, be thwarted, contaminated. There is an oneirism of the defective voice which is every bit as intense and sustained as the strange, sad, stubborn dream of the living voice. As the body's greatest power of emanation, the voice has become the bearer of a fantasy, not just of reach, but of endurance. In going out from the body, we imagine, the voice persists in its absence. But that voice is never entire, and the uploading of body into voice never perfect. It is surprising for example how often animals and other foreign bodies insinuate themselves into less than perfect utterance. Like the deaf, stutterers are compared to animals. As Marc Shell astutely observes, when animals were given human speech in animated film, they often, like Donald Duck, or Porky Pig, suffered from speech impediments.[33] I have a frog in my throat. I have a harelip. I am speaking with a forked tongue – or the cat has got my tongue. To 'buzz' means to speak emptily or unintelligibly, as though with the vociferation of a mere insect – and 'stut' is recorded as a Gloucestershire dialect name for a gnat.[34] There is always the possibility of a fly in the ointment of the voice. Cuckoos were sometimes described as stuttering birds. Robert Arthur's story *The Mystery of the Stuttering Parrot* also suggests that there is an affinity between the voiceless creature and a bestial form of vocality.[35] And the following joke about a stuttering gambler implicates poultry in the stutterer's vocalization:

> A Gentleman who did greatly stut & stammer in his speech, playing at Mawe, laid downe a winning card, and then said vnto his partener: How sa-ay ye now, wa-was not this ca-ca-ard pa-as-assing we-we-well la-a-ayd: Yes (answered

th'other) It is well layd, but yet it needs not halfe this cackling.[36]

Like deafness, stuttering has sometimes been thought of as a kind of alienation from the human – a condition in which one wrestles with what has become a foreign tongue. Its victims, or exponents, are thought of as lispers, babblers, or barbarians, the jeering echolalia with which the Greeks designated those beyond the Hellenic pale. The word 'Hottentot' is an onomatopoeic mockery of stuttering that early Dutch colonists in South Africa thought they heard in the Khoekhoe language of the local people in Southwestern Africa. The speech of others often appears to be not merely unintelligible, but also offensive, a maimed imposture of speech, which mocks the meaningfulness of the *logos*.

Mladen Dolar makes much of the otherness of the voice, of the fact that when we speak, something else – law, desire, the unconscious – speaks in our stead, or midst. For Dolar, the voice is everywhere apparent yet nowhere fully apprehensible as such. 'Phonology' sounds as if it ought to be the science of voices, but in fact the voice evades even its grasp, concerned as it is only with the abstract and ideal patterns of differentiation that can be abstracted from particular voices: the voice 'makes the utterance possible, but it disappears in it, goes up in smoke in the meaning being produced'.[37] But for Dolar, the otherness of the voice is an intact otherness, an otherness with a profile, point and a purpose. There is an ecstatic tradition which embraces this otherness, affirming itself in its own self-immolation. The screams of Antonin Artaud and of Diamanda Galás belong to this tradition of vocal virility defiantly and triumphantly achieved amid the inundation of the voice by animality, noise, dirt. To this tradition too belongs the 'extended voices' work of Trevor Wishart, of Luciano Berio and Pauline Oliveros.

But there is another tradition for which the otherness of the voice may be a much more contingent thing – literally contingent, or touched. Like flypaper, the voice gathers things on the way, lilts, leanings, aches, eccentricities, accents. For the voice to fail is not only for it to wane, weaken, or be broken, to become less itself. It is mixing as well as dimming. For the voice to fail is for it to become adulterated, more than what it was. The voice is interfered with, picks up interference, as though it were an organ of listening as well as of transmission, impression as well as expression. Alongside the tradition of the horrifyingly, heroically failed or maimed voice, there is another tradition, which embraces the voice's condition of what Michel Serres calls a 'mixed body'.[38]

There is no better enactment of this condition than the sound artist Alvin Lucier's astonishing *I Am Sitting in a Room* of 1969. For this piece, Lucier recorded an explanation of the process by which he proposed to make the piece:

> I am sitting in a room, different from the one you are in now. I am recording the sound of my speaking voice, and I am going to play it back into the room again and again until the resonant frequencies of the room reinforce themselves, so that any semblance of my speech, with perhaps the exception of rhythm, is destroyed.[39]

He then left the room, and played the recording he had just made back into the room he had just left, where it was rerecorded. This recording was then played back into the room and rerecorded in the same way. As it is played, recorded, replayed and re-recorded, the voice and the room blend. By iteratively enhancing the resonant frequencies of the room, Lucier manages to let us hear the sound of how the room listens to the voice. What emerges is a new voice, an extraordinary, literally unheard-of 'mixed body', the body of the voice as it always anyway, inaudibly is, amid the things of the world. Sound engineers for film and radio plays will often record silence on the set in order to have available a stock of 'room-tone' into which other sounds may be embedded. Inundated by its own room-tone, the voice in Lucier's piece ends up ventriloquizing the room. In the process, Lucier's stammer, audible in the original recording particularly in the ripple he effects in pronouncing the word 'rh-rh-rhythm', is progressively repaired by the accretions of room-resonance. The mediation that has been seen as a form of wounding or rupture of the voice here gives the voice back to itself, healed, remediation becoming remedy.

In rendering the 'voice' of the river Liffey, by contrast, Joyce's *Finnegans Wake* gives us something like the sound of the voice passing out. There are two remarkable parallel evocations of this process. One is the end of the 'Anna Livia Plurabelle' section, in which two washerwomen are exchanging rivalrous ribaldries across the banks of the Liffey. But, since their voice is also the voice of the river itself, they seem also to be moving downstream, and so moving farther apart as the river widens. The ambient noise of flowing water, along with squeaking bats and fieldmice, begins to drown out their speech. At the same time, they start losing their physical definition; one of them is turning into a tree, and the other into a stone:

> Can't hear with the waters of. The chittering waters of. Flittering bats, fieldmice bawk talk. Ho! Are you not gone ahome? What Thom Malone? Can't hear with bawk of bats, all thim liffeying waters of. Ho, talk save us! My foos won't moos. I feel as old as yonder elm. A tale told of Shaun or Shem? All Livia's daughtersons. Dark hawks hear us. Night! Night! My ho head halls. I feel as heavy as yonder stone.[40]

This movement is repeated at the end of the book, when we hear the voice of the Liffey itself pouring into the sea, gathering density as it loses impetus and direction, and the fresh water of the river swirls together with the brine of the incoming tide:

> I wisht I had better glances to peer to you through this baylight's growing. But you're changing, acoolsha, you're changing from me, I can feel. Or is it me is? I'm getting mixed. Brightening up and tightening down. Yes, you're changing, sonhusband, and you're turning.[41]

The voice is the vehicle and the arena of this agon between dissipation and replenishment. Our celebrations of the voice are too monotonously pitched in the register of fullness, richness, clarity and penetrativeness, the bay is too regularly accorded to the energetic out-loud and 'haute voix'. The autumnal, deciduous voice, which is heard in illness, fatigue, ague and age, is not epically shredded by passion, but rather silted with lilting circumstance. It is a voice becoming distinct in the very accidents whereby it loses its difference and distinctness. As Aristotle wrote, only creatures that have life can give voice, but not everything that is in the voice, or given utterance by it, is alive. In coughs, whispers, drawls, hisses, hesitations, laughs, stammers and other vocal noisings, the voice meets and mingles with what it is not – indeed is, in the end, nothing more than this mingling. The pathos and the finesse of the voice that gives out, gives way, comes not from the virile figure it cuts against the ground of things, but rather from its suggestion of a persona, a being that has its being 'through sound' that, is, like our own bodies, rather than our dream of those bodies, a fluent mélange in which what it is and what it is not commingle and converse. There is a legend that Demosthenes attempted to cure his stammer by filling his mouth with stones and declaiming at the sea's edge.[42] For so much of its history, the stammer has been experienced as a kind of stone-like blockage or fossilization of speech, but the fact that the story links solidity and fluidity provides a telling image of the way in which the animate soul of speech builds and borrows from the inanimate. The voice is nourished by the parasites and imperfections that feed upon it.

THREE

Hiss

All voice is shaped breath. But there are two phases to this shaping. There is, of course, the articulation of the breath, the application of stops and delays, and the chivvying of the voice into particular channels, gates and pathways. Thus is the breath filtered and whittled into diction. But, prior to any of this, there is the primary process that phonologists call 'voicing', which has already transformed the breath into voice. Though this too results from a constriction, in the forcing of air across the vibrating folds of the larynx, it seems like a charging, or enrichment, as though voice were being fuel-injected into the breath by the larynx, as a breeze is infused with the odours of the tangled bank.

We will recall that, for Aristotle, only the ensouled can give voice, that is, give soul to sound or sound out the soul, and yet 'not every sound made by an animal [that is, an ensouled being] is voice.'[1] The example he gives, the cough, is a sound made by the voice that yet has nothing to do with utterance, since its function is merely physical, entirely, as we might say, animal. The cough is an accidental trespass of unensouled into ensouled sound, a mindless or involuntary convulsion in the continuity of the voice, a ravelling of the vocal thread. Though the cough may have elements of voice in it, its function is to expel irritant matter rather than to express thought or feeling.

The cough is perhaps little more than the overtaking of the voice by the unvoiced breath, by a breath that has nothing more than a hydraulic function. Though the cough is often richly 'voiced', in the phonological sense, its effect is not of the breath regulated or tuned by voice, but rather of the breath barging its way intransigently into voice; the cough is voice coerced by breath, not breath tuned and tutored into voice. The cough is closely twinned with and often implicated in the laugh, and we might even say that laughter is the orchestration of the reflex action involved in the cough. Only humans laugh, we humans have made up our minds about that, even though that very laughter has often been viewed, especially in Hellenic and Christian traditions, as bestial or diabolic. There need be no serious contradiction in this. Only humans can laugh, we seem to think, because only humans have the capacity of being ambushed by the animal they dream they no longer are.

And yet the cough is far from inexpressive, and far from inhuman. How disconcerting it is, for example, to hear an animal – a sheep, cat, dog, or even perhaps an ox – cough. The cough is not an inhuman sound, but the sound of the human being overtaken by something else, or even some other creature (a frog, we are wont to say) or form of creaturedness. And for this reason, coughs can become overlaid with meaning and import, to the point of becoming veritable vocal signatures. There is entire thesaurus, a variegated prosody of coughs, from the *tussis nervosa* of the timorous, to the wine waiter's discreetly imperious 'ahem'. And then there are the incipient, exploratory or aborted coughs, along with the plethora of ways of clearing the throat, of which no actor has been more the master than Michael Hordern, who could draw harrumphing symphonies out of his growling trawls of the mucous membrane.

The cough is neither the only nor even perhaps the most conspicuous of these incursions of the raw, errant or otherwise unvoiced air into the economy of voice. Let us convene for the moment only the following crew of creole quasi-locutions: the lisp, the gasp, the sigh, the rasp, the whistle, the hiss, the brrr, the purr, the snore, the sniffle, the crepitus, the croak. In all of these, the meaning comes from the involuntary nature of the sound, a sound not subdued or wholly suffused by the operations of voice. In such sounds, the air is not expressed, pressed out into audibility, impressed into audible shapes and postures, but seems rather to be escaping, as though through a rent or gash. The lisp is no taut suspiration, but a leak or flatulent collapse.

The early anatomists of voice had two competing theories for the structure and function of the larynx. One saw the voice as wind instrument, as reed, flute or organ pipe. The other saw the voice as stringed instrument. Eventually, the explication of the function of the vocal cords meant that the dispute ended in an honourable draw.[2] The voice was a wind instrument in that it employed air, but a stringed instrument in that its sound was produced by the modulation of string-like cords. The voice could therefore be seen as a kind of Aeolian harp, strings plucked by the inner breeze of the breath. These two anatomical alternatives were accompanied by imaginary or ideal forms of the voice. The voice as stringed instrument partook of the lucidity and rational intervals of the Apollonian lyre. The voice as wind instrument was full of reminders of the respiring and expiring human body. In the one, the voice toned the body as tense as a string; in the other, the body, no more than a balloon or saggy bladder, was reduced to wheezing eructation. The lyric voice is virile, virtuoso, inviolate, untouched by human hand; the bagpipe voice is odorous, exhausted and mortal. The story of the contest between Apollo and Marsyas enacts this distinction.[3] T. S. Eliot's lines from the final section of *The Waste Land* – 'A woman drew her long black hair out tight/And fiddled whisper music from those strings' – seems to show the bathetic diminution of the stretched string into scurrying, insect-like susurration.[4]

So, although there is nothing in the voice that is not made of breath, though voice is breath through and through, there is yet a ravine that runs through voice, cleaving the true, transfigured voice from the mere unvoiced breath, and holding voice apart from that in the voice that is yet not voice. It is above all the noise of the breath that has seemed to constitute this shadow song, this whisper music, the voice of the unvoiced in the voiced. It should be observed here that it is the idea or the ideal of an absolute distinction between the voiced and the unvoiced that is here at issue. As one might expect, the increase in physiological understanding and means of observing and measuring the processes of speech production has complicated this simple distinction between the voiced and the unvoiced. Phoneticians now distinguish (and wrangle over) many different hybrid types, such as 'voiced aspirates', 'breathy voice', 'creaky voice' and 'whispery voice'.[5] But my concern, as I have said, is not with phonetics, but with the phenomenological phantom of the voice and its noisy infiltrators and fellow-travellers.

No aspect of phonetics is so overdetermined in this way than the seemingly straightforward and self-announcing distinction between the prime elements of speech. For centuries, Aristotle's metaphysical claim that only those sounds that have been informed by soul are really voice has been cast in phonetic terms, the distinction between soul and the soulless corresponding to the distinction between vowels and consonants. As Roman Jakobson has noted, this division is 'the cardinal and most obvious bifurcation of speech sounds for linguists, for investigators of speech in its motor, acoustic and perceptual aspects, for poets, and finally for the intuition of ordinary speakers'.[6] Vowels are said to be formed in the larynx by the constriction of the vocal cords, producing a musical tone accompanied by harmonics. Consonants are thought to be formed in the mouth, and are the result, as the venerable Henry Sweet describes them, 'of audible friction, squeezing or stopping of the breath in some part of the mouth (or occasionally of the throat)'.[7] Consonants ('co-sounders' – *medeklinkers* in Dutch) are so called because they seem to have no independent existence, appearing always to need to be sounded in combination with other sounds in order to form expressive meanings. Consonants do not seem to constitute viable or expressive sounds on their own. A consonant or consonantal cluster can express a feeling – *tsk*, *ch*, *grr*, *pff* – but there are few consonantal clusters that can singlehandedly express a concept, or perform a specific grammatical function, as 'I', or 'a'.

Vowels, we may say, are identified with an idea of the continuous, the irreversible and the extensive. It is possible to slide, as a trombone slides across its full range of notes, between all the vowels in a single utterance. Vowels are thought of as the motive form of speech, pressing outwards from self to world, and pressing speech onwards from past to future. The vowels have often been thought of as the soul of speech, with consonants serving for its body. When I make the sound zzz, I am said to be 'voicing' a consonant that is otherwise unvoiced; take away this voicing and it is mere sibilance, the random, phantom passage of air. Consonants are accidental, they supervene upon the voice, shaping it from the outside. You can easily identify a person from the quality of their vowel-sounds; vowels are suffused with soul, in Aristotle's terms. Consonants, by contrast, seem anonymous; whispering and snoring and tutting are the mere machinations of the voice, a sort of vocal grit, *gratin* or roughage. Indeed, vowels have sometimes been thought of as the life and soul of speech itself – active, present, yet always in passage as it is presumed to be – with consonants allied more naturally with the letters which fix and represent it (tellingly, both *vowel* and *voice* have *vocalic* as their adjectival form). Benjamin Wells affirmed in 1882 that 'the consonants are the skeleton of a language, the vowels its flesh and blood. While the vowels are more subject to internal change and to influence from without than consonants, they reflect more clearly in their modification the spirit of a language.[8] To sing is to make vowels more prominent than consonants; it is easy to write music for vowel-sounds alone, but difficult and strange to write music for consonants alone. Music seems fundamentally vocalic and that we have had to wait until Stockhausen, Berio and Trevor Wishart for music that takes seriously the musical possibilities of consonants and the unvoiced.

And yet, consonants are in fact more complex sounds than vowels, which is another way of saying that they are noisier. Indeed, there is an alternative tradition within philology which uses the very hardness or immateriality of consonants as the source of secure knowledge about language formation and change. Walter Whiter's *Etymologicon Universale* of 1822 insisted on

> the Principle of Uniformity, by which we are at once supplied with the most important maxim in discovering the origin of words. In these enquiries, the Consonants only are to be considerd as the representatives of Words, and the Vowel Breathings are to be totally disregarded.[9]

Noting the 'higher informativeness of consonants', Jakobson writes that 'In children's language the sense-discriminative role of consonants as a rule antedates that of vowels.'[10]

The distinction between vowels and consonants has also been ethnicized, in terms of a distinction between Hebrew, traditionally regarded by Christian commentators as the primary language, that was closest to the divine, and Greek. This is because written Hebrew does not phonetically represent vowels, while Greek was the first written language to derive a notation for them. It is on these grounds that, in his *Treatise on the Origin of Language* (1772), J. G. Herder distinguishes between the spirit of Hebrew and the dead letter of Greek. For Herder, as for many others, the distinction between vowels and consonants is a distinction within language which is equivalent to the distinction between two forms of language, the spoken and the written. Vowels are the spirit which giveth life, whereas consonants are the letter which killeth. By refraining from writing the vowels, Hebrew is thought to keep them ineffable and inviolate; whereas, by circumscribing the vowels in script, the new Greek dispensation denatures and defiles them:

> With us the vowels are the first and most lively thing and the door hinges of language; with the Hebrews they are not written. Why? Because they could not be written. Their pronunciation was so lively and finely organized, their breath was so spiritual and ethereal, that it evaporated and could not be captured in letters. Only for the first time with the Greeks were these living aspirations unraveled into proper vowels, which, however, still needed the help of breathing [*Spiritus*], etc. – whereas with the Easterners speech was, so to say, entirely breathing, continuous breath [*Hauch*] and spirit [*Geist*] of the mouth, as they also so often name it in their painting poems. It was the life-breath [*Othem*] of God, wafting air, which the ear snatched up, and the dead letters which they painted down were merely the corpse which in reading had to be ensouled with the spirit of life [*Lebensgeist*].[11]

A recent reviver of this tradition of mystical linguistics is David Abram, who finds among various favoured premodern peoples – Aboriginal Australians, Lakota and Navajo Indians, and ancient Semites – a conception of the air as a distributed life force, circulating among and between living beings, an 'unseen presence that flows not just within us but between all things, granting us life and speech even as it moves the swaying grasses and the gathering clouds'.[12] Abram sees the severing or partitioning of this omnipresent mind-force as the sign of a mutilation of being practised by human beings on nature and on themselves. However, he lays the blame less on man in general than on the 'Greek scribes', who, by introducing symbols for the sacred vowels that were left unrepresented in Hebrew, effectively flattened breath into print: '*by transposing the invisible into the register of the visible, the Greek scribes effectively dissolved the primordial power of the air.*'[13] This in its turn encouraged abstraction in all its forms, from the Platonic doctrine of Ideas to the unspeakable horrors of Christian and Cartesian dualism. Abram sees in a reawakened acknowledgement of 'our immersion in the invisible air' the possibility of an undoing of the alphabetic Fall.[14]

But there is another side to breath, the mechanical side, the side that belongs the sonorous engine of the mouth. It is for this reason that, while believing that language derives from animal 'sounds of sensation', Herder insists nevertheless that 'it is no *organization* of the mouth which produces language . . . no breathing machine but a creature taking awareness invented language.'[15] The vowels are given and give life by the addition of tone to air. Though they all depend upon forms of constriction or concussion, the soul of voice is nevertheless imagined as a pure current of air, forming, as it were, its own channel. Voice is thereby identified as pure air in motion; paradoxically, when the noise of voice is removed from the breath, when, that is, we actually hear that breath as mere blind passage of air, this pure and unadulterated current starts to be heard as a kind of noise.

Hiatus

The sound represented by the letter *h* is eccentric to most of the schemes for classifying language. Although *h* is usually thought of as a kind of consonant, it does not perform the function that is often thought to be characteristic of consonants, namely that of stopping, detaining or detouring the efflux of air through the mouth. Aspiration is a feature of all of the consonants, with the sizzle of sibilant *s* and fricative *ff*, or the little detonations of air released in the wake of dental *d* and *t*, or plosive *p*. But the sound supposed to be signalled by the aspirate letter *h* is a kind of pure debouchure, orally unobstructed and minimally modified by the mouth. It approaches, we might say, the degree zero of consonance. It is a consonant in the sense that it is lacking in voice, but vowel-like in that it appears open and unconstrained. Indeed, it has sometimes been described as an 'aspirated vowel'.[16] Aristotle notes that 'we cannot use the voice when breathing in or out, but only when holding the breath; for one who holds his breath produces the motion by its means.'[17] It is the absence or minimal presence of this checking in the case of *h* which means that it belongs wholly neither to voice nor to noise, neither to larynx nor to mouth.

In one sense, the letter *h* represents a perplexing, even a menacing anomaly, its existence being wholly accessory or parasitic. And yet, because of this, it seems to be everywhere, not just at the beginning of English words, where it holds its place of honour, but also secreted semi-silently within them, as in combinations like *ch*, and *gh*, and words like *cough* and *enough*. In this ubiquity, it resembles the sound of the voiced sibilant *z*, to be discussed in chapter Nine. Ben Jonson, who helped make his name by suppressing the *h* in the middle of it, noted the ambivalence of the letter at the beginning of his *English Grammar*, saying that 'H. Is rarely other than an *aspiration* in Power, though a *Letter* in Form.'[18] The slight flicker of meaning in the phrase 'aspiration in power', which seems to allow us to think of the aspiration to power as well as the power of aspiration, is typical of Jonson's wry facetiousness at moments in this text. His later expansion of these remarks turns on a play between biblical letter and spirit:

> Whether it be a Letter or not, hath been much examined by the Ancients, and by some of the *Greek* Party too much condemned, and thrown out of the *Alphabet*, as an *Aspirate* meerly, and in request only before *Vowels* in the beginnings of words. The *Welsh* retain it still after many *Consonants*. But, be it a Letter, or Spirit, we have great use of it in our tongue, both before, and after *Vowells*. And though I dare not say, she is (as I have heard one call her) the *Queene mother of Consonants*: yet she is the life, and quickening of them.[19]

The ubiquity of *h* means that it can also be read symbolically as the principle of conjunction, as the necessity of commixture, which makes it appropriate for discussions of sexual complementarity or conjuncture. Johann Buxtorf tells us, for example, that '*Isch* [Hebrew man] differs from *Ischah* [woman] only by the letter H which is an aspiration, noting that the woman was made of man, and as it were breathed out of his side.'[20] Another, lengthier reflection on the hymeneal conjuncture implied by the *h* goes further by marrying the graphic and the phonic properties of the letter:

> But of *all letters*, it is the *hardest* for the body of man or Woman, alone of it selfe to imitate an H. For it consists of two severall disjunct, parts of *letters*: that is to say of two I I: both which are signes of the *singular* and *first person*; and are of themselves, both good formes of building too, but unles there come some-what, that (after a friendly manner) may *joyne them together*, they *both* still remaine singular and alone: and the building can never come into its desired and beautifull forme. Wherefore, if either man or woman, (being *alone* and built according to the *singular* and *first person I*) doe desire to change for *a better*: There is no better way to establish and make them most firmely grow into this well approved *forme*, then (by the *love of their hearts*) to reach each other their *hands in direct sinceritie*, thus, I--I: And let the *even* and *straight* course of *marriage*, fully and firmely establish them into *one* letter, H. Which not only by *uniting* of two bodies, makes them *eaven*: but by bringing them into the forme of this letter H, makes their *eaven*, *Heaven*: if they continue in the *love*, which first joyned them: which is, *indeed Heaven upon earth*.[21]

The aspirating function of *h* has led to difficulties and disputes for centuries in Europe. Catullus has a poem mocking one 'Arrius' who adds *h*s illegitimately or ridiculously wherever aspiration is possible: '*Chommoda* dicebat, si quando *commoda* vellet/dicere, et *insidias* Arrius *hinsidias*': '"Chomfortable", said Arrius, when "comfortable" was what he wanted to say,/ and "ambush" came out as "hambush".'[22] At the end of the fourth century AD, Augustine regretted the hypersensitivity of grammarians of his own time towards incorrect aspiration: '*si contra disciplinam grammaticam, sine adspiratione primae syllabae hominem dixerit, magis displiceat hominibus, quam si contra tua praecepta hominem oderit, cum sit homo*' – 'if someone should, against the strictures of grammarians, pronounce as '*ominem* the opening of '*hominem*', then he will be abominated by more men than for illicit hatred *ad hominem*.'[23] Jonathan Sheehan has shown the centrality of the letter *h*, which is used principally to lengthen median vowels in German, in words like *Bahn*, to discussions of orthographic reform in eighteenth-century Germany. On the one hand, rationalist reformers attempted to 'tame the overuse of the letter *h*' in the interests of 'a unified pure High German'.[24] Against them stood writers like the critic Johann Georg Hamann, who followed Jakob Boehme in finding a mystical power in the letter; according to Boehme, the insertion of the character signifying the breathing *h* into the five vowels of the tetragrammaton 'shows how the holy name breathes itself out'.[25]

But aspiration has probably never had a more fussed and tussled-over history than in British English. Following the Norman invasion of Britain, *h* sounds, which had often been more guttural than now, and resembled *ch* or *gh*, began to become less marked in English, in line with the tendency for aspirates to vanish in Romance languages like French and Italian. Pronunciation and orthography reinforced each other, with *ostler* replacing *hostler*, for example. This parallels the development of *ch* and *gh*, which have tended either to move forward from the throat into the middle of the mouth, losing much of their scraping attack, or to be hardened into the letter *k*, prior to their being passed over in silence, as witnessed by the mute *k*s at the beginning of words like *knight*, *kneecap* and *knowledge*, and the mute, yet still somehow grinding *g*s of *gnaw* and *gnome*.

But for some reason English began to resist this erosion and a spirited revival of the aspirate *h* set in from the eighteenth century onwards. The effect of this revival was to read the general tendency to drop (or disdain) initial aspirates as idleness or ignorance, and to hear the highlighting of *h*s as a sign of careful and correct attention to the detail of language. The most surprising of the ways in which this has happened is in the pernickety pronunciation of the *wh* of words like *which*, *when*, *whisk* and, of course, *whisper*. Speakers who take care to emphasise these sounds in words spelled with *wh* may well imagine that they are pronouncing the word as it is written, though in fact they are recalling the *hw* of Old English words like *hwy*, or, most notably, the untranslatable calling-to-attention of the word *Hwaet!* ('Oi! Listen up!') that opens *The Dream of the Rood*.

Among some linguists, the h became a sign of the burly native vitality of English speech, as opposed to the effeteness of the French invader. John Spanton writes that 'as England became a stronghold of Norman feudalism, the aspirates and gutturals of the Saxon element were often suppressed; thus diluting the vigour of the English speech by an infusion of the Norman element.'[26] One of the doughtiest defenders of the h was Alfred Leach, whose *The Letter H Past and Present* (1880) promised to show 'the antique origin, the unbroken line of descent, and the rough, sturdy ancestry of our English H'.[27] Leach sees a direct line of transmission from the 'spiritus asper' or 'rough breathing' marked in Ancient Greek – a sign derived from the left-hand half of a bifurcated Greek H – to the guttural aspirates of Celtic and British words. Accordingly, he applauds the revival of the h sound during the nineteenth century – signalled most conclusively in the word *herb*, which was widely pronounced for much of the nineteenth century without an initial aspirate, as it still is in most parts of the U.S. – as a reassertion of the hearty British spirit after the waning of Norman influence: 'when the language of the vanquished began to overcome that of the conqueror, the Aspirate must have entered upon a new era, and H's again have prevailed in the land.'[28] The dropped h, or, more accurately, the indifference to h, that is characteristic of many dialects, especially Cockney, could also be defended on precisely the same grounds, as an expression of a pungently indigenous nonconformism.

Nevertheless, despite the rallying of the fortunes of h, Leach acknowledges the melancholy and in the end perhaps irresistible course towards oblivion on which the sound and the letter are set. Already 'the new H had not the vigour of the old one – the guttural 'of the Anglo-Saxon . . . the powers of H were gradually, surely, and steadily waning, until, at length, its strong guttural sound finally and completely evanesced towards the latter half of last century.'[29]

Leach's book ends with the acknowledgement that

> the tones and modes that constituted nature's primitive eloquence must fall gradually into disuse. The strong breathing and the guttural breathing, having been the most expressive emotional interpreters of the early savage, are repugnant to the artificial sedateness and studied reserve of the modern speaker. In the speech of the well-bred Englishman, the hale old English H has melted into a soft Aspirate, and even this is likely to be soon altogether lost.[30]

Indeed, somewhat improbably, Leach sees in the aspirate sound, not just an individual tragedy, but rather the path to desuetude taken by many sounds

> Any letter doomed to die out of a word or a language, generally attempts to depart gracefully by first acquiring the nature of an aspirate-consonant, and then turns into a perfect H; under this form it relies upon h-dropping mortals to give it quiet burial, and unobtrusively confide it to Oblivion.[31]

The now-you-hear-it-now-you-don't condition of h in English made it the target of heightened vigilance and anxiety from the eighteenth century onwards. The already ambivalent condition of the aspirate is redoubled by its vacillating position in English writing, as a dubious mute. As such, it becomes an authentic shibboleth, so named after the word that the Ephraimite people, attempting to flee from the victorious Gileadites over the river Jordan, could not pronounce, those who betrayed themselves by lisping it as *sibboleth* in the Ephraimite fashion having their gizzards slit by the stickler Gileadites (Judges 12:5–6). Most authorities interpret the word 'shibboleth' as meaning 'an ear of corn', though there is a minority opinion that it refers to a stream or torrent, which obviously has a neat relation to the site of linguistic inquisition. Similarly, there seems to be some subliminal communication here between sound and script in the case of h, for the form of the capital letter H is believed to derive, through Greek, from a Phoenician letter, itself modelled on an Egyptian hieroglyph, having the form of a three-barred fence, and thus picturing the act of regulated passage.

From the middle of the eighteenth century onwards, a stream of popular publications defined and disputed the correct pronunciation of the initial letter *h*, sometimes cast in the form of comic petitions supposed to be uttered by the letter itself. *Poor Letter H* (1854) is an address to the vowels by the letter *h*, punningly appealing for regulation in its use: 'sometimes I have the most *honourable aspirations* to be first and foremost; and then at other times I am so humble that I only want to let my next little brothers speak; but they must speak softly, or maybe I shall be offended.'[32]

One of the many fallouts from this was a minor perturbation in the pages of *Notes and Queries* regarding the pronunciation of the word 'humble', which is so distinctively and rendered as *'umble* by Dickens's hypocritical Uriah Heep, whose equivocal name contains both a voiced and an unvoiced *h*. Dickens's usage was protested against by J. S. Warden, who wrote that

> I was always taught in my childhood to sink the *h* in this word, and was confirmed in this habit by the usage of all the well-educated people that I met in those days . . . but this eminent writer [Dickens] has thought fit of late to proscribe this practice by making it the Shibboleth of two of the meanest and vilest characters in his works.[33]

A number of correspondents seconded the correctness of the pronunciation *'umble*, though one anonymous correspondent replied with verses in favour of retaining the distinctive English *h*, in lines that consciously or unconsciously recall Augustine's quibble on the idea of a phonetic crime against 'humanity':

> Habituated to the sound of *h*
> In history and histrionic art,
> We deem the man a homicide of speech
> Maiming humanity in a vital part,
> Whose humorous hilarity would treat us,
> In lieu of *h*, with a supposed hiatus.[34]

This is in partial imitation of a pedagogic riddle by the poet Catherine Fanshawe (though it has sometimes been credited to Byron), which was frequently reprinted in the second half of the nineteenth century:

'Twas in heaven pronounced, and 'twas muttered in hell,
And echo caught faintly the sound as it fell;
On the confines of earth 'twas permitted to rest,
And the depths of the ocean its presence confest.
'Twill be found in the sphere, when 'tis riven asunder,
Be seen in the lightning, and heard in the thunder.
'Twas allotted to man with his earliest breath,
Attends at his birth, and awaits him in death,
Presides o'er his happiness, honour, and health,
Is the prop of his house, and the end of his wealth.
In the heaps of the miser 'tis hoarded with care,
But is sure to be lost on his prodigal heir.
It begins every hope, every wish it must bound,
With the husbandman toils, and with monarchs is crown'd.
Without it the soldier, the seaman may roam,
But woe to the wretch who expels it from home!
In the whispers of conscience its voice will be found,
Nor e'en in the whirlpool of passion be drown'd.
'Twill not soften the heart; but though deaf be the ear,
It will make it acutely and instantly hear.
Yet in shade let it rest like a delicate flower,
Ah, breathe on it softly – it dies in an hour.[35]

The huffing and puffing and the hectoring of the uneducated about so-called 'dropped aitches', and the apprehension at the impending extinction of the h produced a nervous desire to multiply hs where there was no warrant for them, a 'pervert method of aspirating' that drew even more scorn upon the hapless culprit than the innocent ablation of the h, with all the ferocity reserved for the failed social climber: 'It is not as a rule the very poor who introduce h's, but the small shopkeeper and the villager who reads at home in the evening instead of going to the public-house', sniffs one commentator.[36] Most remarkably, the very name of the letter *h* was subject to this supererogation. The word *aitch* derives from Teutonic *ache* and, by the seventeenth century, was routinely pronounced *ake*, in conformity with the tendency already noted for *ch* and *gh* words to be baked into *k*. Oddly, French, which has almost entirely dispensed with the sound of the *h*, preserves much more of the aspiration in its name for the letter – *asch*. But the recent revival of the aspirate sound in English makes the name for the letter seem like an anomaly – for, unlike any other letter of the alphabet, apart from *w* (*double-you*) and *y* (*wy*), *aitch* contains no announcement of its own sound. There is an ache in the word *aitch*, we may say, for the self-instancing aspiration of which it has been deprived, a fact that encouraged John Heywood in 1550 to make not-very-hilarious hay from *h*'s aches and pains:

> H, is worst among letters in the crosse row,
> For if thou finde him other in thine elbow,
> In thine arme, or leg, in any degree,
> In thy head, or teeth, in thy toe or knee,
> Into what place so ever H, maie pyke him·
> Where ever thou find ache, thou shalt not like hym.[37]

It is in order to make good this imagined mutilation that the word *aitch* has in many quarters been given artificial resuscitation to become *haitch*, a usage which it seems to me is currently gaining ground, or perhaps simply coming out of hiding. The anxious aspirator is like the fetishist, who, according to Freud, goes about patching up imagined amputations of the sexual organ with substitutes, succeeding only in drawing attention to the fact that nothing was missing in the first place. There is perhaps an analogy here between the peephole logic of the *h* and Roland Barthes's reading (which will will encounter again in chapter Nine) of the castration complex embodied in the difference between *z* and *s*, the sibilant half-sisters of *h*, in his brilliantly overblown *S/Z*, a study of Balzac's story of the love between the sculptor Sarrasine and the eunuch singer La Zambinella.[38]

Whisper Who Dares

Until the beginning of the twentieth century, unvoiced consonants were known to phoneticians as 'whisper-letters'. The whisper is distinguished from the lisp, hiss, sigh and whistle. For these are local or accidental occasions of the unvoiced puncturing the flow of discourse. But the whisper is distinguished by being an entire mode of discourse in itself. Whispering is not something that happens *in* speech, it is, like the falsetto, something that happens *to* it. The whisper is a spectre-speaking, a mirror or mode of minority for speech. The consonants were sometimes regarded as a kind of necessary abeyance, an active gap in nature; so Richard Baxter advised his readers that 'the *night* is part of the useful order of the creation, as well as the day. The vacant interspace in your writing, is needful as well as the words: Every letter should not be a *vowel*, nor every character a Capital.'[39] But the whisper is not the chiaroscuro provided by the interplay of death and life in the consonants and vowels; rather, it is entirely nocturnal, the whole of speech transposed into the key of H. The whisper is not the complement of speech, as the consonant is the complement of the vowel; it is its fetch, phantom or facsimile, which doubles without touching on its original.

The whisper is not only voiceless, it is also, and for that reason, mindless. It is perhaps because of this that whispering seems so often to arise as an accidental or imagined locution produced by the passage of air through some merely material obstruction. The wind whispers, especially in leaves and grass. In the story of Midas, the king's counsellor cannot keep the news about his master's ass's ears to himself, and so confides it to a brook, only for the whisper to be taken up by the reeds and bruited across the countryside.

The whisper signifies intimacy and secrecy. It is the mode in which I most naturally speak to or overhear myself. As such, it has religious or supernatural overtones, the whisper being the favoured mode of communication both of angels and of demons. The intimacy of the whisper gives it strong erotic force, too, as in the many popular songs in which whispering features. The practice known as 'horse-whispering' suggests that the whisper allows one to cross the linguistic gulf separating the human from the animal. The successful novel *The Horse Whisperer* of 1975 and the later film have given rise to a series of books with titles like *The Cat Whisperer*, *The Dog Whisperer*, *The Rabbit Whisperer* and, most intriguing of all, *The Tarantula Whisperer*, all promising insights into how to communicate confidentially with one's pets.[40] More intriguing still is the phrase a 'pig's whisper', which is recorded by the OED as being current until the beginning of the twentieth century, and was used to mean a jiffy, or brief instant, or as an emphatic form of the ordinary variety of whisper.

But the whisper signifies not just the keeping but also, as in the Midas story, the incontinent spilling of secrets. The whisper is devious and dangerous and, as such, is allied to rumour. For, if the whisper appears always to be so close as for it to be uncertain whether it belongs to the inside or the outside, it is always also spread abroad. Its very lack of amplitude is what seems to allow the whisper to be so easily amplified, as suggested by Swift's claim to know 'a Lye that now disturbs half the Kingdom with its Noise, which although too proud and great at present to own its Parents, I can remember in its *Whisper-hood*'.[41] The observation, in Shakespeare's *Henry V*, that 'From camp to camp through the foul womb of night/The hum of either army stilly sounds,/That the fixed sentinels almost receive/The secret whispers of each other's watch' (IV.Prologue, 4–7), draws together proximity and propagation in a telling way.

None of the mentions of whispers or whispering in the King James Bible are reassuring or approving. Whispering is the form of conspiracy (which, literally as 'breathing together', hints at whispering); and whispering is another term for the kind of soothsaying or sorcery that is routinely forbidden through the Old Testament. Richard Chevenix Trench observes that 'there lay in "whisperer" once . . . the suggestion of a slanderer or false accuser, which has now quite passed away from the word'.[42] As James Mason's *Anatomie of Sorcerie* (1612) explains, the word 'charmer', against which Psalm 58:5 warns,

> doth naturally betoken one that whispereth, muttereth, or mumbleth, speaking softly as it were betwixt the teeth. And because the charmers, and inchaunters do so, as it is

manifest by experience, and likewise by the 8. cap. of *Esa.* vers. 19. in these words. *And when they shall say vnto you, inquire at them that haue a spirit of diuination, and at the south-sayers which whisper and murmur,* &c. and *Esa.* the 29. cap. vers. 4. *Thy voice shall be also out of the ground, like him that hath a spirit of diuination, and thy talking shall whisper out of the dust.*[43]

Whispering is associated with the forms of speech also specified as 'peeping' and 'chirping' at various point with the Old Testament, terms which are associated with the practice of ventriloquism. Ventriloquism was understood at this period, not as a throwing of the voice into the body or person of another, but as a speaking through the body from some place, or by some means, other than the mouth, and therefore as an improper or displaced form of speaking which might then appear to be coming from elsewhere, and so to be magical or devilish. The whisper is this voice, embodied, but without abode. Indeed, 'whisperer' was occasionally used as a term for a ventriloquist, for example one Mr Fanning, a ventriloquist at the court of Charles I who was known as 'the King's Whisperer' (Edmund Dickinson identifies him as 'Henry King', though nothing else seems to be known about him than that he resided in Oxford). 'On Mr Fanning the Engastrometh', a short poem in celebration of his powers, records:

To speak within, and to ones selfe, and yet
Bee heard, is much, yet Fanning doth it:
So tall and stout a man, 'tis strange to see't
So like a coward should his words down eat:
The belly hath no ears they say; yet his
Hath ears to hear, and tongue to talk, I wis.[44]

The whisper is a speech that appears to be internal, a closet speech or 'speaking within', that has insufficient projective force to get untangled from the thicket of tongue and teeth which gives rise to it. And yet, if it holds back from utterance (a word essentially meaning 'outing', putting out or bringing forth), a whisper also seems to have no interior core or kernel. For, as the shell, shadow or outward semblance of speech, it is a kind of feigning or counterfeiting out of which all colour, body and melody have been drained. The whisper is kept inside, held back from speaking out loud, and yet it has itself no inside. The whisper is like a sketchy blueprint of a voice, an attenuated grisaille or 'fadograph', to use Joyce's delicate minting.[45] Perhaps the fact that the whisper has neither interiority nor exteriority explains why it seems to conjoin the secret and the rumour.

But if the whisper is so spectral and eviscerated, why does it appear so powerfully seductive or so urgently demanding? Why does the whisper have such designs on us? Perhaps it is precisely because it gives us too little, that the almost-but-not-quite nothing of the voice-that-is-not-one thereby craves from us the making of a voice-body of compensatory density and intensity. Perhaps all whispers are kin to the shades of the underworld summoned in Book XI of the *Odyssey*, who must lap from a trench of milk, honey and blood in order to plump their twittering voices out into audibility.[46]

If the sound of raw or unprocessed air suggests contamination or collapse, then the word 'aspiration' should remind us that there is another mode of the unvoiced air. The audibly unvoiced breath is also implicated in expressions of yearning. It is unlikely that any real phonetic difference is signalled in the spelling of 'Oh' rather than 'O', but the visible presence of the *h* serves to signal the transit of the air, unheard, but tangible, through the aperture of the lips. 'Oh' can signify longing, pain, excitement, rapture, intensity of bliss, precisely through the temporary ebb or overcoming of the articulate voice.

So the aspirate air is both carnal flatus and divine afflatus. As such it participates in the duality of air as such, which is never less than double, never unaffected by the ambivalence of the pure and the impure. The unvoiced air moves between the significant and the senseless. In one sense, it is significance broken in upon by the merely phenomenal, unshaped air. But these occasions of incursion are in fact laced intricately through the fabric of speech. In this sense, voice is suffused by the voiceless. Perhaps the secret of *h* is that it is the ultimate mixed body, the Hermes of the crossroads where vowel and consonant, voice and void, sound and sense, soul and machine, meet and have their fluctuant commerce. The errant sign, sounded on the breath, of the unsteady breath itself, that is neither ever absent or present, is never quite held, or ever quite gives out, that is, in Hopkins's words 'needful, never spent', intimates the cryptically indigent affluence of the air in the dreamscene of language.[47] Here, in the twilight epochs of speech's intermission, language gives up the ghost.

FOUR
Hic

Holy Hickops

In most Latinate languages, the word for sob derives from Latin *singultus*. French has *sanglot*, into which some suggestion of the blood seems to have leaked, while Italian stays closer to Latin, with *singhiozzo*, like Spanish with *sollozo*. *Singultus* survives in English only as a posh technical term for a hiccup or retch, though Lancelot Andrewes uses it in a sermon in the sense of a qualm or scruple of conscience: 'For, after we once left our first way, which was *right*, there takes us sometimes that same *Singultus Cordis* (as *Abigail* well calls it) a *throbbing of the heart*; or (as the *Apostle*) certeine *accusing thoughts* present themselves unto us, which will not suffer us to goe on quietly.'[1] The English word *sob* is described as 'of imitative origin' by the OED, which also suggests an analogy with West Friesian *sobje* and the Dutch dialect word *sabben*, to suck. Greek is *lugmos*. German, meanwhile, has the altogether more snuffley *schluchzen*.

Sobbing has at times been closely associated with hiccup and the words for it, for example the sadly obsolete verb *yex*, which is defined in Blount's 1661 *Glossographia* as 'that we do, when we have the Hicket or Hick up; some take it, to sob or sigh'.[2] One sermonist offers 'the hiccough of Conscience' as a translation of *singultus cordis*.[3] Elsewhere, *singultus* is rendered as 'yesking',[4] 'yisking', 'yeasking', 'yolking' and 'yelking'.[5] I imagine that the association between sob and hiccup has led to the Turkish word for 'sob', *hıçkırma*. Yexing had none of the dignity of sobbing. 'What thinkst thou of the Body, that yelpes and yexes, at any small push, at every sudden motion?' thundered John Gaule in his *Distractions, or The Holy Madnesse*.[6] A pamphlet of 1675 by 'A Person of Quality' described the praying style of a religious fanatic as 'a Rapsody of holy hickops, sanctified barkings, illuminated goggles, sighs, sobs, yexes, gasps, and groans, not more intelligible than nauseous'.[7] Christian commentators were keen to point out that Christ died *clamore magno, non singultu*, 'with a loud cry and not a sob' – or, as we may perhaps prefer nowadays, not with a whimper but a bang.[8]

Seat of Convulsiveness

The voice is full of obstacles and incursions that form a repertoire of impediments. For what is voice itself but McLuhan's 'organised stutter', a kind of patterned duress, a straining, stressing or checking of the breath?[9] Some of these unvoiced interruptions of the voice seem to be of some entirely other order, to be sound in the raw, in a zero-degree, 'unvoiced' condition, as linguists might say – clicks, hisses, whistles, pops, palatal burrs and purrs. Others merge their foreignness with that of the voice, and appear mantled in it – as, for example, lisping, whispering, growling, croaking, wailing. The sob does not quite do either of these things. For, rather than being a filter or coloration of speech, the sob is a kind of preemptive assault on it, a gag, clamp, or choke. The sob enacts the sense of a rising constriction, a desire for utterance so intense that it seems to bloat and block the means of it. Oliver Goldsmith in 1774 defined sobbing as 'the sigh still more invigorated'.[10] In his *Sylva Sylvarum*, Francis Bacon put sobbing alongside sighing as the fulcrum or turning-point in a spectrum of reactions to grief between resistance to and the desire for expulsion of the hurt:

> Griefe and Paine cause Sighing; Sobbing; Groaning; Screaming; and Roaring; Teares; Distorting of the Face; Grinding of the Teeth; Sweating. Sighing is caused by the Drawing in of a greater Quantity of Breath to refresh the Heart that laboureth: like a great Draught when one is thirsty. Sobbing is the same Thing stronger. Groaning, and Screaming, and Roaring, are caused by an Appetite of Expulsion, as hath beene said: For when the Spirits cannot

expell the Thing that hurteth, in their Strife to do it, by Motion of Consent, they expell the Voice.[11]

In Latin, *singultus* nearly always seems to be used to signify the breaking or prevention of voice. Ovid writes in his *Remedia Amoris* of Phyllis, lamenting the faithfulness of Demophoon, that '*ruptaque singultu verba loquentis erant*', 'her words were broken by sobs.'[12] Propertius warns his rival that the woman he craves will humiliate him so much that '*tibi singultu fortia verba cadent*', 'your strong words will be lost amid sobs.'[13] This usage is faithfully preserved in Shakespeare's *Venus and Adonis*, where we read of Venus begging Adonis to yield to her desire, 'now she weeps, and now she fain would speak,/And now her sobs do her intendments break'; in *Troilus and Cressida*, Cressida similarly vows to 'Crack my clear voice with sobs' (IV.ii.3).[14]

Countermanding speech, the sob seems nevertheless to cling commandingly to it; it strains for articulation, and is empty and abstract until it has bound itself to it, like the virus with no DNA of its own which must acquire it of its host. The sob is incomplete without the voice it itself fractures and depletes. Sobbing has become a mode of utterance, though it is the utterance of the unuttered, the venting of the fettered. Novelists will often have their heroines speak 'with a barely suppressed sob', but a sob is already suppression, a contraction or holding back of articulation. In the sob, the overcoming of the voice is itself overcome, as it becomes part of the armoury of voice. Sobbing can therefore become a kind of discipline, an exertion as well as an inhibition. The essence of the definite article *the* is said by Laotzu to be comparable to the state of a young boy, who does not yet know of the relations of the sexes, but whose spirit is nevertheless so virile that 'it may sob and cry all day but will not become hoarse.'[15]

There have been few physiological or psychological studies of the sob. However, some assistance is given by a study of crying conducted by G. Stanley Hall and Alvin Borgquist of Clark University in 1906, based on 200 returns of a questionnaire, supplemented by ethnological data from the Bureau of American Ethnology and the Archives of Aboriginal Knowledge, and responses to questions put to missionaries regarding the peoples of the Pacific. The questionnaire included enquiries and exhortations such as the following:

> Describe each symptom of 'a good cry' in order . . . Describe lump in the throat and its repression, effects on respiration, on the voice, complexion and circulation . . . What is a sob? Describe its frequency and culmination. Is there physical pain and where; in throat, thorax, abdominal walls? Where is the seat of convulsiveness? Is sobbing the climax of the cry? Are there cry-fetiches, i.e. special acts, thoughts, experiences or scenes that have pre-eminent power to cause it in you?[16]

Borgquist devotes a substantial section of his discussion of the physiology of crying to the sob. The definitions of the sob offered by his informants are interestingly various, including 'a convulsive catching of the breath', 'a convulsive choked drawing of the breath' and 'a convulsive contraction of the diaphragm'. Some informants saw the sob as a muscular phenomenon and made no mention of its sound. Others defined it in terms of its sound, as 'a short, quick sound, which indicates the cessation from [sic] prolonged weeping', or 'a choking sound made in the throat'; one respondent even defined it as 'the vocalisation of the cry'. Some saw the sob as the prelude to crying: others, by contrast, defined it as the residue or diminuendo of the act of crying, one affirming that 'not weeping but the sob comes late.'[17]

Sobbing's relation to crying exhibits the same indeterminacy as its relation to speaking and, as we will see later, singing. On the one hand, sobbing is simply a particularly intense feature of crying, and so is often to be found as a synecdoche for the act of crying as such, especially in the formula, which seems to have been particularly common in medieval English, 'sobbing and sighing'. And yet sobbing is also to be distinguished from crying. It may be regarded as the tense overture or onset of tears, the damming or welling of the tension that will spill over into the unloosed inundation of full-blown howling or roaring. Equally, it may be thought of as the depleted hiccuping into which the wail proper decays. In either case, the sob is the obverse or inside lining of crying, as seems to be indicated in Indamora's words in Dryden's *Aureng-Zebe*: 'Break, heart; or choak, with sobs, my hated breath;/Do thy own work: admit no forreign death.'[18]

Borgquist offers the suggestion that sobs are absent in the young infant, whose crying is sobless (this is wrong, surely?), and describes the typical adult cry as 'sobs and gasps only', the explanation being that 'the sob persists at a time of life when other elements of the cry have been inhibited.'[19] An eighteenth-century commentator writes, by contrast, that 'grown persons *sigh*; children *sob* . . . *Sighs* are the language of sorrow and *sobs* the convulsive throes of heart-felt distress.'[20] Borgquist holds strongly to the view 'that a reaction so uniform in its characteristics and so widespread over the human race is instinctive in its actions', yet will not confirm the universality of the sob, saying only that 'There is little explicit mention of the sob in the ethnological returns. Its absence has not been observed among savage peoples.' Borgquist will characterize the physiology of the sob as resulting from the dual function of the diaphragm, as involved both with respiration and with vomiting; a sob is the effect of a long intake of breath labouring against the convulsive efforts of the diaphragm to expel matter.[21]

Lump

The sob seems to requisition a kind of visual or material form, a blubbing sob-stance. It rises like a kind of knot, clot or blob, the 'lump in the throat'. Borgquist's informants explained that 'it cracks the voice', even sometimes 'entirely cuts off the voice'. Most saw the lump increasing or becoming more uncomfortable with the effort to suppress tears, while the flowing of tears by contrast had the effect of dissolving it – 'must cry to get rid of the lump'.[22] During the long heyday of the affective conditions described as hysteria, spleen and hypochondria, these symptoms of an irresistible interior rising and swelling recur frequently, along with reports of actually visible abdominal lumps or tightenings. It was believed by some (though by no means as many as historians of hysteria like us to think) that this was the result of a rising or otherwise vagrant womb. It was sometimes characterized as 'the suffocation of the mother', implying thereby both the asphyxiating effect of the mother (*matrix*, or womb), and an effect of suffocation applied to or suffered by it. The uncertainty implied in that unfixed genitive 'of' in 'suffocation of the mother' (is the mother suffocating or suffocated?) in fact points us to a larger, engendering principle of uncertainty that is at work in the sob: the paradoxical sound in the voice of the voice's own undoing or abatement.

The sob is at once a mangling of speech by inarticulate crying and the interior ligature or constriction whereby speech deprives the sob of its natural expression. The sob is the substantial form of a kind of hollowness or vacancy: thus it is often thought of as dry and empty, the lament for unvented lament: 'my empty heart will sob out in music like a hollow reed, and the stone will melt in tears.'[23] Mark Twain complained about the facile lachrymosity of heroines in popular fiction, who are forever bursting into tears:

> This kind keep a book damp all the time. They can't say a thing without crying. They cry so much about nothing that by and by when they have something to cry *about* they have gone dry; they sob, and fetch nothing; we are not moved. We are only glad.[24]

The Latin *singultus* is unrelated to *singulus*, but the latter seems to exert a kind of pressure on its use. Sobs are paradoxically singulative – paradoxically, because they tend to come in chains, but, as with chains of hiccups, they are chains of unique and uncoordinated eructations, that form no connection with each other. The French expression *Il a parlé entre deux sanglots* – he spoke between sobs, literally, between two sobs – dramatizes this isolation clearly. The singulative sob is in evidence in Whitman's extraordinary use of the word to describe the swallowing of a ship by the ocean in the poem 'Thought':

> of the steamship Arctic going down,
> Of the veil'd tableau – Women gather'd together on deck,
> pale, heroic, waiting the moment that draws so close – O
> the moment!

A huge sob – a few bubbles – the white foam spirting up –
and then the women gone,
Sinking there, while the passionless wet flows on – and I
now pondering, Are those women indeed gone?
Are souls drown'd and destroy'd so?
Is only matter triumphant?[25]

Since the whole point of the poem is to describe an unwitnessed and therefore unmourned tragedy, the word 'sob' consumes and cancels itself; it evokes a single, paradoxically dry gulp, giving way to the 'passionless wet' of the indifferently and undifferentiatedly heaving ocean. Indeed, we might describe the sob as essentially dry or desiccated, in that it is the sob which checks or interrupts the flow of tears. This makes Keats's early morning buds, which 'Had not yet lost those starry diadems/Caught from the early sobbing of the morn' in 'I Stood Tiptoe' or the 'sobbing rain' of 'Endymion' moistly oxymoronic.[26] On the other hand, though, the usage might be thought to be supported by the appearance of the word 'sob' as a form of the word 'sop', meaning to soak or saturate – Helkiah Crooke refers to the 'sobby and waterish places of the body', and John Evelyn to the 'sobbing *Rain*' that produces moss.[27]

Sob Sisters

The sob instates a complex calculus between the voluntary and the involuntary. One sobs in large part as one sneezes, without being able to originate or oversee the process. But there have been those who have seemed to be able to summon sobs as easily as others sniggers. The champion sobber in the damply lachrymose Middle Ages was the mystic Margery Kempe, who seems to have missed no opportunity to dissolve into gales of tears and sobs. These were, it seems, predominantly, sobs of rapture rather than grief or distress: 'sche schuld so wepyn & sobbyn þat many men wer gretly a-wondyr, for þei wysten ful lytyl how homly ower Lord was in hyr sowle. Ne hyr-self cowd neuyr telle þe grace þat sche felt, it was so heuenly, so hy a-bouen hyr reson & hyr bodyly wyttys.'[28] It is quite clear that this was a source of perplexity and annoyance to Margery's neighbours:

> sche wept bittyrly, sche sobbyd boistowsly & cryed ful lowde & horybly þat þe pepil was oftyn-tymes aferd & gretly astoyned, demyng sche had ben vexyd wyth sum euyl spirit er a sodeyn sekenes, not leuing it was þe werk of God but raþar sum euyl spiryt, er a sodeyn sekenes, er ellys symulacyon & ypocrisy falsly feyned of hir owyn self.[29]

She seems to have sobbed her way around every pilgrimage site in Europe and the Middle East, which so got on the wicks of her fellow-pilgrims that they insisted that she take her meals apart, in grizzling privacy. There is a strange dissonance between the voice of Christ, 'whos melydiows voys swettest of alle sauowrys softly sowndyng in hir sowle, seyd, "I xal preche þe & teche þe my-selfe"', and the convulsive effects that being so suffused with divine grace produces in her:

> þan was hir sowle so delectabely fed wyth þe swet dalyawns of owr Lorde & so fulfilled of hys lofe þat as a drunkyn man sche turnyd hir fyrst on þe o syde & sithyn on þe other wyth gret wepyng & gret sobbyng, un-mythy to kepyn hir-selfe in stabilnes for þe vnqwenchabyl fyer of lofe whech brent ful sor in hir sowle.[30]

Margery's cultivated ecstasies of sobbing have found a mass-media correlative in the cynically mechanical tugging of heart-strings in the twentieth century. The 'sob-sister' arrived on the scene in 1907, when the four female reporters who were covering the trial of millionaire Harry K. Thaw for the murder of his wife's lover were given this name because of their tendency to focus on the more pathetic and sentimental aspects of the case.[31] A piece of music from 1934 entitled *Tabloid* by Ferde Grofe is described on its inside cover as 'an intensive study of the getting out of a daily periodical, set to music' It includes 'Run of the News' and 'Comic Strips' and 'Going to Press'. The second movement, 'Sob Sister' is described as

> a ballad of bitterness. Its central theme tells of a heart that aches even as it mocks at cowardly emotion; of a laughing

> retort that is obviously manufactured gaiety. It is colorful, alive, vibrant with the emotions of a paradoxical image whose prototype can be found in any newspaper office.[32]

From 'sob-sister' comes the parallel 'sob-brother', 'sob-raiser' and the pleasingly cynical 'sob-squad'.[33] As the century wore on, these were followed in short order by 'sob-story', 'sob-act' and 'sob-tune'.

Tears in the Voice

There are close associations between music and acts of lamentation, whether it is in the stylized ululations of Africa and the Middle East, the groaningly bent notes of the blues or the operatic swoops and croons of a piece like 'While My Guitar Gently Weeps'. Not surprisingly, sobs have also found their way into music and song. Organs have stops designed to suggest or imitate the sound of weeping, in particular the 'tremulant', which, in medieval music, was used only in penitential seasons 'to represent the sighing and sobbing of men'.[34] The term was also used to evoke the effect of a sudden muting in playing the lute. In a manual of 1676, Thomas Mace urges players of the lute to

> give each Crochet Its due Quantity; And [illeg] Prittiness; Cause Them to Sobb, by Slacking your Stopping Hand, so soon as They are Struck; yet not to unstop Them, but only so much as may Dead the Sound on a sudden. This gives Great Pleasure in such Cases.[35]

The sob has a number of musical allotropes, for example the Austrian yodel and the catch in the voice characteristic of vocal styles in the Middle East and Eastern Europe. The sob is also the ur-form that lies behind the trills, leaps and catches of the voice characteristic of traditional Scottish, Irish and other Celtic singing, which either imitate the grace-notes of bagpipes or are their original. These may be the source for the more masked but still sob-like clucks that are de rigueur in American country singing. There is even a version of this technique practised by opera and classical singers, and described in one contemporary account of the singing of Mario Lanza as 'the famous "tears" in the voice, that small pretence learned from the sobbing of the nightingale'.[36] In fact, all of these forms of musical sobbing seem less like tears (drops) than tears (rips), and thus seem to suggest a passion redoubled by its suppression, which fissures the smoothness and steadiness of the melody.

The sob also features strongly in forms of religious incantation, especially in the singing of Jewish cantors. An account of popular religion, collected from oral testimony in coastal Georgia in the 1930s describes the climax of a performance by a preacher:

> Noticing that the hour is growing late, the Bishop abruptly ends his talk. There follows a prayer, led by one of the deacons and chanted rather than spoken. At the end of each line the man's voice catches on a high sob verging on hysteria, and those in the congregation murmur an almost inaudible echo of the speaker's plea. The other deacons join in the recital and in the wild sobbing. At the conclusion of the prayer a high pitch of excitement is reached.[37]

Jug Jug

The heightened apnoea that characterizes the sob can also have strong sexual suggestiveness. A book of instructions for magical adepts explains that the ecstasy of intimacy with one's Holy Guardian Angel will often produce a kind of sexual rapture – though this is deprecated:

> The intensity of the consummation will more probably compel a sob or a cry, some natural physical gesture of animal sympathy with the spiritual spasm. This is to be criticised as incomplete self-control. Silence is nobler.[38]

There is, of course, considerable voluptuousness in the sob, as is apparent in Baudelaire's sumptuous, sensual evocation of the delights of Lesbos:

Lesbos, où les baisers sont comme les cascades
Qui se jettent sans peur dans les gouffres sans fonds,
Et courent, sanglotant et gloussant par saccades,
Orageux et secrets, fourmillants et profonds;
Lesbos, où les baisers sont comme les cascades!

Lesbos, where the kisses come in cascades
That throw themselves fearless into bottomless gulfs
And flow, sobbing and gurgling in spasms,
Stormy and secret, teeming and deep;
Lesbos, where the kisses come in cascades![39]

As with many other terms for the breaking in of the voiceless to voice, the sob is often characterized as a kind of natural or animal utterance, which seems odd in the light of Alvin Borgquist's perhaps incautious assertion that the sob 'seems to be essentially human [and] seems to be always absent in the cries of animals'.[40] Borgquist may be relying here on Darwin, who notes in his *The Expression of the Emotions in Man and Animals* (1872) that keepers in London Zoo 'have never heard a sob from any kind of monkey' and concludes that 'sobbing seems to be peculiar to the human species'.[41] One of the sounds that come at the end of Wordsworth's 'Evening Walk' is 'The tremulous sob of the complaining owl.'[42] Bram Stoker refers to the 'cooing sob of doves' in his *Lair of the White Worm*.[43] Elsewhere, readers are urged to hear the coyote 'sob'.[44] Among the most remarkable of the animals that seem capable of or drawn to sobbing are the turtles described by Thomas Blount in 1693:

> I remember that in a place called the Camanas, which lyeth to the Lew-Ward of Jamaica, the Sea TORTOISE (of which there are Five Sorts) or TURTLES, as some call them, those Triple-Hearted Amphibious Creatures (for they have each of them three distinct Hearts) being entangled in a S[k]ain or Net, which was usually set for the taking of them, or else being turned on their Backs on Land (for then they cannot turn themselves on their Feet again) did always Sigh, Sob, shed Tears, and mightily seem to Lament, as being most

> sensible of their Destruction, and that they were in their Enemies hands.[45]

This belief may very well have suggested to Lewis Carroll the moping, melancholy figure of the Mock Turtle, who has to be shaken and punched in the back by the Gryphon to help him overcome the 'sobs [that] choked his voice' – '"Same as if he had a bone in his throat," said the Gryphon.'[46]

But, of all creatures, it is the nightingale that is most frequently said to sob. As with all birds, there is a kind of rupture in its phenomenal being, since the bird is most often heard rather than seen and nightingales are anyway rather inconspicuous; it is this which prompted Plutarch's Spartan, on plucking a nightingale and finding almost no meat on it, to remark that it was '*vox et praeterea nihil*'.[47] This is true of many birds, but there is a particular reason for the nightingale to be associated with the constricted lament of which sobbing is characteristic. In poetic tradition the nightingale is identified with Philomela, who is raped by her brother-in-law, Tereus, who then cuts out her tongue to prevent her blabbing. But Philomela manages, by weaving the story of her ravishment into a tapestry, to communicate it to her sister Procne, with whom she effects revenge, by killing Tereus's son Itys and feeding the body to his father in a pie. Tereus flies into a murderous, and doubtless dyspeptic, fury on the discovery of what he has eaten and is about to slaughter the two women when the gods arbitrarily but elegantly transform the whole cast into birds: Procne into a nightingale, Philomela into a swallow, Tereus into a hoopoe. In Latin versions of the story, Philomela becomes the nightingale. This is a distinct improvement, for it allows a Just-so Story conclusion, along the lines of: 'and still today, when you hear the melancholy song of the nightingale, you can hear Philomela, sobbing out her woes.' Leonard Lutwack finds this twist of the tale rather unintelligible, though, since 'the tongueless Philomela is hardly fit to sing the elaborate song of the nightingale' and thus the songless swallow might seem better adapted to her condition.[48] But the whole story seems to be about inarticulate expression, about a melancholy expressed, not in direct utterance, but in the suffering attempt to give utterance, struggling against impediment. Suffering mutes and muffles articulation, which produces a further intensification of suffering, in the incapacity to give it voice; but that impeded voice then becomes the authentic voice of suffering. It is, in other words, the very structure of the sob in its relation to the voice that it breaks and remakes as broken. This is what makes Philomela's an 'inviolable voice', as it becomes in T. S. Eliot's *The Waste Land*; it has taken wounding into itself, it is an apotropaic self-violation.[49] This is given a further twist in the many versions of the story in which the nightingale is represented as intensifying its pain by singing with its breast pressed against a thorn. It is a further confirmation of the paradoxical constitution of the sob as the simultaneous eliciting and inhibition of voice.

The Philomela story makes sobbing the standard metaphor for the nightingale's song. Here, for example, is Frank S. Williamson's poem, 'The Magpie's Song':

> Where the dreaming Tiber wanders by the haunted
> Appian Way,
> Lo! the nightingale is uttering a sorrow-burdened lay!
> While the olive trees are shaking, and the cypress boughs
> are stirred:
> Palpitates the moon's white bosom to the sorrow of the bird,
> Sobbing, sobbing, sobbing; yet a sweeter song I know.[50]

Gerard Manley Hopkins's evocation of the bird's song has a woman hearing it from her bed as she thinks with apprehension of her lover at sea. Although the 'mighty stops' of the bird's song are so forceful that they 'shook/My head to hear. He might have strung/A row of ripples in the brook',[51] there is mortal premonition embodied in the song, the liquid gurgles of which seem mockingly to prefigure the gasps of the drowning man:

> I thought the air must cut and strain
> The windpipe when he sucked his breath
> And when he turned it back again
> The music must be death.[52]

Mathilde Blind also draws the nightingale into a drama of release and restraint. The sobbing song of the nightingale seems to be animated by the imminence of the very death that will consign it to dumbness:

> As between clenching teeth I hissed
> Our irretrievable farewell.
> And through the smouldering glow of night,
> Mixed with the shining morning light
> Wind-wafted from some perfumed dell,
> Above the Neva's surge and swell,
> With lyric spasms, as from a throat
> Which dying breathes a faltering note,
> There faded o'er the silent vale
> The last sob of a nightingale.[53]

John Clare unusually evokes the sight of the bird, writing in his 'The Nightingale's Nest':

> Her wings would tremble in her exstasy,
> And feathers stand on end, as twere with joy,
> And mouth wide open to release her heart
> Of its out sobbing songs.[54]

Here the impediment of 'sobbing' is no more than implied, though it gives a pleasurable eddy in the outpouring from the splayed beak of the bird. Rercalling that, in Elizabethan slang, nightingales are prostitutes, W. H. Auden's 'Song of the Master and the Boatswain' in his *The Sea and the Mirror* evokes the sob of the nightingale as part of a hard-boiled biting back of meretricious melancholy:

> The nightingales are sobbing in
> The orchards of our mothers,
> And hearts that we broke long ago
> Have long been breaking others;
> Tears are round, the sea is deep:
> Roll them overboard and sleep.[55]

D. H. Lawrence wrote back against the singultive tradition of the nightingale and could not believe that any of the poets who had written about the nightingale could ever actually have heard it 'silverily shouting'.[56] He reminds us of the 'jug-jug-jug!' used by medieval writers to represent 'the rolling of the little balls of lightning in the nightingale's throat . . . They say that with that jug! jug! jug! – that she is sobbing. How they hear it, is a mystery. How anyone who didn't have his ears on upside down ever heard the nightingale "sobbing" I don't know.' Lawrence suggests that the forlornness and lamentation that poets like Keats hear is actually the poet's own, in a 'sadness that is half envy' at the 'pure assertion', of the nightingale's 'intensely and undilutedly male sound'.[57] Instead of the broken gulps heard by the poets, Lawrence hears, and exultantly rebroadcasts

> A ringing, punching vividness and a pristine assertiveness that makes a man stand still. A kind of brilliant calling and interweaving of glittering exclamation such as must have been heard on the first day of creation, when the angels suddenly found themselves created, and shouting aloud before they knew it.[58]

'Perhaps', he surmises, 'that is the reason of it: why they all hear sobs in the bush, when the nightingale sings, while any honest-to-God listening person hears the ringing shouts of small cherubim.'[59] Of course, as always with Lawrence, there is his own projection: for this glorious sound has to be male, and the implicit criticism of the sob-story of the poets is that it is female, passive, suffering. Lawrence ends the essay celebrating the triumph of the cock who is 'utterly unconscious of the little dim hen' when he sings.[60] In fact, Lawrence seems to have seen sobbing as the great threat to virility to be found in the depleted sentimentality of modern life. His poem 'Now It's Happened' blames the Russian Revolution on the excess of soul and sentimentality to be found in Russian culture, concluding that 'our goody-good men betray us/and our sainty-saints let us down,/ and a sickly people will slay us/if we touch the sob-stuff crown/ of such martyrs'.[61]

Interjection

It is as though sobbing were so much a surrender of the voice to some other mode of utterance, or the utterance of some harboured other, that it more easily becomes detached from a human subject or channel, and transferred to an outside source. But where the human is unhumanized by the sob, it is precisely the sob that humanizes the inhuman world. Among the auguries of wind collected in his *Natural and Experimental History of Winds* Francis Bacon offers us the suggestion that 'Crows as it were barking after a sobbing manner, if they continue in it, do presage winds, but if they catchingly swallow up their voice again, or croak a long time together, it signifies that we shall have some showrs.'[62] In the universal weeping of Shelley's waterlogged lament 'Adonais', we are told that 'The wild Winds flew round, sobbing in their dismay.'[63]

Bells are particularly apt to be heard as sobbing. In a poem entitled 'A Passing-Bell' Lawrence catches the automatic or unconscious nature of the sob by running together wind and child: 'The rain-bruised leaves are suddenly shaken, as a child/Asleep still shakes in the clutch of a sob.'[64] Bells are perhaps prominent in the life of the sob because their physical form is so suggestive of the mouth, with the clapper (usually internal in British bells, often externally applied elsewhere in Europe) performing the office of the tongue, or possibly the uvula. But bells also seem possessed of throats; even though there is nothing beneath or behind this throat producing the sound, bells nevertheless seem to suggest something rising or climbing to it. Thus we have Whitman's poem, 'The Sobbing of the Bells':

> The sobbing of the bells, the sudden death-news
>   everywhere,
> The slumberers rouse, the rapport of the People,
> (Full well they know that message in the darkness,
> Full well return, respond within their breasts, their brains,
>   the sad reverberations,)
> The passionate toll and clang – city to city, joining,
>   sounding, passing,
> Those heart-beats of a Nation in the night.[65]

Transference is characteristic of the nightingale's song, or its effect. Coleridge evokes a kind of disembodied sobbing at the beginning of his 'Dejection: An Ode', a poem about the constriction or impossibility of poetry; longing for the good, boisterous inspiration of a storm, there is only 'the dull sobbing draft, that moans and rakes/Upon the strings of this Æolian lute.'[66] Rochester, telling Jane Eyre that she must leave Thornfield and go to Ireland, suddenly finds the key to unlock her reserve:

> 'Jane, do you hear that nightingale singing in the wood? Listen!'
>
> In listening, I sobbed convulsively; for I could repress what I endured no longer; I was obliged to yield, and I was shaken from head to foot with acute distress.[67]

Indeed, the sob seems never to be exactly in its place. Walter Savage Landor's poem 'The Death of Artemidora' gives us another sob that seems suddenly to be snatched from the one who might have uttered it:

> Again he spake of joy
> Eternal. At that word, that sad word, *joy*,
> Faithful and fond her bosom heav'd once more,
> Her head fell back: one sob, one loud deep sob
> Swell'd through the darken'd chamber; 'twas not hers.[68]

We recall that the OED tells us that the word *sob* is 'probably of imitative origin'. But what precisely does the word *sob* imitate? Certainly, it is very far indeed from the Latin *singultus* and its derivatives, which seem to place the sob firmly amid the tonsils. We seem sure that we can hear the sound of the sob in the word for it, and can hear the sound of sobbing in a wide range of animal and material sounds, even though we may have no very clear idea of what that sound is. The sob is like the phenomenon known as 'referred pain', a pain experienced in a site adjacent to, or distant from the site of a lesion, sometimes because that site does not have the nerves that would make the sensation of pain possible, meaning that referred pain is always felt to be somewhere else than where it is. Our sobs are always apart from as well as a part of ourselves. They take us apart, we find them in the voices of our unlikes, like bells and birds. In a similar way the sob always makes itself heard as something other than it is, for it is the sound of sound consuming itself. It is the jeopardy of that imaginary entity I have called the voice-body – the phonoplasm or bodily imago we build out of every voice, the body with which every voice clothes itself, a body that is almost always at variance with the actual body from which the voice emanates.[69] It is Whitman again who catches the indecorousness of the sob, its capacity to reform and deform the entire body, turning it into what we might call a 'sob-body' of pure convulsion. Whitman's poem 'Tears' never allows us actually to see or name its subject, which is therefore not a crying person, but the persona of crying itself:

> O who is that ghost? that form in the dark, with tears?
> What shapeless lump is that, bent, crouch'd there on
> the sand?
> Streaming tears, sobbing tears, throes, choked with
> wild cries;
> O storm, embodied, rising, careering, with swift steps
> along the beach!
> O wild and dismal night storm, with wind! — O belching
> and desperate![70]

The unexpected 'belching' seems just right, for the sob is eructive as well as interruptive. The indelicate breaking of wind makes the desperation of the sobber seem just a little ridiculous, even as the sobber's incapacity to defend against ridicule intensifies the desperation.

But sobbing is also the making of the voice-body, in what Giorgio Agamben follows Aristotle in calling an *impotential*, the ability to be unable, from which so many of the voice's resources are made.[71] What rends the voice also renders it up, for the voice is nothing but the mixed economy of these injuries, condemnings, indemnities and redemptions. What are voice-bodies made of?

Breath, spit, gristle and desire in equal parts – in other words, sonic scar-tissue. Byron finds in the fifteenth canto of his *Don Juan* an image of existence itself in this kind of inarticulate eruption or interruption of the voice:

> All present life is but an Interjection,
>   An 'Oh!' or 'Ah!' of joy or misery,
> Or a 'Ha! ha!' or 'Bah!' – a yawn, or 'Pooh!'
>   Of which perhaps the latter is most true.
>
> But, more or less, the whole's a syncopé
>   Or a singultus – emblems of Emotion,
> The grand Antithesis to great Ennui,
>   Wherewith we break our bubbles on the ocean.[72]

In the sob, the voice catches its breath, and therefore both corrupts and captures itself.

FIVE

Mmmm

The primary signification of the bilabial nasal sound m across many languages is repletion, with a particular reference to a filling of the mouth with food or, in the infant, milk. It has often been suggested that the commonness (though not universality) of initial and medial m-sounds in words for mother in different languages is a testimony to the strong and primary association between the maternal and the mammary. When the infant's mouth is pleasurably plugged with the breast, the only way for sound to get out is through its nose, an effect recalled in the nasality of the m, or the n, or their combination in the sound rendered as mn.[1] Oral satisfaction is similarly signalled through sounds that recall this crammed condition – 'mmm', 'yummy'. Bilabial m-sounds therefore allow, and so connote, more than any other sound the enactment of the cooperation of eating and speaking.

But this is a vexed association, since eating and speaking are mutually exclusive actions, as indicated in the hiccup, the product of their interference with each other. This means not only that bilabial nasal m is the only sound one can make when one's mouth is otherwise fully occupied, but also that it may be drawn on to express the gustatory delight in something that is actually beyond words. The closing off of the mouth to language is therefore signified in a way that opens up to language a means to signify what escapes it. The assimilative mm is the way in which speech assimilates itself to, and assimilates to itself, not-speech. Though mm is thought of as a labial, the sound produced is a cooperation between nose and throat, since a nasal sound requires air to be directed into the nose from the back of the throat, that can also easily fall back into an animal rasp or snort of delight.

Even apart from the direct mimicking of speech baulked or bulked by oral pleasure, the *m* sound may be regarded as a primary phoneme – one which human children across many different cultures produce earlier and more easily than many other sounds. Accordingly, it is one of the commonest sounds in the world's languages; indeed, there are hardly any languages that do not have some version of it (though, pleasingly, there is no such sound in the language we, but obviously not they, exonymically call 'Mohawk'). The vocable *um*, which functions in English as a linguistic placeholder, is a kind of silence made audible – the sound of not speaking, that keeps the channel open when where there is no communication. It is a vocal noise that impersonates voice. It is a neat coincidence that the *em* is the name for the dash that has the width of the *m* in a given typeface, which, since the *m* was usually cast in such a way as to take up the whole of the block of type, is exactly the width of the square space known to printers as an *em-quad*, or, more familiarly, *mutton-quad*.

By a logic of approximation, the sound that signifies speech impeded by repletion also comes to signify the holding back from speech altogether, or the imposition of silence. To keep mum, or stumm, and therefore to voice the unword *mum* as one does when 'mum's the word', is to say nothing, to say the thing that is nothing, making oneself deliberately dumb. As Jonathan Rée has shown, the history of the word *dummy* illustrates the stupid and cruel association between being unable to speak, or unpossessed of a voice, and being lacking in intelligence or even soul.[2] A 'dummy' is therefore not just a stupid person, but a kind of substitute or changeling being, the soulless shell or effigy of a person. A dummy is a placeholder, a human pause or pantomime, the mimicry referring specifically to the act of miming, or what was known as 'dumb-show', showing dumbly, or showing dumbness itself.

Miming is also close to *mumming* and *mummery*, words which were often applied to empty or ridiculous religious ritual, as in the 'mumchances, mumries & unknawin language wherein they pudled of befoir' of Catholic ritual into which the people were in danger of relapsing, according to one Scottish preacher in 1590.[3] No doubt a large part of the disdain that has attached to acts without words has been due to the fact that such performances suggested the wordless significations of the animal, the infant – or the deaf and dumb. Mummery may be thought of as close to *mammering*, a state of hesitation or vacillation; such 'mammering doubtfulnesse' may be accompanied by heming, humming or stammering.[4]

The plumped out pause that is the *um* is perhaps a minor form of the Big Nothing embodied in the mystical vocable *Om*, or *Aum*, that is supposed simultaneously to saturate and evacuate the thoughts of the meditator. In both the *um* and the *Om*, the sublexical word is a kind of abstract of speaking itself, a reduction to its essentials of the two operations of the mouth, a simple opening, and a simple closure, the oscillation of freeing and stopping that programmes and patterns the whole complex choreography of lips, tongue, teeth, gums and palate. This most elementary opening and closing is most obvious in the puppets who are often associated with mummery or dumbshow, the word *puppet* sliding easily into *mommet*, or halfway towards it in *muppet*. The primary sound of the mouth, the sound of the cry, is the *oh* or the *ah*, that seems to want to mimic the orb of the mouth. But the cry can also seem like the neutral passage of air, the gush of the open gullet, mere force without form. In Vedic Sanskrit, the sound *om* was originally a continuous, uninflected sound, which was intended to signify the totality of all coming into and dissolution of being. Without the turning of the air backwards and inwards that is provided by the compression of the lips, there would be no closure to the sound, nothing to mark it off as a completed form. By stopping off the cry, the *m* seals it into a circle, giving it back, bringing it round to itself. As one writer has observed, 'Im Lautlichen des m spricht sich ein Sich-Einfühlen, ein Eintauchen aus' – 'In the sounding of the *m*, an empathy towards, an immersion in oneself speaks out.'[5]

The twelve verses of the Mandukya Upanishad are devoted to the explication of the AUM. According to verses nine, ten and eleven, the three letters evoke (A) the waking state, (U) the dreaming state and (M) the state of deep sleep, without consciousness:

> *Prājna* whose sphere is deep sleep is M . . . the third part (letter) of *Aum*, because it is both the measure and that wherein all become one. One who knows this (identity of *Prājna* and M) is able to measure all (realise the real nature of the world) and also comprehends all within himself.[6]

The fourth condition of the AUM, signified by the sounding together of the three parts of the word, is soundless, because it no longer has any parts or distinctions:

> That which has no parts (soundless), incomprehensible (by the aid of the senses), the cessation of all phenomena, all bliss and nondual *Aum*, is the fourth and verily the same as the *Ātman*. He who know this merges his self in the Self.[7]

A commentary on this verse by Sri Śankarāchārya explains that '*Aum* is the beginning, middle and end of all; that is, everything originates from *Aum*, is sustained by it and ultimately merges in it.'[8] The Khândogya Upanishad begins with another explanation of the universal power of the Om:

> 5. The Rik indeed is speech, Sâman is breath, the udgîtha is the syllable Om. Now speech and breath, or Rik and Sâman, form one couple.
>
> 6. And that couple is joined together in the syllable Om. When two people come together, they fulfil each other's desire.
>
> 7. Thus he who knowing this, meditates on the syllable (Om), the udgîtha, becomes indeed a fulfiller of desires.
>
> 8. That syllable is a syllable of permission, for whenever we permit anything, we say Om, yes.[9]

Perhaps in part because of their associations with melding and immersion, *m*-sounds may often seem to evoke states of drowsy numbness or meditational trance. There is a connection between the primal satisfactions of the infant's appetite, the hypostasis of the 'sensation of "eternity", a feeling as of something limitless, unbounded – as it were, "oceanic"' evoked by Freud, and the particular sounds with which they may be associated, accounting for some of the narcotic charge of the bilabial nasal.[10] The magical thinking expressed through the letter *m* is reinforced by the fact that a large group of words in the lexical field related to magic employ it: *myth*, *music*, *meditation*, *magic*, *mysticism*, *dream*, *imagination*, the *mantic*, the *numinous* (indeed, something of the incantatory power attaching to the words *phenomenon* and *phenomenological* indicate their affinity to this phonaesthetic cluster, despite the fact that the phenomenon is the opposite of the noumenon). It is perhaps the prominence of the *m*-sounds in Coleridge's 'five miles meandering with a mazy motion' in 'Kubla Khan' that makes this line seem mimetic, the suggestion perhaps being that mazes and maziness that are confusing to the eye have a stupefying effect.[11]

M words are also prominent in mathematical language, and are implicated in various kinds of measure of quantity, dimension and number (*much*, *more*, *most*, *miles*, *millions* and *millimetres*). Perhaps gratified by the echo of her own name, Margaret Magnus writes that '/m/ is the phoneme of Maya, of that which can be measured. What is 'major', 'minor' and in the 'middle' are all /m/'.[12] Yet, for that reason, they can also be adapted to connote the amplified and the immeasurable, the immortal, the immemorial, the mighty and the majestic, and so, boomingly, on. Freud called magical thinking 'omnipotence of thoughts', for the belief in magic is a belief in the magical power of thinking to make the world conform to it.[13] But magical thinking is also often characterized by its conviction, or at least assertion, of the limits to thought, along with the irrational curtailing of the powers of reason, and the deliberate projection of mysterious powers or realities that lie beyond it: if you cannot know what you cannot know, you can still relish the delicious assurance that you cannot know it. Words that rumour of the numinous and the mysterious are often the carriers of this thought that assiduously keeps itself at a distance from itself, while remaining serenely confident nevertheless of its power to take the measure of the immeasurable, imagine the fact of unimaginability, name the unnameable. Magical thinking operates in the mode of amplified murmur, of assertion without articulation, of mime and intimation, lullabied by the slumberous humming of these nasals.

William James uses *m*-sounds at a crucial and memorable moment in his discussion of the nature of discrimination in perception. James argues that discrimination requires a conscious act, such that we can easily relapse from learned discrimination into non-discrimination: 'Such anæsthetics as chloroform, nitrous oxide, etc., sometimes bring about transient lapses even more total, in which numerical discrimination especially seems gone; for one sees light and hears sound, but whether one or many lights and sounds is quite impossible to tell.'[14] James sees such innumerate fusion as a primitive condition to which there is always a tendency to return: 'The law is that all things fuse that *can* fuse, and nothing separates except what must.'[15] James's famous example of this confusion of sensation is the baby who, 'assailed by eyes, ears, nose, skin, and entrails at once, feels it all as one great blooming, buzzing confusion'.[16] Swayed by the sonorous jam that James makes of the baby's sensation, the phrase has often been misheard, or perhaps improved, as 'booming, buzzing confusion'. It may lie behind Forster's rendering of the terrifying 'ou-boom' to which everything is reduced in the resonant, mouth-like space of the Marabar Caves in *A Passage to India*,

> The echo in a Marabar cave is entirely devoid of distinction. Whatever is said, the same monotonous noise replies, and quivers up and down the walls until it is absorbed into the roof 'Boum' is the sound as far as the human alphabet can express it, or 'bou-oum', or 'ou-boum' – utterly dull. Hope, politeness, the blowing of a nose, the squeak of a boot, all produce 'boum'. Even the striking of a match starts a little worm coiling, which is too small to complete a circle but is eternally watchful. And if several people talk at once, an overlapping howling noise begins, echoes generate echoes, and the cave is stuffed with a snake composed of small snakes, which writhe independently.[17]

James's boom may also reverberate through the humiliating misprint whereby Leopold Bloom is rendered as 'L. Boom' in the newspaper report of the funeral he attends in *Ulysses*, turning him from accredited presence to the mere noise of rumour.[18]

In this sense, the *um* is another diagram of the mouth as such, abstracted to its twin actions of opening and closing. The noises of the voice are the voice of the vocal apparatus itself heard in parallel and in excess to the voice. Where the voice seeks to shape the mouth and the speaking voice in accord with meaning, these noises seek to pull the meaning back into the shape of the speaking apparatus, to draw the whole round world into the hollow O of the mouth. And the most mouthy sound of all is the one that seems to draw everything back into the mouth, the *m*.

The *m* has a cardinal place also in Kabbalistic meditations on the magical powers of sound and script. The *Sefer Yesira*, or *Book of Making*, one of the earliest formulations of Kabbalistic word-magic, makes *mem* one of the three principal letters, standing for water and earth, while *alef* stands for air, and *shin* for fire. Section 36 explains that:

> There was formed with Alef: spirit, air, humidity, the chest, law, and the tongue (or language). There was formed with Mem: earth, cold, the belly, and the scale of acquittal. here was formed with Shin: heaven, heat, the head, and the scale of guilt.[19]

The most developed, not to say demented, Kabbalistic reading of the mystical properties of the elements of speech and script is probably that undertaken by Francis Mercury Van Helmont in his *Alphabet of Nature* (*Alphabeti vere naturalis hebraici brevissima delineatio*) of 1667. Van Helmont sought to show that the characters of the Hebrew alphabet were actually gestural diagrams of the actions of the mouth performed in sounding them. The M sound has a particular importance for Van Helmont. He wrote his *Alphabet of Nature* in the form of a discourse between 'H' and 'M', which may be regarded as standing for the two syllables of his surname. H asks the questions, while M provides the authoritative answers and explications. Van Helmont gives mystical phonologies for both of these letters. The Hebrew *He*, corresponding to English *h*, is described as 'an aspirated guttural, made from air, which reveals its energy through exhalation'.[20] He goes on to suggest that

> A certain mystical meaning concerning generation seems to be hidden in this letter, for all animals produce this sound when panting from the heat of lust. And for this reason it is probable that a *He*, but no other letters, was added to the names of Abraham and Sarah because many people were descended from them.[21]

Where *He* stands for fertile openness, *Mem* signifies a closing together:

> M. *Mem* is a mute labial. Its sound consists of a hollow, interior, and enclosed murmur and is easily recognised by the common letter M. The tongue touches the palate lightly and the lips kiss each other lightly . . . [I]f anyone wishes to look more closely at its mystical meaning, especially for the final *Mem*, when the mouth is filled with air and living seed, as it were, one can easily note a certain analogy: for through this letter every kind of multiplication and plurality is indicated. Then, the figure closes like a pregnant mother, who encloses her propagating power firmly within her womb.[22]

Van Helmont repeated and elaborated these readings in his unfolding of the significance of the letters of Aelohim in his *Thoughts on Genesis* (1697):

> As for *He*, it is, and denotes *Respiration*, *Breath*, *Life*, *Vegetation* or *Growth*, *Fruitfulness*, the *Air* and *Heavenly Influence*, and therefore was vouchsafed to *Abram* and his Wife *Sarai* . . . so that from henceforth he was no more to be called *Abram*, but *Abraham*, and she no longer *Sarai*, but *Sarah*; and according to what is there added, this Change was to signifie to him, that God had *appointed him to be the Father of many Nations*. Whence it appears, that O, H hold forth to us a sublime exalted *Life*, *Fruitfulness* and *Vegetation* or *Growth* . . . on the

> other hand, M denotes a *Mother*, the *Womb*, and the Multiplicity of Births: for by its comprest and stifled Sound, from a shut Mouth (as appears in the pronouncing of this Letter) the Conception of Births is plainly presented to us.[23]

So *he* and *mem* embody the two principles that recur through Van Helmont's reading of the Hebrew characters, those of opening and closing, or seminal force and form. He saw speech as generative in a literal sense, believing it to be suffused with the fertilizing powers of air and semen: 'our voice depends significantly on our reproductive power, and . . . this reproductive power comes from nothing but the semen.' Semen expresses itself in a radiating force or force of emanation: M. says that 'every man radiates from himself his entire vital power without stop . . . ideas flow forth . . . from a man, either through his voice or through the emanations of his entire body.'[24] One proof Van Helmont offered of the link between seminal force and the voice was the difficulty that sexually immature boys have in pronouncing the Hebrew letter *Resh* (R): 'if a young boy is compelled to pronounce the letter R, we often see him grow pale and sick. For this letter completely depends on the perfected power of the semen, for which reason eunuchs cannot fully express it.' He even thought that there was a special spiritual force contained in and expressed through the hair.[25]

For Van Helmont, who believed that 'the articulation of the right names will summon up understanding of the essential natures of things', Hebrew was the root of, and route back to, clarity and unobstructed primal force in language.[26] He prefaced his *Alphabet of Nature* with a Latin poem, which affirms that 'Hic Linguae motus proprio sub nomine surgunt/ . . . Natura haec CLARO nos jubet ORE loqui' (Here the motions of the tongue emerge with the names that belong to them . . . Nature orders us to speak about these things with a clear mouth).[27] The 'clear mouth' – '*helle Mund*' in German, in which language *The Alphabet of Nature* was also published – slyly alludes to Van Helmont's own surname. And yet, Van Helmont was less than confident about his ability to reconstitute the generative power of Hebrew, writing that 'My own tongue becomes speechless [*obmutescere*] in the presence of that Queen of all languages, and I am deeply ashamed to reveal publicly my inadequacy in this sort of discourse. For this language is not simply human like every other language in the world but divine and celestial.' Later on, M. admits 'I labor under the infirmity of those who stutter [*balbutientium*] and . . . a great number of things rush into my mouth at the same time, so that everything appears to burst out in one breath without order.'[28] This seems the very opposite of the clear mouth that the speaking of Hebrew seems to promise.

But if the *m* sound signifies a kind of elementary closing together into form, it is also strongly associated in English and related languages with indistinctness. A single *m* closes off and gives definition; a doubled or multiplied *m* signifies a loss of definition, and oscular oscillation. To mumble means both to utter words in a jumbled fashion and also to chew ineffectually, as though with toothless gums. Not only are one's words indistinct when one mumbles, but the distinction between eating and speaking is also blurred, mumbling being a kind of speech in which one imperfectly eats one's words as they are uttered, like the men whom Bloom hears in the restaurant in *Ulysses*: 'I munched hum un thu Unchster Bunk un Munchday.'[29] The result of mumbling is a kind of mash or mess, itself without definition. Joyce tried to evoke the woozily sentimental quality of Gerty MacDowell's interior style in the 'Nausicaa' chapter of *Ulysses* by calling it a 'namby-pamby jammy, marmalady drawersy . . . style with effects of incense, mariolatry, masturbation'.[30] A similar observation about the associations of *m* was made by John Wallis in his *Grammatica linguae anglicanae* (1653). Having observed that words like *jingle*, *tingle*, *tinkle*, *mingle*, *sprinkle* and *twinkle* indicate the idea of fluctuating faint movements, Wallis says that the 'obscure and obtuse' vowel u and the crowding of consonants in the *-mble* of words like *mumble*, *grumble*, *jumble*, *tumble*, *stumble*, *rumble*, *crumble* and *fumble* 'gives the sense of a confused convolution' [*confusam quasi convolutationem innuunt consonarum congeries mbl*].[31] As Margaret Magnus says, fancifully as usual, but, as usual, suggestively too, 'The texture of M is overwhelmingly mushy. M can also unmake; it can mangle, mash, massacre. Or it can mix things together to create something new.'[32] It is the mouth that is the most regular exponent of this action of mulling, moiling and mashing, and it is not surprising that the lexicons of slang and cant have multiplied bilabials in the figuring of the mouth. These include *mummer*, the mouth, *muns*, the face, or mouth, *mums*, the lips, *mongee*, food and *mungarly*, bread, with *mungarly casa*, a baker's shop, *muff*, vulva and *muff-diver*, cunnilingist, *mumping*, begging, and *mumper* or *mumbler*, someone who feigns indigence for gain.[33]

The mumble represents the ellipsis or eclipse of the teeth, those makers of hard and fast distinctions. To mumble is not to tear but to soak, not to bite but to chew and suck. In Bloom's memory of a love-token passed between himself and Molly Bloom, mumbling attains an erotic charge:

> Ravished over her I lay, full lips full open, kissed her mouth. Yum. Softly she gave me in my mouth the seedcake warm and chewed. Mawkish pulp her mouth had mumbled sweetsour of her spittle. Joy: I ate it: joy. Young life, her lips that gave me pouting. Soft warm sticky gumjelly lips.[34]

Later on in *Ulysses*, in the 'Circe' chapter in which so many inanimate objects and ideas are made into ventriloquial dummies, Bloom's kisses are themselves given gooey, dreamy words to mouth: 'THE KISSES: (*warbling*) Leo! (*twittering*) Icky licky micky sticky for Leo! (*cooing*) Coo coocoo! Yummyyum, Womwom! (*warbling*) Big comebig!'[35]

The labial exchanges within and across Bloom's erotic memory and the onomatopoeic kisses themselves meet and mingle with the scene in which Stephen attempts to bring about a magical exchange between oratory and osculation, miming in air the words that are meant to summon up the act of kissing, and making it hard for the reader not to feel his and her mouth being sucked into the air-kiss:

> He comes, pale vampire, through storm his eyes, his bat sails bloodying the sea, mouth to her mouth's kiss.
>
> Here. Put a pin in that chap, will you? My tablets. Mouth to her kiss. No. Must be two of em. Glue em well. Mouth to her mouth's kiss.

> His lips lipped and mouthed fleshless lips of air: mouth to her moomb. Oomb, allwombing tomb. His mouth moulded issuing breath, unspeeched: ooeeehah.[36]

Other writers have been drawn to the strong implication of the lips produced by m sounds. Dylan Thomas's 'The Force That Through the Green Fuse Drives the Flower' mimes different kinds of mouths at work in speaking, sucking, leaching and finally, devouring. There is a force that 'dries the mouthing streams'; the speaker is 'dumb to mouth' to his veins that 'the same mouth sucks' as sucks at a mountain stream and is equally 'dumb to tell' (unable to tell, or dumb in order to indicate dumbly) how 'the same crooked worm' (tongue, finger, pen, penis) is at work in his writing.[37] Joyce's 'allwombing tomb', the equivalence of life and death, is carried through the poem's humming labials. To be 'dumb to tell' implies both that the speaker is unable to tell, and therefore dumb, and also that being dumb might itself be a kind of telling, mutism being assimilated to utterance.

A word like *murmur*, the internal doubling of which seems to mime the kiss-like compression of the two lips on each other, has often suggested something of this opulence in interchange. Charles Nodier thought that the word *murmure* was a perfect example of onomatopoeia, that was shared across all the Romance languages, though he found the French pronunciation of the word more subtly liquid than that of other languages, in accordance with the principle that everybody finds their own language more richly onomatopoeic than anybody else's. The reduplicated *m*-sounds of murmur 'perfectly depict for the ear the gentle, confused sound of a brook tumbling in tiny ripples over pebbles, or foliage gently rocked by the breeze to which it tremulously yields. The vague, almost imperceptible movement of waters and woods stirs in solitude a rumour that scarcely interrupts the silence, so delicate and exquisite is it.'[38] The fact that the Phoenician character from which the *m* derives not only meant water, but figured its ripples in its form, no doubt helps confirm these voluptuously undulant associations.

But bilabial nasals do not always have the dreamy richness of Keats's 'murmurous haunt of flies on summer eves'.[39] They can also connote the secret or the sinister, as in Fritz Lang's *M* (subtitled *Eine Stadt sucht einen Mörder*), in which murder and murmuring are twinned, or in the ominous fact of a 'heart murmur', a usage that recalls the conspiratorial early uses of the word in English, in which to *murmur* was often used in the sense of to complain or to whisper against.

Erotic mingling is often also presented as a mangling or marring. The articulation that makes nothing articulate, but simply turns and churns on itself, is often associated with the meaningless mutterings of religious ritual. In Protestant England, *mumbling* became a preferred term for the Latin incantations of priests, suggesting, like *pattering*, as we will see in chapter Seven, the idleness of mechanical formulae uttered without belief or conviction – 'Mumblying up a certayn nombur of wordys no thyng understonde'.[40] The term *mumbo-jumbo* may well derive from *maamajomboo*, a masked dancer, and also has reference to a god or spirit said to have been worshipped by West African peoples, but it has quickly come to refer to the meaningless or empty utterances associated with superstitious reverence. In the eighteenth-century anti-Catholic poem *Mumbo-Chumbo*, the figure has become an embodiment of terrifying oral menace, standing for the preachers who terrify credulous women with their talk of hellfire and damnation, and swallow up the young lives who are sacrificed to them:

> But oh! what Shrieks! what horrid doleful Cries!
> As this dread Image still approached near,
> With hollow bellowing Sounds, infernal Noise!
> That the rude Herd almost distract with Fear:
>
> They beat their Breasts, they teare their 'shevilled Hair,
> With agonizing Grief, tormented sore;
> To MUMBO CHUMBO loud they make their Prayer,
> And with sad Plaints his Fury do deplore.
> But th'Idol stern, inexorable, wild,
> Spreading its brawny Arms, and crooked Claws,
> Seems as it would devour each Mother's Child,
> And all englut them in its rav'nous Jaws.[41]

There is little of the mumbling magic of the priest here, and the poem's title-page illustration suggests that the breath of the creature issues in a mephitic blast rather than displaying the deceitful secretiveness of the magical incantation. But behind the figure are seen the menacing silhouettes of its puppet-masters, one of them making the sign of the cross, whose utterance is much less manifest. In the end, though, the horror of the idol is diminished to mere humming clamour, which is all show (he stands on a wheeled trolley, which emphasizes the fact that he is being operated by the shadowy figures behind):

> Then when they mount the Pulpit's high Ascent
> Thundering Damnation in the stounded Ear,
> Their Voices hoarse, with Clamour almost rent,
> Striving to harrow up your Souls with Fear . . .
>
> Still let them rave, and their loud Throats uprear
> As if the Walls they'd crack, and split the Doors:
> Be not dismay'd, nor ought give Way to Fear;
> Only think this – *That* MUMBO-CHUMBO *roars*.[42]

The monster who is at once ravening and ridiculous is kin to Lewis Carroll's Jabberwock, that has the jagged threat of jabbering talk, though the actual sound of its approach reveals how much of a stage dragon it is, tricked up out of myths and stories – 'The Jabberwock, with eyes of flame,/Came whiffling through the tulgey wood,/And burbled as it came!'.[43]

Murmuring, muttering and mumbling involve a kind of maceration or mastication of one's own words, which may then seem to form an imaginary speech-stuff, a colourless, tasteless but slightly glutinous blancmange, which it is tempting to identify with the 'sweet-tasting, white, and viscous phlegm' that Van Helmont believed was necessary for the production of all speech and that if diminished weakened the body and voice alike (*Alphabet*, 83). Van Helmont enlarged upon this idea that there is a kind of seminal pabulum necessary for all speech in his *Paradoxal Discourses*:

> It's known by experience, that when some strong men in a fiery driving earnestness, by long and intense speaking about weighty matters, have tired themselves, so that their Voice hath grown low, and their Speech at last quite failed them: which in some hath been known to continue for three weeks together, and afterwards upon the return of their Speech, they have been sensible of a sweet slimy matter which came in their Throat, of the same taste and smell with Wheat-flower and water mingled together (which in the Great World is the true Seed of the Earth) and of much the same scent as the Seed of Man hath; and that when they have chanced (with a light coughing) to spit out this sweet slimy matter (which comes into the Throat both from above and from beneath) before it was fully perfected and united, they have again totally lost their Speech, and become dumb, until a like slimy matter hath afresh been gathered again.[44]

This imaginary uttering-magma, half-matter, half-mutter, may be embodied in the interesting fortunes of the word *mummy*, which has deathly as well as maternal associations. The common use of the word mummy to refer to an embalmed corpse derives from a word used in medieval Europe for a tarry substance, perhaps bitumen or what was called *pissasphalt* or *earth pitch*, which was either used in the process of embalming, or was believed to be exuded by or extractable from such bodies. There seems to be a curious glide of logic here: where the mummy derived from the ground flesh of corpses was perhaps originally held to be valuable because of the precious embalming agents that had been used in preserving the corpse, it came to be thought of as embodying a kind of healing spirit that inhered in the dead flesh itself, following the common pattern of value-inversion to be found in much magico-medical thinking, in which the nastier the medicine the more sovereign its virtue. Joseph Blagrave's *Astrological Practice of Physick* (1671) followed Paracelsus in suggesting that the ideal composition for the infamous 'weapon-salve', said to be capable of curing all wounds, should include two ounces of moss from a dead man's skull, two ounces of 'man's grease' and half an ounce of mummy.[45] It also offered instructions

'How by the Magnet of ones Body to extract a Spiritual Mummy whereby to cure most Diseases incident unto the body of Man', which consisted of taking one's own dried excrement and applying it to one's body in order to replace the spiritual essence exuded in one's sweat.[46] The word *mummy* as a contraction of *mama* is thought by the OED not to appear until the early eighteenth century, but the insulting association between desiccated corpses and ladies who have outlived the bloom of their moister years is apparent in a poem like Robert Herrick's 'Upon a Bleare-ey'd Woman': 'Wither'd with yeeres, and bed-rid Mumma lyes; Dry-rosted all, but raw yet in her eyes'.[47]

The word *mummy* gradually underwent a decline in dignity. Probably because of the process of pulverization or emulsification that produced mummy-like substance, *mummy* came to signify, no longer a precious essence capable both of preserving and of redeeming the body, but a baser kind of stuff, a mere pap or paste, or living flesh regarded in this unflattering light. The passage from precious to contemptible in the status of the word *mummy* was no doubt accelerated by the growing suspicion of medical charlatanry during the seventeenth century, as found for example in an anonymous squib of 1676 entitled *The Character of a Quack Doctor*:

> I cured *Prester Johns* Godmother of a Stupendious Dolor about the *Os Sacrum* . . . by Fomenting her Posteriors with the Mummy of nature, otherwise called Pilgrim Salve, and the spirit of Mugwort Terragraphocated through a Limbeck of Chrystalline transfluences.[48]

Violent characters in seventeenth-century fiction and drama might threaten to beat, or thrash others 'to mummy'. Complaining, in *The Merry Wives of Windsor*, of being ducked in the Thames, Falstaff reflects on the increase in his already substantial mass that the immersion might have effected: 'the water swells a man – and what a thing should I have been, when I had been swelled? I should have been a mountain of mummy!' (III.v) Charles Goodall's vengeful 'An Epitaph on Old Oliver' about Oliver Cromwell asks the earth to lie light 'on Noll's *soft* Noddle;/His *Corps* in *Putrefaction* coddle', in order 'That

Dogs may lay his *Carcase* bare,/And *Messes* of his *Mummy* tear'.[49] The insult levelled by Mr Oldwit against his vain, elderly wife in Thomas Shadwell's *Bury Fair* (1689) runs together the meanings of a desiccated corpse and a sort of substitute flesh-filler: 'you, for your part, are fain to fill up the Chinks in your rivell'd Skin, as House-painters do the Cracks in Wainscot, with Putty. Pox on 't, you wou'd by Art appear a Beauty, and are by Nature a meer Mummy.'[50] The insult that closes John Donne's 'Loves Alchymie' depends upon the traditional unwillingness of men to believe that women have souls: 'Hope not for mind in women; at their best/Sweetnesse and wit, they are but Mummy, possest'.[51]

Nozy

When one hems and hums, mutters, mumbles and mammers, it may seem to muffle utterance. When the lips close, sound can escape only through the nose. Nasality has a poor reputation among speakers of English; voice and singing coaches see nasality as something to be diminished or eliminated in the interests of fullness and clarity of vocal tone. One of these avers that

> Genuine resonance can only be achieved when the technique is open-throated and free of interfering tension, never by 'placing' the tone 'forward' or into the nasal passages . . . Without exception [nasality] is associated with throat constriction, and the proportion of nasality always corresponds exactly to the degree of constriction present in the tone.[52]

One who speaks through the nose may be regarded as snooty, censorious, small-minded, nit-picking, whining, cowardly and treacherous, or, in another field of meanings, dull and doltishly adenoidal – Coleridge writes that a government agent overhearing him discussing Spinoza with Wordsworth thought he heard the name 'Spy Nozy'.[53] The fact that English is less provided with nasal sounds than other European languages, and markedly less so than French, the traditional cultural antagonist of the English, means that nasality comes also to stand for the disgusting corporeality the

English found in the French, which is only a slightly more polished form of gutturality. Indeed, with the lips sealed, there is a close, backstairs communication between throat and nose – one may as readily grunt and snarl through the nose as hum.

Nasality is also, for eighteenth-century etymologists, strongly associated with negativity; according to Charles de Brosses, this is the proof that sound-meanings 'are not the effect of a voluntary or reasoned choice, but the consquence of a secret analogy, resulting from the physics of the mechanism of speech'.[54] A decade or so later, Antoine Court de Gébelin offered a clearer, if no more convincing explanation of the link between nasality and negation. Nasality, he writes, signifies preeminently the ideas of rejection, refusal and denial 'because in the language of gesture and in imitative language, one closes one's mouth and pushes the air out forcefully through the nose when one does not wish to accept something and wishes by contrast to put something displeasing at a distance'.[55] It is this that accounts for the remarkable fact, Gébelin claims, that the letter *n* gives rise to no onomatopoiea – 'it is, in fact by its nature absolutely proper to humans.'[56] Oddly, and despite the fact that *m* and *n* are so closely associated (along with their similarity of sound, they are often paired, in words like *autumn* and *mnemonic*, for instance, and are adjacent letters in many alphabets derived from Phoenician script), this puts the associations of *n* in stark contrast to those of *m*, of which Gébelin writes that:

> its pronunciation is so gentle, so mobile, so easy, that it has become the name of mobility and that of the first object which we meet in infancy, the tenderest and most precious, and that to which we owe everything: the name of the MOTHER who brought us into the world and whose breast provides for us nourishment that is so abundant and as healthy-giving as it is agreeable.[57]

Nor is it just European cultures who hear the nasal as negative. Nasality is associated with death and the uncanny in a number of other cultures. The Dogon people of West Africa associate the nasal voice with mortality and putrescence, seeing it as matter that has been unnaturally trapped in the nasal passages rather than having free and natural issue through the mouth.[58] A. W. Howitt reported a similar association between nasality and death among indigenous Australians of the Brabra clan:

> At another séance by Mūndauin [a medicine man of the Brabra clan] the ghosts said finally, speaking in hollow muffled voices, which my informant imitated by holding his nose when speaking, 'We must now go home, or the west wind will blow us out to sea.'[59]

Folk-understandings of speech are never more mistaken than when hearing or attributing nasality. For what one hears as a 'nasal voice' is in fact one in which sound has been prevented from resonating in the nasal passages, for example by inflammation, the effect typically being to condense nasals into punctual plosives and dentals, so that *mother* becomes *buther* and *don't* becomes *doad*. So speaking through your nose is actually, as Charles de Brosses observes, an 'antiphrasis', since somebody without a nose would actually sound as though they were speaking through their absent organ.[60] Far from debasing and diminishing speech, the nose is its ideal acoustic silhouette, giving speech its depth, subtlety and tonus – de Brosses thought that the nasals were particularly 'fitting for lyric poetry', a judgement an English critic is unlikely to have made.[61] The nasals are inherently ambiguous, acting both as obstruents (blocking the air), and as sonorants (releasing it enriched). If the lungs are the loudspeaker of speech, the nose is its tuning-dial. You need unblocked nasal passages to say the word 'tune', which otherwise gets chewed up into 'chood', a fact exploited by the advertisement for the menthol sweet which traded on the performative promise that 'Tunes help you breathe more easily.'

For this reason, the phonoplasm of the *m* that offers itself to the material imagination as a mangled, jumbled substance can also be conceived as magically metamorphic. It is hard to mark a limit to the range of meanings that are capable of being conveyed wordlessly, or through the range of imaginary quasi-words provided by it – um, hum, hmm, ahem. Indeed, it is very hard to think of any expression of attitude for which there is not a corresponding nasal. The different varieties of nasal hum easily allow for the expression of entreaty, assent, accusation, reflection, excitement, amusement, enjoyment, disgust, derision and many others beside. The polymorphousness and omnicompetence of nasal sound means that it approaches the condition of a universal, though nonlexical, language that operates entirely through the modulations of pitch and intensity, rather than through the production of distinct phonemic elements. It is a kind of semaphore or audible dumbshow in the voice, a symphony performed on a two-holed nose-flute. In one sense a kind of shadow or semblance of the voice, in another it is something like an ur-voice, a pure, continuously variable tone, as though voice had been sublimated by being relieved of speech.

Humming

It is said that human beings are named from the humus, the ground, but their name might just as well derive from the practice of humming that is almost universal among them. Just as the nasal hum represents a kind of linguistic stem-sound, which can be used to express almost any kind of feeling, so, when employed musically, it can be seen as a kind of all-purpose instrument, that can be used to play any melody.

What is distinctive about the hum is its indistinctness and lack of clear location. The effect and function of the hum seems to be to spread out and to make uniform, smoothing out the jagged spikes of particularity. This is why humming, the ideal form or apotheosis of the bilabial nasal, seems to come from everywhere, and perhaps why certain Protestants, so wedded to the ideal of bearing witness and face-to-face testimony, found the hooded, impersonal mutters and murmurs of Catholic ritual so unnerving and objectionable. Humming is also associated with insects and machinery, and, in both cases, the hum seems to have a general rather than particular source, where it is possible to determine it at all. The mechanism of humming or buzzing in insects has for centuries been regarded as enigmatic, with different observers attributing the production of the sound to different parts of the insect's body, mouth, legs, wings, abdomen. The association of humming with insects is of a piece with their characteristic lack of faciality – insects have heads and mouth-parts, but not *faces*, exactly. Humming in humans seems similarly displaced, not just from the mouth into the nose, but into the chest, throat and skull, all of which appear to resonate more energetically during humming. Because one not only can, but must hum with closed lips, it is always a species of ventriloquism, or thrown voice, that comes from everywhere and nowhere. More than an undertone, it is also overtone, paratone, epitone.

The hum, like the whisper, or, as we will see, the buzz, seems expressive, but impersonal. Humming is a background rather than foreground phenomenon. We hum distractedly and as accompaniment rather than with full and conscious intent, humming typically being something we do when pleasurably absorbed in something else. Like chewing, humming might be thought of as a way of tuning us in to different kinds of activity. It certainly seemed to be for the pianist Glenn Gould, who not only liked to practise with a hoover going in the background, perhaps because it forced him to bring more attention than usual to the sound he was trying to produce, but also hummed along compulsively to his own playing, which gave recording engineers great difficulty. The preposition 'along' that is so often twinned with humming indicates its distinctive role as accompaniment, Sean Malone, who has studied Gould's humming, concludes that, rather than humming along, he seems to have hummed 'an independent contrapuntal part'. Malone maintains that:

> Gould was not only aware of the surface material, that is, the notes themselves, but was also aware of a larger framework of background structure manifested in the independent lines of his humming. Gould may have visualized a large-scale, amodal image of the composition's structure – an abstract conception of themes, climaxes, and form, etc. – transcending the tactile and physical requirements of performing the piece.[62]

This would certainly accord with the thickly mixed textures of Gould's radio documentaries, such as *The Idea of North*, which merges and mingles voices, at some points without allowing any one of them to be clearly audible over the others, and indeed employs the drumming of a railway carriage as a unifying underdrone.

Exposure to mechanical hum has become an almost universal experience for modern human beings, especially those living in urban circumstances and surrounded by machines employing fans and other rotary devices that tend to produce steady drones or buzzes. Murray Schafer even went as far in his *Tuning of the World* as to identify the frequency of this urban *om*, noting that when, during meditation exercises, American students were asked to sing the tone of 'prime unity', they were most likely to sing B natural, which he claims is that of the frequency of 60 hertz that can be heard 'in the operation of all electrical devices from lights and amplifiers to generators'.[63] Schafer claims that in the UK, where AC current alternates at 50 hertz, students naturally hum the tone of 'primal unity' as G sharp (415.3 hertz).[64] More intriguing still, he suggests that the revived interest in modal forms of music, which tend, as, for example, in Indian music, to be stabilized by continuous drones, may be accounted for by the particular kind of listening, which tries 'to relate all sounds to one sound that is continuously sounding', that is prompted or corroborated by the ambient hum of the mechanized world.[65]

The grounding function of such sounds may be borne out by the fact that we notice them much more when they stop than when they are in operation, The glorious relief that we feel when suddenly the air-conditioning or the fridge or the thrum of some other continuous, automatic process suddenly gives way to silence is evidence of how far such humming background noises reach into our attention, and how much fatiguing work they require to keep them from penetrating through to awareness. It is scarcely surprising that such sounds should be so good for lulling infants to sleep, and can sometimes provide effective relief for sufferers from tinnitus, by masking or drowning the noises in their heads. Indeed, the nasal hum may be regarded as the background noise of all speech, a background which becomes the foreground when we hear large numbers of voices simultaneously, and in which the jags of particularity are rounded up into what we call a hum of conversation. The word *humdrum* implies a low, monotonous kind of noise, without distinction or variation, which is opposed to articulate speech. Joseph Addison wrote in 1711 that

> The *Hum-Drum* Club, of which I was formerly an unworthy Member, was made up of very honest Gentlemen, of peacable Dispositions, that used to sit together, smoak their Pipes, and say nothing 'till Mid-night. The *Mum* Club (as I am informed) is an Institution of the same Nature, and as great an Enemy to Noise.[66]

Another important ambivalence of the hum is that it seems both agitated and static, a feature captured neatly in Shakespeare's 'From camp to camp through the foul womb of night/The hum of either army stilly sounds' in *Henry V* (IV.Prologue.4–5), a phrase I quoted in chapter Three to demonstrate its mobile sibilance. This may be related to the affective ambivalence of the hum, which, like the murmur, can be both soothing and alarming, depending on whether it is perceived as a continuous, suppporting background, or as sinisterly eroding or intruding on the foreground of sound. Thus 'venous hum', also known as 'nun's murmur', or '*bruit de diable*', is a sound of turbulence heard by an examining physician during ausculation of the veins of the chest or neck, which may also be heard by the subject.

Not surprisingly, the fact that humming often acts as a filler for songs the words of which are not known has attracted the attention of psychoanalysts, who tend to interpret it as a deliberate suppression or avoidance of compromising words or ideas, and therefore the expression of unresolved psychological conflict.[67] Perhaps there are circumstances in which the hum can indeed function symbolically as a saying which is simultaneously an unsaying, but this seems to formalize an action that seems considerably more various in its purposes and functions. The hum might better be regarded as the articulation of the nasality that otherwise lies hidden beneath and within all articulation, as its binding and enlivening principle. The hum is the the melodic inner lining of all speech, a song that never quite bursts into song, nor ever fully differentiates individual melodies (which all sound much of a muchness when they are hummed), but is rather the song of songs, the average and aggregation of all the tunes that lie latent within the voice.

Bull-roarer

A number of musical instruments try to imitate the diffusive effects of the hum, though perhaps there is a certain resistance to the idea of music, as formally articulated sounds, in every form of humming noise. The instrument or sonorous object that meets these conditions most obviously is the bell, which, especially at lower frequencies, is densely populated by undertones and overtones that can distort and even inundate the principal tone in a wash of harmonics. This may have a great deal to do with the sacredness of bells, as it does of other instruments that make such diffuse kinds of noise. Of these, one of the most widespread is known as the 'bull-roarer'.

The bull-roarer is a simple instrument, usually consisting of a slat of wood on a string which can be whirled around the head, creating a low, pulsing, humming drone. This object, which is found in many different parts of the world and was well known in Europe as a child's plaything, was a source of deep fascination to European anthropologists in the second half of the nineteenth century. E. B. Tylor described it in a letter of 1880 as 'one of the enigmas of ethnology', while for A. C. Haddon, writing in 1898, it was 'the most ancient, widely-spread and sacred religious symbol in the world'.[68]

The growling hum of the bull-roarer may seem to intimate the terror not just of imminent assimilation, but the more diffuse menace of earthquake or volcanic eruption conveyed by low-frequency humming sounds, the characteristic of which is that, coming from all directions at once, they seem to surround the hearer. Andrew Lang surmises that 'the windy roaring noise made by the bull-roarer might readily be considered by savages either as an invitation to a god who should present himself in storm, or as a proof of his being at hand.'[69] He would have been encouraged in this interpretation by reading about the South African verion of the bull-roarer, known as the *nodiwu*, in the writings of George Theal, who notes that 'there is a kind of superstition connected with the nodiwu, that playing with it invites a gale of wind. Men will, on this account, often prevent boys from using it when they desire calm weather for any purpose.'[70] J. G. Frazer emphasizes the sympathetic magic involved in swinging the bull-roarer, suggesting that 'by making a noise like thunder with the help of bull-roarers they probably hope, on the principle of imitative magic, to bring on a thunder-storm and with it a fertilizing deluge of rain.'[71] The 'deep whirring noise' made by the twirling of a sounding slat which Frank Cushing records in his account of a procession in around 1880 of the Zuni people of New Mexico to their 'mountain of Thunder', during the season in which fire is particularly honoured, seems to evidence a similar kind of sonorous premonition.[72]

When humans produce such sounds and, even more, when they produce them from their own mouths, they seem to put themselves reassuringly outside the kind of sound that is ordinarily diffusely exterior to them. The ambivalent place of the hum with regard to the mouth – it may be called 'paravocalic' since it seems to come from the vicinity of the mouth but not directly from it – is probably important in enacting this ambivalence. The import of the hum is that it is a sound that does not quite or wholly inhabit the mouth, yet at the same time, never quite quits it either. The hum is emitted rather than uttered, as though from the whole body of the creature making the noise, and in all directions, rather than from the heart, or soul, or whatever else the punctual source of vocal sounds is thought to be. The hum seems to have no direction, development or position; it seems to be everywhere at once and all at once. Because it does not obviously come from a verifiable source in a singular mouth, and because it is not a sound that comes wholly or exactly from the mouth, the hum may be thought of as itself a kind of open, yet enclosing cavity, as itself, in other words, a kind of mouth. There are mouths that give rise to sounds; but there are also, as here, sounds that give rise to the idea of a mouth.

The word *hum* is not intended to convey precisely the sound involved in the bull-roarer. Indeed, the sound has also been called a roaring, rushing, whirring, whizzing, droning or drumming. Lorimer Fison and A. W. Howitt wrote in 1880 of the Australian 'turndun' (another name for the bull-roarer) that, 'when whirled round, or whisked backwards and forwards, it makes a peculiar and slightly humming noise, which also approximates to the sound of the word "whew."'[73] Describing a performance on the bull-roarer at the Royal Institution, Andrew Lang wrote that it produced 'what may best be described as a mighty rushing noise, as if some supernatural being "fluttered and buzzed his wings with fearful roar".'[74] He had previously described the sound of the domestic version made by young country boys as 'a most horrible and unexampled din, which endears it to the very young but renders it detested by persons of mature age'.[75] A.S.F. Gow says that the instrument 'emits a muttering roar which rises in pitch as the speed is increased'.[76] J. G. Frazer identifies the 'screeching noise' made by Canadian indigenous peoples as emanating from a bull-roarer, which he says is made 'so as to produce a droning or screaming note according to the speed of revolution'.[77] The versions of the instrument made and used in Britain had a variety of different names suggesting the different ways in which the sound they made was heard: it was also known as a 'hummer', a 'humming buzzer', a 'swish' and a 'bummer'.[78] Humming is an approximation, a lexicalized onomatopoeia, rendering a sound the characteristic of which is to hover and shimmer around articulation. The kinds of sounds that the bull-roarer may seem to imitate are themselves approximations to words, in the quasi-utterance of the animal's growl or the as-if vocality of the wind. And yet, that approximation is the very thing that the hum enacts – only in the imitated, there is an approximation to the word, while in the imitating word, there is approximation to or hovering round the sound (which is itself an approximating shimmer across several different possible words). The hum approximates to this approximation.

The most conspicuous and consistent feature of the use of the bull-roarer is in forms of initiation ceremony and rites of passage, most particularly that of adolescent boys into manhood. Of course, many other objects and actions are also involved in such rituals, but it may be possible to suggest some of the reasons why the kind of object the bull-roarer is and, more particularly, the kind of sound it produces might be particularly appropriate to such passages. Among many indigenous Australian peoples the bull-roarer was said to be the voice of a spirit who, at the time of initiation of young men, eats them up, and then disgorges them again, as adults.[79] Howitt reports that, more specifically, in one part of Queensland, 'the sound of the Bullroarer is said to be the noise made by the wizards in swallowing the boys and bringing them up again as young men.'[80] Baldwin Spencer and F. J. Gillen record that, among the Kaitish people of Northern Australia, the sound of the bull-roarer is thought to be

> the voice of Twanyirika, who is supposed by the Kaitish to live in a particular rock, and that when a youth is initiated he comes forth in the form of a spirit and takes the boy away into the bush. He is further supposed to hobble along carrying one leg over his shoulder. Both women and children believe that in some way Twanyirika kills the youth and later on brings him to life again during the period of initiation.[81]

Among the Kurnai, the voice is said to be that of Tundun (who gives his name to the bull-roarer itself), while, among southeastern coastal tribes, it is the voice of an ancestral spirit known as Daramulum.[82] Frazer describes a particularly vivid enactment of this process of eating and ejection in the formation of a ceremonial hut about 100 feet long:

> It is modelled in the shape of the mythical monster; at the end which represents his head it is high, and it tapers away at the other end. A betel-palm, grubbed up with the roots, stands for the backbone of the great being and its clustering fibres for his hair; and to complete the resemblance the butt end of the building is adorned by a native artist with a pair of goggle eyes and a gaping mouth. When after a tearful parting from their mothers and women folk, who believe or pretend to believe in the monster that swallows their dear ones, the awe-struck novices are brought face to face with this imposing structure, the huge creature emits a sullen growl, which is in fact no other than the humming note of bull-roarers swung by men concealed in the monster's belly.[83]

What Frazer describes as the enactment of the mystical 'deglutition', involves a man who takes a gulp of water and ejects it with a gurgling noise over the novice to signify his delivery from the belly of the monster.[84]

Many of the myths concerning bull-roarers, especially among Australian peoples, emphasize that they are a gift or legacy to mortals from the original created beings of the Dreamtime. The sound of the bull-roarer seems to suggest supernatural power or presence, perhaps because of the haunting, paravocal relationship it has to mortal speech. Noise has often been used both to summon the supernatural into human life and also to keep it at bay. The peculiarly pregnant noise of the hum seems well adapted to suggest some utterance that lies beneath or to the side of speech, the whirrs, thrums, buzzes and whizzes that seem to belong to the animal, the mechanical, the demonic and the divine rather than the self-knowing human speaker. It may therefore suggest a crossing between the animal and human worlds, and equivalently between the world of things and the world of living creatures.

The extreme secrecy attached to the bull-roarer emphasizes the fact that the (somewhat mundane) source of the sound is not to be known. This may be assisted by the fact that, as it is whirled, the string and to some degree even the slat of wood will disappear into a blur of movement, as though the material object were itself literally being dissolved into sound. This may further enact the particular ambivalence of the bull-roarer, that it is held to be a gift to created beings from self-created beings, or beings who, in indigenous Australian mythologies, are held to have made themselves. The sound of the bull-roarer, a sound apparently without a source (and also, unlike human speech, having no direction, and no beginning or end), helps to confirm this origin in what is apparently self-originating.

The rites of initiation in Australia involve a symbolic wounding. As in many other circumstances, the death and rebirth of the young man is enacted through circumcision or subincision, or both. There is also another kind of symbolic wounding, rendered with his customary dryness by Frazer, who speaks of young boys who 'had been raised to the dignity of manhood by an old man, who had promoted them to their new status by the simple process of knocking a tooth out of the mouth of each with the help of a wooden chisel and hammer'.[85] This wounding of the mouth seems to be associated with the act of utterance, for F. J. Gillen reports a more specific kind of mutilation among the Arunta people. A man who has the idea that he might become a Railtchawa or medicine-man visits a cave inhabited by a spirit called the Iruntŭrriña, and sleeps at its mouth:

> At daylight next morning, the *Iruntŭrriña* appears at the mouth of the cave and throws at the prospective *Railtchawa* an invisible lance called *atnóngara*, which pierces the neck from behind, penetrates the tongue making a large wound, and escapes by the mouth. The tongue remains perforated in the centre with a hole large enough to admit the little finger – and this hole is the only permanent effect of the *Iruntŭrriña*'s treatment.[86]

Following Spencer and Gillen, Frazer reports a more specific kind of mutilation among the Arunta people. In this, a medicine man is initiated by falling asleep at the mouth of a cave:

> as he sleeps one of the ancestral spirits steals up to him and drives an invisible spear through his neck from back to front. The point of the spear comes out through the man's tongue, leaving a hole through which you could put your little finger, and this hole the man retains for the rest of his natural life, or at least so long as he retains his magical powers; for if the hole should close up, these spiritual gifts and graces would depart from him.[87]

The avulsion of the tooth seems to be the same kind of very specific wounding as the hole in the tongue, for it suggests that the initiate now has a kind of gap or gulf in his being, through which spirits and higher powers may make entry and exit, a gulf which is identical with and confirmed by a gulf in his speech. To speak with a wounded tongue or with a missing tooth is to testify in one's very articulation to a defect in articulation, and therefore to the workings of a purer, less articulated utterance, through the impersonal, all-meaning whirl of the air in the mouth, within or underneath articulate speech. Ultimately this hole in the tongue or the mouth is a redoubling of the hollow O of the mouth itself, which is itself what René Spitz has called a 'primal cavity' in the body, the magic cavern or cauldron in which mere wind becomes sound and meaning.[88] The sound of the bull-roarer is itself just this kind of mystic nothing, a nothing that can become something.

The opposition between something and nothing is often explicated psychoanalytically in the contrast between possession and nonpossession of the phallus. Given its role in maintaining strict divisions between the sexes, it is easy to see the bull-roarer as a kind of phallic symbol. This has been held to apply as much to its sound as to its physical form. I. J. Dunn associates the terrifying noise of the bull-roarer with other sounds that seem to mark violent divisions: 'The horn blast, the Shofar, or the bull-roarer cleave the stillness. They make a point in time, a sound in eternity.'[89] In his investigation of the history of the idea of sound and breath as impregnation, Ernest Jones also associated the bull-roarer with mythical 'thunder-weapons', such as the hammer of Thor, the trident of Poseidon or the trisula of Shiva, concluding that 'there are innumerable connections between the idea of thunder on the one hand and ideas of paternal power, especially reproductive power, on the other.'[90] William Niederland also distinguishes between the immersive maternal sound of the lullaby and the violent interruptions of the cry, seeing the two sounds as related to each other as sleeping is to waking:

> From here it is only one step to the soothing lullaby of the mother on the one hand and to the father as the 'disturber' and 'waker' on the other hand. The soft feeding noises which the infant produces during nursing merge with the mother's voice to constitute good sounds, whereas the 'waker' (originally the baby's own loud cry at awakening thirsty, hungry, or otherwise in a state of tension) now becomes the father who is the emitter of bad sounds . . . The

> precursor of this equation, in my formulation, may be traced to the infant's own awakening cry which gets fused with the father's loud 'cry' (voice, thunder, bull-roarer) and makes him into the threatening figure of the child's dreams as well as into the roaring hungry giant or angry deity of so many myths and fairy tales.[91]

And yet there does not seem to be anything particularly rupturing or penetrating about the sound of the bull-roarer. Indeed, J. Layard connects the bull-roarer with the figure of what he calls the 'Female Devouring Ghost . . . who lives in a cave intent on devouring the souls of men as they make their journey to the land of the dead'. He suggests that 'the noise of the bull-roarer swung to imitate them [sacrificed boars] and frighten women and novices is said to be her voice.'[92] And, if the bull-roarer is supposed to be threatening and associated with pain and danger, it also has a kind of protective function, ensuring safety. Spencer and Gillen report that the Kaitish people of Northern Australia believe that the spirit Atnatu is always listening closely to ensure that the bull-roarer is sounded properly during the initiation rite; failure to perform the incisions without the proper accompaniment can result in Atnatu hurling down his spears lethally on those performing the ceremony.[93] So the interior meaning of the bull-roarer may appear to be a kind of soothing appeasement or apotropaism.

Perhaps we should say that the space of the bull-roarer's sound is one in which difference itself and as such – with sexual difference standing as its representative – arises. The bull-roarer establishes the difference between fusion and separation, or the difference between indifference and difference.

The function of the bull-roarer also seems precisely to figure the complexity of magical belief itself. Nearly everywhere in Australia and in many other places besides, the bull-roarer was regarded as taboo for women to see, or, in many cases, even to know about. The passage of young men into adulthood may involve imparting to them the knowledge that the bull-roarer is the source of the noise that is believed by women to be that of a devouring monster.[94] There seems to be a parallel between the secret interior place of the giant's or monster's stomach and the humming or growling of the hungry sound he makes. Having returned, the initiate is made to understand that the sound is really just that of a slat of wood on a string. But with this unveiling comes the responsibility of keeping the secret from the women and children of the tribe.

To believe, or to pretend to believe, in the reality of the invisible monster is to be inside the belly of belief, the sonorous abdomen performed by the whirring, placeless sound, which, if it keeps the uninitiated at bay, also keeps the initiates safely apart. To understand the physical source of the sound is to have been delivered from the belly of belief. But now the keepers of the secret have something inside them. Only a few of those who have discussed the bull-roarer seem to acknowledge the very probable fact that, as J. Van Baal says, 'the uninitiated who are said to be frightened (and certainly the older people among them) only pretend to be scared, being perfectly well aware of the true character of the secret.'[95] A. C. Haddon also finds it curious that in one island of New Guinea the bull-roarer was too sacred to be shown to a woman, while in another, it was openly employed as a plaything.[96] It seems very likely, at least to me, that the secret of the bull-roarer was and is an open secret, one in which the different parties have most of all to keep secret from each other the fact that they know the secret (namely that there is no secret power, and therefore, in a sense, that there is nothing to keep secret), and perhaps even know that the other knows it. Perhaps the fact that the secret of the bull-roarer was not in fact secret is the secret about which the late Victorian ethnographers who were so swallowed up in their self-woven myth of the bull-roarer, have felt most compelled to keep mum. The noise seems to be implicated in this inside–outside alternation.

I have evidently moved some way from the very specific kind of vocal sound, the bilabial nasal, with which I began. Indeed, I have been discussing a class of sounds that have the form and feeling they do precisely because they are anoscular, seeming not to belong to or issue from the human mouth. And yet, these unmoored, mouthless sounds retain their implicit reference to the mouth precisely through their quasi-vocality, and their link to that familiar of the mouth, the resonation of the nose, and all the forms of impersonal or sacred noise which nasals can consequently evoke. Outside the voice, such sounds nevertheless resound with all the noises that are not purely or wholly voice, but with which voice is nevertheless compounded – all the things in the voice, that, by not being voice, by being a kind of not-voice, make it what it is. The noise of the nose haunts, and is haunted by, the voice.

As with the discussions of the other oral performances discussed in this book, it would be very easy to mistake the case that I have been trying to assemble about the meanings accreting or attributed to the bilabial nasal for the very kinds of magical thinking on which I have had to depend for my evidence. If it is true that language is in essence and in itself fundamentally arbitrary, with no given or necessary relationship between particular sound-forms and particular areas of reality or experience, it is also true that human users of language, who are also, by that very token, human producers and transformers of it, are powerfully influenced by conscious and unconscious assumptions about the relations between sound and sense, many of them magical. As a theory of the essential nature of language, phonosemantics may be – no, certainly is – erroneous, but the error has a distinctive form and force. Like many other forms of magical thinking, it is a form of error that bends things into its image, insisting itself into a kind of truth. So I am arguing, not for the simple actuality of the effects of the bilabial nasal, considered as what Margaret Magnus calls a 'god in the word', or consonantal 'archetype', but for the reality of the fact that we seem, in our uses of and attitudes towards language, to assume this actuality.[97] Rather than a mythic actuality, it is therefore a mimic or as-if actuality. Possibly swallowing, or myself being taken in by phonaesthetic fantasy, I have had to assimilate myself to the mimic magic, the magical mimesis, of this taking-to-be-true. The magic of sound iconicity and its associated forms of mouth-mysticism are ultimately founded on – nothing; founded, that is, on the fact that the source of this magical power is just noises made by air, cartilage and saliva. The mouth is magical because, as the vehicle of speech, it constantly translates hardware into software, making something (meaning) out of nothing (mere sounds), and nothing (idea) out of something (matter). But is the fact that people believe in something that has nothing to it itself something, or nothing? If the primal cavity of the speaking mouth has indeed so often seemed to be full of magic, this may be literally enough because there is nothing in it.

SIX
Grrr

The nineteenth-century physician James Yearsley, whose book *Throat Ailments* went through many editions after its first appearance in 1842, distinguished between voice, as the production of sound from the larynx, which animals as well as humans have the capacity to produce, and speech, the meaningful articulation of those sounds by the organs of the mouth, which only humans can produce. Yearsley develops a familiar comparison of the speech organs as a kind of musical instrument, with the lungs as the source of air, the different tones of the vocal cords corresponding to the holes of the instrument and the channels of the voice and nose corresponding to its pipes. But then he adds a level to the analogy:

> we cannot proceed further with the simile, if we confine ourselves to the organ alone. The power of articulation possessed by the tongue, palate, lips, and other parts under the direction of the mind, is not comparable to any parts of the organ itself, but rather with the hand and intellect of the performer on the instrument.[1]

We might recognize in this move the Aristotelian introduction of the element of soul, which is not only in the voice, but also acts upon it, in that act of imagination which produces meaning as opposed simply to sound. But here, it is the external modification of the sound rather than its internal production that is to be regarded as soul.

Yearsley's particular interest was in diseases caused by inflammation of the tonsils, along with what he described as 'elongation of the uvula'. He seems to have regarded these portions of the mouth as forming the gateway between voice and speech, and described the deleterious effects upon speech that enlargement of the tonsils and elongation of the uvula could bring about:

> the clear resonance of the natural voice is changed for a harsh and disagreeable tone. This deterioration is known by the term thick speech; the voice cannot be understood at anything like the natural distance; either there is an unpleasant drawl, or the words are mumbled together in a confused manner; the variations and flexibility of the voice, which add so much to its expression, become altered to an unvarying monotony.[2]

The uvula marks the point where the throat emerges into the mouth, as the river into its delta. Here, the body of the voice might be regarded as entering into form, through articulation and differentiation.

The whirr of the fricative is a sort of small, insentient frenzy, as though it were blind, stalled, undirected force. The sound of the fricative is the sound of a turbulence, a miniature anticyclone of air turned back and round on itself. Of all phonations, the fricative appears most to detain the passage of the sound. And yet, unlike the other consonant sounds, which are restricted to the particular portions of the vocal apparatus that produce them, the teeth for the dentals, the lips for the labials and plosives, the fricative also has a kind of mobility and adaptability, which enables it to take up residence in other regions of the mouth – wherever the air can be forced through a narrow channel, for example in the sibilants, where the front of the tongue sends the air over the teeth, or, in Welsh, the side of the tongue against the molars, as in *Llanelli*.

Since sounds are produced by the coordination of movements and spaces, there is a tendency when attempting to read the meanings of sounds to focus on the position of the mouth or the quality of the movement of the vocal organs. In phenomemic mimesis, it may be recalled, sounds seem expressive, not because of any obvious or direct resemblance to sounds in the world, but on account of a kind of kinetic rhyming between the process of forming the sounds in the mouth and a corresponding process in the world. The mouth becomes a tactile cinema – a *kinematograph*, precisely – of the world. Socrates in Plato's *Cratylus* is struck by the agitation of the tongue involved in the trilled letter ρ, *rho*, which may be regarded as the lingual equivalent of the velar or uvular fricative, especially at the beginning of the word, where it is sometimes marked with a diacritic to indicate a 'rough breathing':

> Well the letter rho, as I was saying, appeared to be a fine instrument expressive of motion to the name-giver who wished to imitate rapidity, and he often applies it to motion . . . for he observed, I supposed, that the tongue is least at rest and most agitated in pronouncing this letter.[3]

This sound, and some of the associations with motion that Socrates discerns survive in English spellings like *rhythm*, *rheumatic* (incorporating *rheum*, which originally means a flowing of mucus), *catarrh* and *diarrhoea*. The Platonic hypothesis with regard to the rough sound of *rho* has inaugurated a durable and seemingly unextirpatable conviction, and especially among French writers, about the dynamic qualities of the *r* sound.[4]

As sounds move forward in the mouth, they tend both to become more distinct, that is, to involve less abrasive friction and reduced turbulence, and to lift in pitch, producing the sense of diction, punctuality, division and precision. Higher-pitched sounds tend to be associated with distance and particular positions in space, partly because they provide a lot of sonic information of that kind (you can always pick out the beeping of the ringtone or the triangle's tinkle amid the surgings of the symphony). High-pitched sounds not only seem to come from the front of the mouth, they also seem to put us in front of things, since we tend to face the source of sounds. Low-pitched sounds, by contrast, seem less located, more circumambient. The selective hearing loss that affects all human beings as they grow older returns them to something like the blurred hearing of the infant, because it tends to erase the consonants that are the least redundant portions of speech, that is, the portions of speech that give the most information by narrowing things down: that is why abbreviations use consonants rather than vowels – *txtng* is much more easily readable than *ei* as *texting*, and partially solved crossword clues with consonants in them are easier to fill out than when there are only vowels. Following some sudden hearing loss some years ago, I had to get used to the experience of looking at people speaking to me whose voices nevertheless sounded as though they had their backs towards me.

There used to be a fashion for calling these velar fricatives 'guttural', a word that has markedly negative associations for English speakers, mostly because these sounds do not feature very much in modern English. As we saw in chapter Three, English used to be as rich in guttural sounds as German and Dutch, and the presence of *gh-* forms in words like *light*, *knight*, *brought*, and *daughter* testify mutely to the once-active employment of the pharynx and uvula in their earlier pronunciations. English no longer has many guttural sounds, though they are often heard in non-standard dialects or in the pronunciations of non-English speakers. The particular historical accident which accelerated the slow recession of such sounds (though it was, as it were, a retreat forwards, into phonic frontality), was the Norman Conquest, which encouraged the spread of Romance forms, in which all these guttural sounds first tended to be softened, into a simple aspirate *h*, and then to vanish altogether. This furnishes the essential meaning (though it arises historically, which is to say, by accident) of the guttural or of sounds that come from the throat: namely that they seem *early*.

The vocal apparatus of the English speaker thereby becomes not only a mimetic theatre of physical actions and forces, but also an orographic chronotope, a weaving together of places and times in the mouth. Sounds that are made early, that is, at the initiation of the sound-making process, before the intervention of the tongue and its work of articulation, may seem primitive, even (literally) prelinguistic. They seem to come from deeper and further back in time, both the time of the particular utterance, and the time of utterance in general.

Since they are produced at the back of the mouth, guttural sounds are also hidden from view; it is much easier to demonstrate the production of dentals, plosives and aspirates to the deaf or to speakers of other languages than gutturals. The fact that guttural sounds seem sonically hard to place means that they can come to signify the cryptic or concealed as such – not just a hidden sound, but the sound of secret or mysterious intent. The seventeenth-century natural philosopher Kenelm Digby writes of a deaf and dumb Spanish prince who had been taught to lip-read, which Digby represents as the seeing of sound. Digby is particularly impressed by his capacity to make out the sounds of Welsh and Hebrew, which appear much less visible than those of Spanish:

> He could discern in another, whether he spoke shril or low: and he would repeat after any body any hard word whatever. Which the Prince tryed often; not only in *English*, but by making some *Welchmen* that served his Highness speak words of their language: Which he so perfectly ecchoed, that I confess I wonder'd more at that, then at all the rest . . . for, that tongue (like the *Hebrew*) employs much the guttural Letters; and the motions of that part which frames them cannot be seen or judg'd by the eye, otherwise then by the effect they may happily make by consent in the other parts of the mouth, exposed to view.[5]

The associations of guttural fricatives can be powerfully positive. The sound appears notably in the Hebrew word *ruach*, which means spirit, or wind of inspiration, and features in the second verse of Genesis: 'and the spirit of God moved on the face of the waters'. Michel Serres evokes the sound to suggest the animal delight in the breath in running and exertion, and asks us to hear in the rough aspiration of the word, something like the raw, pure audible-sensible of the breathing body, before it has been consigned to the prison house of language:

> The first utterance of Genesis, at the dawn of the world, above the hubbub, says God, *ruagh*, a hoarse, alliterative breath, on the soft palate, at the back of the throat, before language, in front of the root of the tongue, where the

> gasping intake of breath acknowledges the divine; *ruagh*, breath, breathing, wind, breeze of the spirit.[6]

But, for the most part, the associations for English speakers of the gutturals and especially the guttural fricatives, are negative. Some commentators have pointed to the fact that English words beginning with *gr-* seem frequently to have negative or unpleasant associations. Three clusters of association have been suggested: 1) unpleasantness (*grim*, *grisly*, *gritty*, *gross*, *grotty*, *gruesome*, *greasy*, *gristly*) 2) complaint (*grumble*, *groan*, *grieve*, *gripe*, *grimace*, *grizzle*, Scottish *greet*) and 3) relating to undesirable friction or rubbing, or its products (*grind*, *groove*, *grate*, *grout*, *grub*, *gruel*, *gravel*, *grave*, *grit*).[7] One might easily see all of these as combining into the expression of what might be called negative friction – being rubbed up the wrong way. The complaint words with initial *gr-* might equally be thought of as a kind of articulate speech that has been broken or deformed by violent or painful pressure. Guttural sounds are routinely said by English speakers to sound 'harsh', a word that seems to imitate some of the asperity suggested by the sound and experienced in making it.

Linda Waugh quotes a *New Yorker* cartoon in which one tiger is saying to another 'griping, greedy, grasping, grotesque, gruesome, grisly – do you know any other good grr words?'.[8] The comic idea that a creature like the tiger, whose very name is an encoded growl, would find positives where we tend to find negatives, is embodied in Tony the Tiger, the emblematic burning-bright animal who declares that the breakfast cereal Frosties are 'grrreat', turning friction into energetic *frisson*. Like other vocal noises, the gutturals often suggest the animal in the voice, the animal being the chiasmic principle that is both within and against the animate, in Aristotle's sense. Underlying all the negative *gr*-s is almost certainly the growl, which may be regarded as a kind of subvocal or prevocal utterance. In an animal, the growl is also prior in time, but not just because it precedes language, but rather because it is a rumbling premonition of a roar. Leibniz called the *r* the canine consonant, for obvious reasons (*Mimologics*, 47) – the dog not only is, but says, *rough* (though the name *canis* was sometimes explained as a derivation from *canere*, to sing.) When a girl asserts her not-to-be-messed-with aggressiveness, she may accordingly be called, or style herself, a *grrl*.

There are many other animals that appear to be invoked – called up by, but also into voice – in the guttural fricatives. There is the frog that famously gets caught in the throat, and also crows that caw and other birds that crow. Hawking is the action of noisily and energetically clearing the throat of phlegm. Sometimes the sounds of the throat combine animal and supernatural overtones. Inuit shamans would sometimes have themselves harpooned in the back like walruses and then, in trance, go round every igloo in the camp 'uttering guttural sounds like a walrus and spitting water and blood'.[9] The nasality that is often associated with guttural fricatives gives it a porcine grunting or snuffling cast.

Often, death is embodied in the idea of other peoples, or in the lethal or deathly sounds that seem to us to issue unwitting from their mouths. Coleridge comments, somewhat cryptically, in the course of an admiring passage of talk on the fineness of the two English *th* sounds – as displayed in a phrase like *the ether* – on the comparative lifelessness of German when it comes to the articulation of the word *death*: 'How particularly fine the hard *theta* is in an English termination, as in that grand word – Death – for which the Germans gutturize a sound that puts you in mind of nothing but a loathsome toad.'[10] I find it difficult to divine what might be going through the mind, or the mind's mouth, of the sage of Highgate here. For one thing, Coleridge seems to hear a voiced (if that is what is meant by 'hard') *th* at the end of English *death*, which, while possible, would be a surprise, and for another, he seems to hear something guttural in the German *Tod*, death. I have played a few times with the sound, and find that it is just about possible, if you snort it as though you were a tank commander, to impart to it a little interior rumble that seems to implicate the throat, and therefore to introduce into the voice the mortuary toadish visitant, inducing the hallucination of a croak in the animal's name.

The bestiality of guttural sounds may also give them a reference to eating, making them the site of interchange between the animal act of eating (an act which largely debars speech, or restricts it to guttural grunts) and the definitionally human or even divine act of speaking. This interchange is implicated in one of the most obviously echoic words in English, *hiccup*, which is an endstopped form of the word *hiccough*. One might reasonably infer that *hiccup* is a later, lexicalized version of the somewhat more diffuse-sounding *hiccough*, though the judgement of the OED is that *hiccough* in fact is a later spelling, that puts 'back' a sound which had not in fact previously been audible in the word. As we saw in chapter Three, such *hysteron proteron* is often to be found in relation to the letter *h*, and we will see something similar happening a little later in relation to the word *ghost*. A hiccough is caused by a disturbance of the mechanism that normally separates the functions of swallowing and breathing, the epiglottis moving by reflex to seal off the trachea when food is moving into the oesophagus. In hiccough, involuntary movements of the diaphragm suddenly close off the trachea as though food were passing. The sound is produced by a sudden involuntary intake of air which meets the obstructed trachea, causing the *hic-* sound, followed by the *-cup* or *-cough* aftershock of eructation. A hiccough may therefore be seen as a kind of chiasmic spasm, as swallowing and breathing threaten to cross over into each other's domains. Sadly extinct now is the word *yex*, encountered in chapter Three, from Old English *ȝeocsian*, *ȝiscian*, meaning to sob or hiccup, which implicates the velar fricative in the sound of the hiccup.

The fricative may be said to be negatively associated with eating, in that it strikes the ear as an expectorant sound that relates it to the magically potent actions of spitting and vomiting. The guttural is at work in this way in the *eecchh!* and *urghhh!* of digust. 'Eating the Wind', by 'Claude Searsplainpockets' of the *Speculative Grammarian*, the 'premier scholarly journal featuring research in the neglected field of satirical linguistics', is an account of the elaborate 'gastro-pulmonic' system of an imaginary tribe called the Xoŋry, which sets out their elaborately particularized designations and phonic enactments of compound activities of eating, speaking, spitting, snorting, devouring and vomiting, including words for 'to eat while talking', 'to snort up the nose while talking', 'to projectile vomit, while talking'.[11] Such associations are memorably dramatized in a passage from Samuel Beckett's *Molloy*, in which the title character describes his attitudes towards his names for his mother: 'I called her Mag, when I had to call her something. And I called her Mag because for me, without my knowing why, the letter g abolished the syllable Ma, and as it were spat on it, better than any other letter would have done.'[12] Here, the *m* sound seems to suggest acceptance and assimilation, the closing of the lips on what has come in from the outside: Roman Jakobson proposes that the nursing infant, whose mouth and lips are monopolized by the nipple, will automatically associate the contentment of the maternal breast with the 'slight nasal murmur [which is], the only phonation which can be produced when the lips are pressed to the mother's breast or to the feeding bottle and the mouth is full' – though, actually, a guttural gurgle is also possible during suckling and is also of course sometimes to be heard in eating.[13] The *g* is, by contrast, a convulsive casting up and out of what has been within. In English, 'spitting' is a labial matter, but Beckett's original French, 'crachait dessus' is an altogether more disgusted and disgusting.

Sylvia Plath articulates an inverted form of this 'phlegmatopoeia', in Luke Thurston's phrase, in her violent father-loathing poem 'Daddy'.[14] At the centre of the poem is the sense of constricted speech, a speech that finds in the German of Plath's father an obstructedness itself:

> I never could talk to you.
> The tongue stuck in my jaw.
>
> It stuck in a barb wire snare.
> Ich, ich, ich, ich,
> I could hardly speak.
> I thought every German was you.
> And the language obscene.[15]

The poem pushes itself repeatedly forward, and back, to this sticking point of stifled utterance, the alternative of tongues and feet suggesting a bizarre literalization of putting a sock in speech, or putting your foot in your mouth – or, as the poem has it, 'the boot in the face'. 'Daddy' finds release from the glutinous 'gobbledygoo' – 'I'm through' being its final words – if it does, in an utterance that, by mimicking the asphyxiating chokehold, tries to empty itself of it, even though the release it finds is itself a kind of muffling or amputation: 'So daddy, I'm finally through./The black telephone's off at the root,/The voices just can't worm through'.[16]

The otherworldly and even the diabolical have also been thought to be audible in such voices. Ventriloquism, in its archaic form of 'speaking from the belly', without the involvement of the tongue and lips, has often been regarded as a kind of impious or irregular speech, a speech that has been corporeally displaced, or even, according to one popular theory, produced by drawing in rather than pushing out the breath, which produces a characteristically growling, hollow kind of utterance.[17] The particular kind of turbulence of the airflow in the fricatives is an accelerated form of this reversal, in which, rather than being pushed unidirectionally, from inner to outer, sound is detained and thickened in the throat.

The suggestion that the guttural fricatives are primitive, even prelinguistic, and the accidental fact that English (like other languages) has tended historically to move such sounds from the back of the mouth to the front, can make the language of the barbarian seem transitional, between noise and voice, still turning the corner from the throat to the mouth. There are two kinds of archaism involved in the English apprehension of gutturals. The first associates them with the so-called Gaelic languages of the margins of Britain, where guttural fricatives survive – in Scots and Irish *och* and *loch*, for example – and with words of Germanic origin. The relative forwardness of Latin compared with the guttural backwardness of German is emblematized by the very words for language employed by the two languages, the seemingly liquid *lingua* and the clogged *Sprache*. Derek Attridge has laid out the logic that produces the contrasting associations of the sunny, Mediterranean letter *c* and the suspicious Germanic *k* that it often pairs, inviting us to reflect on the marked difference of value between *Caesar* and *Kaiser* or *America* and *Amerika*.[18]

The second kind of archaism associates the gutturals with Hebrew, Arabic and other allegedly primal languages. Though Hebrew has had the credit of being believed to be the language spoken by Adam, it could, and can, be regarded as an occult precursor of the daylight, classical clarity of Greek and Latin. The so-called Semitic languages could then be regarded as equivalent to the Germanic undercurrent of English, proximate yet at the same time remote. Lancelot Addison, who spent some time living in the Maghreb, or what was then known as the 'Barbary coast' of Northwest Africa, instructed his readers of the derivation of 'Barbary' from the way in which they pronounced their language, their accents thereby coming to serve as their names, like the tiger, or the allegedly stuttering Hottentots:

> For if we listen to the Moors language, *Barbary* seems to be descended from Barbar, which signifies an inarticulate murmur and grumbling noise without accent or harmony, for their speech is harsh, being very guttural: which is esteemed an argument of its Antiquity. And indeed it hath gain'd the vogue of no less antient a pedigree, than to be bred of the old *Punic* and *Arabian*.[19]

The word from which *Barbary* derives is the Arab *barbara*, to talk noisily and confusedly, a word that surprisingly appears to have no relation to the Greek *barbaros*, even though this too involves a mocking echo of indistinct or unintelligible speech. Greek and Arab, both of them speaking a language richly provided with gutturals, seem to have heard labials as primitive babble or hubbub (the latter derived perhaps from the Gaelic cry of aversion or contempt *ub! ub!*). For Addison, by contrast, it is the guttural which sounds barbaric.

Kabbalistic tradition has taken a more positive view of the gutturals. The Hebrew letter that corresponds to Greek χ, *chi* is ח, *chet*. Annick de Souzenelle draws a contrast between this letter and the *hey*, the simple aspirate in Hebrew, suggesting that 'Whereas *hey* signifies wind, breath, *chet* signifies a barrier'.[20] Souzenelle identifies the *chet* with the paradoxical hymen of sin, that both obstructs the passage to the divine and yet also marks the gateway to it – the serpent, the barrier, is called נחש, *nachas*, a word which has the phonic obstacle at its heart.[21] Other contemporary interpreters emphasize the oscillatory function of the *chet*. Yitzchak Ginsburgh associates it with the principle of 'life itself as pulsation, the secret of "run and return"'.[22] The shape of the *chet* is traditionally understood as being formed from the two previous letters in the Hebrew alphabet, *vav* and *zayin*, joined by a thin bridge or roof. Ginsburgh tells us that this enacts a kind of hovering energy, made up of 'touching yet not touching'.[23] The principal reference here is to Genesis 1:2, *ruach Elohim . . . meraphehet 'al*, which has often been translated 'The spirit of God moved on the face of waters', but which means, literally, to 'flutter', 'flap' or 'shake'.[24] But there is a more metaphorical understanding of this tremor enacted in the *ruach*, the word for spirit or life which ends with the *chet*, which is the brooding of an eagle as it hovers over the young in its nest. In Ginsburgh's interpretation

> by 'hovering' over created reality, G-d continues to sustain and nourish His Creation while simultaneously allowing each creature . . . the ability to grow and develop 'independently.' The letter *chet* thus hints at the delicate balance between the revelation of G-d's presence to us (the *vav* of the *chet*) and the concealment of His creative power from his Creation the *zayin* of the *chet*).[25]

The rhythm of paradoxical pulsation is also emphasized in Lawrence Kushner's reading of the letter, which makes more of the parallel between sound and image:

> In the Torah the Chet . . . is written with a sharp jagged notch on its forehead. It is almost as if there were two separate letters barely joined together. They need each other to stand. But they wish they did not. So they barely touch. Chet is the agony of a soul torn apart from itself. The top of your throat and the bottom of your throat fighting against one another create the sound of the chet.[26]

It is for this reason that the *chet* is supposed to give rise to many 'strange and conflicted word-pairs'.[27] Thus sin, *chait*, suggests 'A soul torn against itself because it is sure that it is pious', while *chasid*, a pious person, 'is a soul convinced that it commits many sins'. Pain is *chavel*, sonically and graphically twinned with *chayim*, life, suggesting 'almost dying from birthwork. Bringing forth life'; while destruction is *churban*, but linked with *chuppa*, the marriage canopy which the letter is often said to resemble.[28] Theories of sound symbolism, or sonorously performative language, often involve the crossing of image and sound. There are two interpenetrating forms of this. In one, the shapes of the mouth dance out what will become the tensile shapes of letters. As we saw in chapter Four, according to Francis Mercury Van Helmont, the tongue 'naturally forms the Hebrew Letters in the Mouth'.[29] The semaphoric fantasy of letters danced out by the mouth is mirrored by the choreographic suggestiveness of the shapes of the letters on the page, which 'begins to teem with little mouths opening, or closing, with gullets, with upside-down noses, with pointed or curled-up tongues – more or less recognisable, always both open to the view and hidden away in the thicket of letters' (*Mimologics*, 57).

Edward Sapir told 500 subjects that the words *mal* and *mil* were words for different sizes of table in an unnamed foreign language, and asked them to decide which was which: an overwhelming majority (96 per cent of the adults) assumed that *mal* would designate the larger table, and *mil* the smaller.[30] This example recurs frequently in the critical literature on iconicity, no doubt in part because the results obtained seem so compelling. There are other studies which try to find similar correlations between sounds and spatial values. The values implied by and correlated by the *i*/*a* contrast may be tabulated as follows, to suggest a general set of regular homologies between the values of what are felt to be closed and open sounds:

i	*a*
front (mouth)	back (throat)
closed	open
high	low
light	dark
bright	dull
definite	indefinite
exterior	interior
distant	proximate
located	placeless

articulate	inarticulate
form	force
image	sensation
word	cry
human	animal
protasis (*tic*)	apodosis (*tac*)
filling space	filled with space

The essential difference here seems to be between a conception of closed or definite space, and vaguer, more indefinite space, with the primary locale being the semi-imagined spaces of the mouth and throat. Sounds made in the front of the mouth seem to partake in the strong and precise familiarity that most people feel with their own mouth's topography. It is an awareness with which Vladimir Nabokov plays in the opening words of *Lolita*, which featly foots a little phonetic dance from the elements of the infant siren's name, and in the process also wittily dramatises the relative lowness of *o*, from the back of the mouth, and the lightness of *i*: 'Lolita, light of my life, fire of my loins. My sin, my soul. Lo-lee-ta: the tip of the tongue taking a trip of three steps down the palate to tap, at three, on the teeth. Lo. Lee. Ta.'[31] It is a movement of advance, ascent (despite the fact that the steps come down to the front) and emergence, from loins to teeth, from desire to articulation.

Sounds from elsewhere in the vocal apparatus may be strongly felt, but felt nevertheless as belonging to a vaguer, more undefined *elsewhere*. It is much more disturbing to have a portion of one's mouth numbed by anaesthetic than one's throat, since one's throat is any case less clearly outlined in one's oral self-image, and so, as it were, already more 'numb'. In a curious way, since I am able to visualize the different areas of my mouth so well, it is as though I were in some sense outside it, looking in. That perceptual vantage point seems not to be so available to me in thinking of the throat and the even more occult parts of the bronchial apparatus, from which few sensations are likely to be reported, unless I swallow something hot or sharp, or have an inflammation. My mouth is an inside that is perceivable from an outside – I seem at times to work it by remote control. My throat is an inside that I am, that is only perceivable from inside. I am in my throat without somehow quite feeling able to look in on it.

This contrast between defined and undefined space, at an even greater level of abstraction, is a distinction between matter and the immaterial. Although matter exists familiarly in three progressively more attenuated states – solid, liquid and gas – matter means for most of us matter in its solid state. The characteristic of such matter is to be dense, concentrated, and definite, which is to say, with clearly defined boundaries between a material form and its outside. Matter, that is to say, occupies space; a material thing is a thing that has a certain extension in space (a 'body'), but an extension that goes only so far, such that the thing can be distinguished from the space around it and from other things in that space. The immaterial does not in so clearly apprehensible a way divide space; rather it tends to occupy space, spreading into and blending with it indivisibly. Hence the fundamental distinction enacted by *i* and *a*, and by the physiological processes we feel and imagine (and imagine we feel), is that between matter in space and matter as space.

There is one more step of abstraction that it is possible to make, which may deliver to us an essential feature of the experience of language. The distinction between frontal and posterior sound values is finally a distinction between matter and immaterial, or between something and nothing. The mouth is a furnished room, with items disposed in an orderly way in its space; the throat, and all the other inner compartments on to which we may feel it dimly and indistinctly give, is vacuity itself. The mouth is a place that can be selectively and sequentially lit up by the flashlight of the tongue – even the craggy absence left by a missing filling is turned into a positive by the tongue's haggling at it. The throat is a dark place, a space therefore of indeterminate shape and extent. The throat is a gulf of nothingness. It is the place in the mouth in which the nothingness of pure gurgling, the pure agitation before articulation, can be heard as articulation. The sounds that issue from the throat, however, do not, insofar as they are sound, entirely belong to it. They function as sounds in a language, even though not belonging entirely to articulation, meaning that they do not wholly inhabit the nocturnal realm of noise either. They are a place where darkness and light, though not yet fully distinguishable, alternate: they form an oscillating chiaroscuro, in which the distinctness and the indistinctness of light and dark chiasmically cross and recross.

Of all the vocal sounds, the guttural, and especially the fricative, is the aptest to suggest the agitation of the mucus membrane and its associated substance, the phlegm, that is always present in the throat. Phlegm is, as it were, the paradoxical embodiment of this nothingness, a glutinous sort of space-stuff, a stuff that clings to its space, that is never distinct enough from the space it occupies. The desire to clear the throat, which can become pathologically intense and unremitting, is a desire to move from the tangled thicket of the throat into the clearing of the mouth, or from the turbid glottal thickness of the phlegm to the fluting lucidity of the saliva, and by getting 'it' up and out ('better out than in') to make it a something rather than a something-which-is-not-a-thing, and therefore something that can be fully expelled, and in the process rendered absolutely nothing.

The throat marks the point of transition at which the slimy, semi-solid quasi-nothingness or space-stuff of air is mantled in articulate speech, the point at which the animal becomes animate in becoming articulate. It is the point (even though it never exactly comes to a point) at which the nothing of pure, purblind guzzle or gargle becomes the something, or rather, the many different distinguishable things, of speech. Nothing becomes something. And yet, in thus becoming more definite, more articulate, speech also seems to become less material, less bodily. The glutinous, clinging ur-plasm of speech is sublimated in the crucible of the mouth into mobile sense and meaning. It is now, in Aristotle's terms, 'a particular sound that has meaning, and not one merely of the inbreathed air, as a cough is'.[32] So, in becoming language, something (bodily matter) becomes nothing (meaning); but it is also the case that nothing (mere matter) becomes something (meaning). This transition has the classical cross-your-heart shape of the chiasmus:

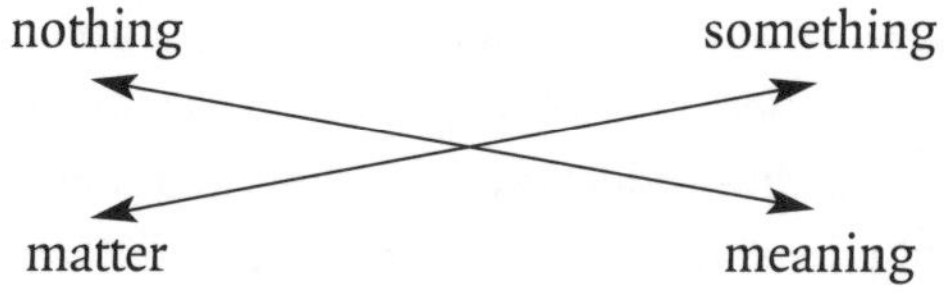

It is for this reason that the guttural sound is not just the sound of the beginning of life and meaning, the rasp of the *ruach* that gives form to what is *tohu-va-bohu*, without form and void, dividing the light from the dark. For the throat is also that part of us from which issues the death-rattle, that, like the snore, can never be uttered wittingly, or with the full present-and-correct assent of the soul on the *qui vive*, but is nevertheless the sound we make when we give up the ghost. Who ever believes their bedfellow when told that they have been snoring for hours? Certain kinds of heavy metal bands, notably Napalm Death, but also Necrophagia, Master, Hellhammer and Cannibal Corpse (vocalist Chris Barnes), cultivated a growling, kind of vocal style, described somewhat impolitely, though informatively, in 2004 by Will York as the 'Cookie Monster style' in order to embody their preoccupations with 'death, decay, and other such existential dilemmas'.[33]

The association of the guttural with emptiness is assisted by many other associations. One of them is the figure of the Gorgon, who may be regarded as something like the embodiment of gutturality, not least because she ends up decapitated, the blood gushing from her throat.[34] But this fate seems to be anticipated in her name, deriving from the Sanskrit root *garg*, which according to Thalia Feldman, signifies 'a gurgling, guttural sound, sometimes human, sometimes animal, perhaps closest to the grr of a growling beast'.[35] The word *garg*, and the name *gorgon* to which it gives rise, means to make a noise which is neither a word or a name – a name that means nothing except *that*, that it means nothing. The apotropaic gorgoneion, or gorgon's face, traditionally represented her with her tongue stuck straight out, as though to indicate the surrender of the functions of the mouth to those of the throat. Her legacy is to be found in the grotesque gargoyles which decorate churches and cathedrals throughout Europe, which are the facializations of gurgling gutturality. The Gorgon or Medusa was interpreted by Freud as a figure of castration, as the threat of nothingness, though his focus, somewhat literalistically, was on the pubic tangles of her snaky hair.[36] But there is horrifying enough vacuity in the notion of a head devoted to the production of headless and voiceless utterance. Remembering the Latin *vox et praeterea nihil*, Jane Harrison remarks that the Medusa 'is a head and nothing more; her potency only begins when her body is severed, and that potency resides in the head; she is in a word a mask with a body later appended'.[37] But it might just as well be said that this is a body facialized, an acephalic body that has not so much grown a head, as grown into one.

The horror of that which is there and not there takes a milder, more civic form in the idea of the ghost. Here, once again, gutturality cooperates in the compounding of something with nothing. In any case, the letter *g* has often been read and heard as connoting vacuity. Charles de Brosses wrote in his *Traité de la formation méchanique des languages* of 1765 that 'gaping things are painted by the letter of the throat (g), such as *gouffre* (abyss), *golfe* (gulf) or even better by the aspirating letter, as in *hiatus*' (quoted *Mimologics*, 71). This sense of a being that is compact with nothingness is well conveyed by a visible sound which cannot in fact be heard, though there seems nevertheless to be a hollow kind of resonance with words like *ghoul* and *ghastly*, which according to Ernest Weekley, are made more ghostly by the phantom presence in them of the unsounded *h*.[38] These seem to be specifically Germanic ghosts, named with a word from the Germanic language that still hangs anachronistically around English. But, as Weekley points out, this ghostliness is itself a doubly spectral effect. Though giving the appearance of a haunting survival, the *h* in *ghost* is in fact a relatively new arrival, and one, what is more, that derives from the predilections of the eye as much as the ear. In Old English the word is spelled regularly as *gaest*, and in Middle English as *gost* or *gast*. *Ghost* first appears in Caxton, perhaps, the OED surmises, influenced by Flemish *gheest*. And yet, the ghost still haunts, for *Geist* seems at home, and *ghost* still wanders abroad; so, 'I get your gist', but 'I haven't the ghost of an idea.' The vagrant or homeless *h* also seems implicated in the fortunes of the word *guest*, which, in forms like West Aryan *ghosti-s*, comes close to Latin *hostis*, enemy, and *hospes*, guest, host. As J. Hillis Miller concludes, of this linguistic intertwining, 'A host is a guest, and a guest is a host.'[39]

Something similar seems to have been at work a couple of hundred years later when, needing a name for the mysterious, unpredictable, airy stuff that nevertheless was not air given off when he heated coal, Jan Baptiste Van Helmont invented the word 'gas', explaining that 'by the Licence of a Paradox, for want of a name, I have called that vapour, Gas, being not far severed from the Chaos of the Ancients.'[40] We should remember that, for the Flemish Van Helmont, *gas* and *chaos* would have sounded much more similar than they do in English today. The primary meaning of the Greek word *chaos* is a gulf or chasm, from the stem χα – to yawn, or gape – a sound made, according to Dwight Bolinger's suggestion, when one's jaw sags open and one looks 'aghast'.[41] The 'spiritus silvestris', or 'wild spirit', for which Van Helmont sought a name was not much different from a pure chaos, a *tohu-va-bohu*, a nothing, The wild spirit is a chiasmic crossbreeding of gaseous nothingness and what Helmont called 'the thingliness of a Gas'.[42]

Linguistics tends to assume the coherence, autonomy and continuity of a language, and for that reason has tended to treat individual languages as closed and self-sufficient systems. This makes it hard to account for the status of the guttural in English, from which it is largely absent. However, language is never entirely reducible to 'a language', for languages are constantly influencing and entering into one another. In the case of the gutturals, we have a class of sounds that have an impact on English precisely because they are felt not to, or no longer to belong wholly to it. In one sense, the phonology of German, for many reasons the reference language for English phantasms of gutturality, is separate from and therefore outside English. But, insofar as a kind of phonaesthetic memory (or mnemonic phonology) seems to exert an influence on English, and to have an oblique but emphatic presence-in-absence within it, German is also in some sense inside English. So the guttural fricative both is and is not a sound in English, this chiasmic judder between presence and absence being like an accelerated form of the guttural fricative itself.

The question at issue raised by the kind of 'mimological reverie' (*Mimologics*, 309) which I have both documented, and have myself been indulging here is, as Genette puts it, 'whether or not natural language respects and invests these imitative capacities in its functioning' (*Mimologics*, 323), whether it is a generative magic that language itself performs, or the effect of a kind of magical thinking that we perform upon language. But the further question this raises is whether it is possible to keep language 'itself' apart from the work of phonaesthetic phantasy. If language is not just what is abstractly given in structures and relations, but also what is historically made of those structures, or of what we profoundly seem to wish to be true of language, whether on rational or irrational grounds, then what Janis Nuckolls describes as 'a kind of sound-symbolic creativity that is protracted through generations, below the threshold of awareness for most, yet assented to and thereby engineered by entire communities of speakers' must be regarded as something language is as well as something we do to it.[43]

I am not entirely opposed to the suggestion that sounds begin to gather a kind of magical significance, though this comes about as all magical effects do, not by inherence but by a kind of supervenience. The number thirteen has no power to bring luck or misfortune. But the attention paid to the number thirteen by superstitious people, or by people (like me) who are determined not to surrender to superstition, actually gives it a supervenient power of being fearfully attended to and having its effects scrutinized. This implies that when we examine the magic embedded or enacted in words, we are examining the aptitude to read those words in that way – the magical effect being an effect of magical attribution, or according of magical power.

The difficulty here is that the two strains, of magical belief, and the sceptical anatomy of it, are hard to keep completely separate in practice. In fact, there might be said to be a chiasmic oscillation between them, which is the same oscillation as is to be found in thinking about magical thinking. Magic does not exist in that there really is no omnipotence of thoughts. But the thought that there may be omnipotence of thoughts is a powerful and a dangerous thought (dangerous because it can itself become omnipotent). There is nothing to fear from magic, but plenty to fear from thinking there might be such a thing. Rationalists like me have a hard time keeping our thinking about magical thinking free from magic – especially, perhaps, when we irrationally deny or forget the force of magic in rationality.

This oscillation between the magical and the rationalist is mimicked in the oscillation between iconicist or mimological theories of word formation and conventionalist theories. For one does not need to give credence to the claims made by most iconicists that certain sounds have essential and archetypal meanings to accept that beliefs or hunches about such meanings might often put pressure on the formation and function of words. In such cases, the iconicity is not preformed but performed, not given but made. The fact that the performance depends upon a mistaken theory need not prevent the repeated error having a considerable generative force. Language comes to consist of what is done to it, meaning that language is always inside and outside, behind and in front of itself.

The engine of this inside–outside alternation, this outering of language, is the fact of utterance, the fact that there is no language without the putting of language into play and at stake. Voice and language envelop and exceed each other. Voice contains language, for there is nothing in language that cannot be given voice to or taken up into voice. But language also contains voice, since what we call a language is the sum total, or the imaginary horizon, of all possible occasions of speech. Voice is the soul of language, but, as Aristotle is at pains to assert, language is the soul of voice, what gives it its essential meaning (for without language and without meaning, the voice is merely noise). But voice is also a kind of noise within, or parasite upon, language. As Mladen Dolar observes, the voice is precisely that which is never audible to phonology – which is why phonology, from *phone*, may also be thought of as *phonos*, murder, the assassination of voice.[44] The voice is accent, accident, occasion, all of them signifying etymologically the way in which things fall out. We can gloss the word *accent* as 'essential accident'. Everybody has an accent as everybody has a point of view; voice is the necessity of this contingency, the way it has to happen to have fallen out. Voice is the necessary disturber of language's peace, that will not leave it one piece.

Voice is the friction of language, that rubs it against the grain, and fricatives are the emblem and occasion of the action of vocality as such. How are we to understand friction or frication? Friction encompasses a spectrum of actions. At one end, there is the caress, that conserves and curates that which it touches. The caress is a non-appropriative touch. It is also generative; in the words of Jean-Paul

Sartre, 'the caress is not a simple stroking; it is a *shaping*. In caressing the Other, I cause her flesh to be born beneath my caress, under my fingers.'[45] The caress is both a touching and a keeping intact; like the moving or brooding of *ruach* on the waters, it seems to imply the suspiration, or the insufflation, the tenuous, tremulous touch of breath alone. The caress illuminates and accentuates the form of what it touches, giving it its distinctness and integrity. At the other end of the spectrum from this lightest of all touches is the violent abrasion, that abrades, rips, pulverises, reducing its object to atomized multiplicity. The voice moves between these two extremes in its relations with itself. Sometimes, the voice seems to touch itself with the most erotically delicate of touches, a touch that withdraws from and in the process yields place to itself, a doubling that consolidates, like an echo or an aura. But sometimes the voice also seems to turn on itself, shaking itself to pieces as though gripping itself terrier-like in its own teeth. It is cooling zephyr or wrathful whirlwind. When voice delicately doubles itself, it seems to shape for itself an ideal and serene body, made out of nothing but sound. When voice rancorously grates, scrapes or abrades itself, it seems to want to grind itself down into a different kind of nothingness, the nothingness of dross, detritus, of mere empty rubbing. Guttural frication performs voice's self-relation, or language's relation to itself via the scratchy intercession of voice. Voice is nothing more or less than this friction between the two extremes of frication, that make the voice something out of nothing, or nothing in the midst of something.

SEVEN

Pprrpffrrppffff

The lips, the most visible portion of the vocal apparatus, are the last part of that apparatus to shape speech. Since they seem to give the parting touch to vocal sounds, they can seem to have a special role in marking its passage from inner to outer. We have seen that the occlusive function of the bilabial nasal *m* relates it to a kind of protracted innerness, or indirect emission. The class of sounds known as 'plosives', and typified by the sounds of English *b* and *p*, have the opposite function. For, by temporally retarding the current of air and then releasing it in a little puff, pop or explosion, plosives seem to suggest some sudden and even violent separation of outer from inner. Where the *m* pleasantly or excitingly maintains tension in equilibrium, *p* and *b* produce a sudden release of tension through an abrupt differential of pressure. *Abrupt* seems a good adjective to figure this, since it contains both *p* and *b* and because they seem to exert their force in different directions, unlike, say, the words *erupt* or *corrupt*. The prefix *ab-*, 'from', suggests some kind of drawing in or backwards from the outside, while the second part of the word seems to explode outwards, through the double obstruction of the *b* and *p*.

The plosives are often associated with bodily explosion. In swearing, in which *b* features with well-known and conspicuous force – Blast! Blazes! Blow! Bugger! Bother! – the willed nature of the act of speech borrows from the spontaneous and unwilled eruptions of the spit, the spew, the belch, the fart and similar semi-voluntary actions of eruption or eructation. Much of the force of these expulsions comes from the sense of bad or toxic contents being violently expelled. In this respect, they may perhaps be related to the actions of violent splitting off that W. R. Bion sees as part of the repertoire of the subject in the 'psychotic stage', which is characterized by an inability to tolerate the internal tension arising from states of ambivalence, and the violent desire to split off or spit out from the self contents that are designated as bad.[1] The expulsive force of the plosive recruited to the action of swearing suggests the intolerability of ambivalence, of 'bad' contents being harboured within the 'good' space of the mouth, and the necessity for putting the bad aside, thereby restoring the integrity of the good.

Ernest Jones suggests that there is a close association between such expulsions and a fantasy of more benign emanations, that may be thought of as fertilizing and impregnating. In 'The Madonna's Conception Through the Ear', Jones used the etymology of various plosives to chart a connection between anal flatus and childbirth. I cannot summarise his etymological reasoning more economically than by reproducing it:

> the more generic word 'pigeon' comes from the Greek πιπιξειν = to chirp; from the latter also comes the word 'pipe', which has the meanings of a tube . . . an instrument for making smoke, to chirp or sing, and, in slang, the male organ. A whole series of words are derived from the same root (probably of onomatopoeic origin), which mean 'to blow', 'the back parts', or 'child', and Jung has pointed out the connecting link of these three apparently disparate ideas is to be found in the common infantile notion that children are born from the rectum. Thus: (1) 'pop', 'puff', 'to poop' (= to pass flatus). Compare the French 'pet' = flatus, the same word in English meaning darling, little dear, and the German 'Schatz', = darling, treasure, which also comes from a vulgar word for defaecation); (2) French 'poupée' and Dutch 'pop', both meaning doll (German 'Puppe'), Latin 'pupus' = a child, 'pupula', = a girl, and English 'puppy' and 'pupa', meaning the young of the dog and the butterfly respectively. That words of such widely different significations as 'pupil', 'fart', 'peep', 'fife', 'pigeon', 'puff', 'petard',

> and 'partridge' should all be derived from the same root illustrates the astonishing propagating power possessed by sexual words.[2]

These etymological convergences testify to the fondness for and continuing attachment to what might be seen as incomplete evacuations, or what seems to lingers after evacuation. They rest upon a paradoxical association between what is violently expelled or set apart from the body and the new, separated form that results from that partition. The action of evacuation is therefore at once an absenting and a presenting, the annihilation of what is spat out and the recreation or preservation of the form that it seems to precipitate. These seem to come together in the word 'pop', which is itself literally a something made of a nothing – a sign that is made out of the sound of something violently dissolving, the noise made by something becoming nothing. It is not for nothing that plosives are so often involved in the idea of bubbles.

The most important and conspicuous way in which *p* and *b* work together is in the evocation of the baby and its associated blubbings and burblings, from both ends of the alimentary tube. This is summed up for me in the soapy poutings of Marilyn Monroe, to whose alleged sexual allure I have always been resistant (I have always thought that if one could have embraced it, her body would have turned out to be a balloon giving off a faint odour of blancmange), and most especially in her song 'I Want to Be Loved By You' in *Some Like It Hot*, with its baby-refrain 'Boop-boop-be-doo'.

In this sense, the blowing and bursting of bubbles might furnish an image of speech itself (it does so literally in the case of cartoon speech-bubbles), reduced to the primary action of first piling up and then dispelling air. Not surprisingly, the plosives *b* and *p* are often employed in locutions intended to convey empty or noisy speech, especially in the idea of a bag of wind rapidly alternating between a superbly englobed and dribblingly deflated condition. The word to *blather*, and its close cousins *blether*, *blether* and *bluster* (*blother* is currently unemployed), are all renderings of the action of the bladder, the medieval emblem of the empty-headed fool. Plosive-rich words feature regularly in slang and dialect, especially to signify the disorderly or meaningless. A 'bobbery' or 'bobbely' is a riot or disturbance, for instance, and a 'barbly' is pidgin for babble or racket.[3]

The forceful violence of excremental *b* and the empty flapping of ventilated *b* can be combined for satiric intent, as in the use throughout Joyce's *Ulysses* of plosive sequences to signal the ludicrous, dunderheaded violence of colonial militarism. John Bull is represented by voiced labial plosives consistently through the book: Private Compton threatens that he will 'Make a bleeding butcher's shop of the bugger'.[4] The British Empire is scornfully reduced in the 'Oxen of the Sun' chapter of the novel to 'Beer, beef, business, bibles, bulldogs, battleships, buggery and bishops', a phrase that is transmogrified in the dreamy delirium of the 'Circe' chapter into a mock benediction of eight 'beatitudes', which bumps the earlier sequence into new configurations:

> STEPHEN: In the beginning was the word, in the end the world without end. Blessed be the eight beatitudes.
>
> *(The beatitudes, Dixon, Madden, Crotthers, Costello, Lenehan, Bannon, Mulligan and Lynch in white surgical students' gowns, four abreast, goosestepping, tramp fast past in noisy marching.)*
>
> THE BEATITUDES: *(incoherently)* Beer beef battledog buybull businum barnum buggerum bishop.[5]

If speech can be reduced to the alternation of flows and stops – the distinction between vowels and consonants being the most familiar form of this contrast – then the plosive provides the most forceful and definitive of all these forms of stoppage. One may suggest that the general force possessed by the plosive is that of creating definition, through a narrowing of focus. This constriction is particularly in evidence in words that imitate the compressed sound of words that seem to imitate exact units of time – the *beep*, *pip*, or *bleep*. In a word like *bit*, the plosive obediently chops up the stream of speech, and even more emphatically with the word *but*, which can indeed appear to butt in to the flow of meaning, blocking or redirecting it.

The plosive both exploits and emphasizes the difference between the inner and the outer, and the lips that make for their meeting and demarcation. The plosive enacts the sudden appearance, in a world of continuously varying qualities, of discontinuity, of the difference between inside and outside, for example.

Margaret Magnus suggests that the field of reference of English *p* may be differentially related to the violent expulsions of the *b*. *B* is pronounced by 'blowing' up the mouth, making a 'bulge' and then letting the air 'burst' out. *P* is pronounced by 'pushing' which produces a 'puffing' up and 'pouring' out. The result in *p* is 'not an explosion, but a more precise "placement."'[6] Magnus would like us to believe that this is a result of a kind of particle physics of sound formation in the mouth, but there may be a more contingent reason why English words involving the letter *p* often suggest the making of precise distinctions, which is that English inherits from Greek a considerable number of specifying prefixes that begin with this letter – *pro-*, *per-*, *pre-*, *para-*. It is partly this inheritance that accounts for the fact that p is the third commonest initial letter in the lexicon of English. Words employing *p* tend to suggest the making of precise claims or distinctions, or the establishment of exact relations, as in the self-designating word *preposition*, which both specifies a spatial position, and seems to suggest the position of priority that such a specification should have. The doubling of *p* in a word like *principal* or, even more, the tripling of *p* in a word like *appropriate*, gives a certain extra pointedness to the word – and therefore can also, at times, suggest hair-splitting or pernickety over-niceness. I have known several speakers of English who regularly substituted the word *pacific* for the word *specific* and even *pecificity* for *specificity*; this may have been partly because of the difficulty in forming the word *specific*, which, like quite a few words with *p*, seems conspicuously and even purposively difficult to say, but also because of the feeling that a word the function of which is to make a point of particularity is given an extra little specifying prod with the preciseness of an initial *p*.

This effect seems to be intensified by the silent *p* of words formed with initial *ps-*, preserving the Greek ψ, psi. There are scarcely a dozen such word-families in English, including such delicate exotics as *psephologist*, *psoriasis* and *psittacosis*, though the abundance of the class of words formed from *psyche* gives them extra prominence in modern English. Perhaps there is a logic of the intensified minimal in this. If *p* represents a reduction and concentration of the more energetically and chaotically diffusive force of *b*, then reducing the sound even further, to the point of inaudibility, making the *p* of *psychology* a virtual *p* that sounds only for the eye of the mind, or the mind of the eye, perhaps concentrates the particularising force. Following a similar logic, P. G. Wodehouse's 'Psmith' is a comic mockery of the English habit of conferring or claiming pseudo-distinction with names the spellings of which provide little guide to their pronunciation (Mainwaring, Beauchamp, Worcester and the like), as is Leopold Bloom's fantasy in *Ulysses* of the prissy upper-class English invitation 'Do ptake some ptarmigan.'[7]

Here, as in many other places in this book, it may seem as though I am supposing that certain meanings are somehow packed or locked into particular sounds, such that *p* must always imply pin-prick particularity. But, of course, the very fact that *p* is such a common sound in English means that it will be found in a very large range of semantic contexts, and doing a great number of different kinds of job, most of which derive no assistance from the putative tendency of *p* to denote precision. If there is any plausibility (from *plaudire*, to clap the hands, with an approvingly plosive sound) in the meanings I have made out for the plosive, or the sibilant, or the nasal, as it may be, it is not because the sounds are possessed of these meanings. It is because they operate within a subtle field of probability, which they themselves affect. The fact that there may be quite a few familiar words available to a speaker or hearer in which particularity seems to be associated with the plosive makes it more likely that such effects will be selectively amplified in use and in analysis. This does not in the least prevent *p* being able to be used in other contexts and with other meanings entirely – of poetry and pleasure, or pus and puke, for example, in which ideas of precision and particularity may no longer seem to be in the picture. It is just that we will, no, steady on, *may* be more likely to pick out those patternings in which picking-out or patterning seem to be the issue. It is not a matter of meaning, but of leaning. We may not be able to reckon up these probabilities by mere counting, though sometimes, as with the surprising number of words having to do with light that begin with initial *gl-*, the numbers seem to be illuminating. For, even if we were able to show that there are more words with *p* in which particularity is not the principal point (and there almost certainly are, I would guess), what we have to reckon with is the force and effect of the desire to make out these regular patternings and associations, where it may exist (or arise – since this present discussion may actually be changing the odds for you as you read it). Hence the fact that, as I write, I cannot seem to stop the plosives in the words I am using from obtruding in precisely the ways that seem to make the points I am making, even if I am trying to make an opposite point. Something in language, or our use of it, or our attitudes toward our use of it, seems to resist the most probable arrangements of sounds, which would be wholly random arrangements, and prefers the improbability of ordered or regular arrangements.

There is a loose analogy with a contemporary understanding of genetics. It has been clear for some time now that being haemophiliac, homosexual or hot-tempered are not going to turn out to be determined once and for all by the presence of certain chromosomic arrangements, but it may well be that these arrangements will impart some measure of likelihood to a particular outcome, given the convergence with other conditions. We have a very vague understanding of these probabilities, given the huge range of variable parameters that might bear upon the outcome. Probably the word *probably* itself is implicated in some of this thinking. Since I am preoccupied by questions of probability, I find myself using the word a lot, and have become quite expert in articulating it, having a particular fondness for the word *probabilistically*, repeated practice of which means that it now trips pat off my tongue (I have developed a similar facility with the word *phenomenological*, which I can rattle off like a Gatling gun). But every successful performance of the word contains, or, rather, has as its background, or, rather more, produces as its background, the possibility of messing the word up, as in the words 'specificity' and 'appropriateness'. The successful performance of the word, in other words, depends upon the apparently augmented chances of its failure, or, inverting this, the relative improbability of its successful articulation. This gives the word *probabilistic* a highly probabilistic profile in phonetic terms.

Like the *b* phoneme, *p* is also often recruited to represent empty, mindless, or mechanical speech. Only a small excess is required to tip sense into nonsense and significant sound into noise. The fact that the eminently grown-up word *probabilistic* has such a high risk of collapsing into babble or baby-talk (a fact accentuated for me in the present context by the fact that I almost hear the explosive word *ballistic* in it) means that pulling it off successfully has something in it of a Peter-Piper accomplishment. In his burlesque of the Fall in 'Apple Tragedy', Ted Hughes has God getting Adam, Eve and the serpent drunk on cider squeezed from the apple, with the serpent trying to protest against the ensuing violence: 'The serpent tried to explain, crying 'Stop'/But drink was splitting his syllable', perhaps recalling the tipsy Caesar in *Antony and Cleopatra*, who says 'mine own tongue/Splits what it speaks' (II.vii.123–4).[8] *Blathering*, *blattering* and *blithering* have near relations in *prating*, *prattling* and *pattering*, the last-named being derived from the first word of the *Paternoster*, and implying the kind of rapid, inattentive utterance characteristic of mechanical recitation of prayer; Palsgrave's *Lesclarcissement de la langue francoyse* of 1530 defined the French word *papelarder* as to 'patter with the lyppes, as one dothe that maketh as though he prayed and dothe nat'.[9] The fact that such recitation of prayer may often in fact have taken place in an undertone, or even a whisper, in which stopped consonants become more prominent, also emphasises the drift of voice into dry noise. There is a very fine line between the precision of a word which requires the clear articulation of multiple *p*s and *b*s in close proximity, and the blurred, scattergun effect of a kind of rapid repetition in which the vowel sounds are lost in the repercussive rat-a-tat-tat of plosives.

Nowhere is this more prominent than in the action known as 'blowing a raspberry'. The action is an imitative dismissal, and seems to have been associated in particular with theatre audiences and the action known once as 'exploding' an act from the stage, as in this account from 1894:

> Mrs Bangers came on, dressed as a Venetian doctor of laws, and scarcely had she spoken the impressive sentence: –
>
> 'It droppeth as the gentle rain from Heaven' . . .
>
> – when a loud and offensive noise, like the rending of glazed calico, made by obtruding the wet tongue between the closed lips, and by low cabmen and persons of that class, called a 'raspberry,' came from the gallery.[10]

A rather curious account of this action is quoted from the *Sporting Times* by Barrère and Leland's *Dictionary of Slang* of 1890:

> One gentleman I came across had a way of finding out the cussedness of this or that animal by a method that I found to be not entirely his own. The tongue is inserted in the left cheek and forced through the lips, producing a peculiarly squashy noise that is extremely irritating. It is termed, I believe, a raspberry, and when not employed for the purpose of testing horseflesh, is regarded rather as an expression of contempt than of admiration.[11]

The word clearly makes reference to the much older word 'rasping', which was used to mean belching or farting. Francis Bacon uses the word in the course of a discussion of the way in which eruptions of air produce sound:

> All *Eruptions* of *Aire*, though small and slight, giue an *Entity of Sound*; which we call *Crackling*, *Pussing*, *Spitting*, &c. As in *Bay-salt*, and *Bay-leaues*, cast into the Fire; So in *Chesnuts*, when they leape forth of the Ashes; So in *Greene Wood* laid upon the *Fire*, especially *Roots*; So in *Candles* that spit *Flame*, if they be wet; So in *Rasping*, *Sneezing*, &c. So in a *Rose-leafe* gathered together into the fashion of a Purse, and broken upon the Fore-head, or Backe of the Hand, as Children use.[12]

Such sounds are illustrative of a central principle for Bacon, that all sound involves some resistance:

> It is certaine, that *Sound* is not produced at the first, but with some *Locall Motion* of the *Aire*, or *Flame*, or some other *Medium*; Nor yet without some *Resistance*, either in the *Aire*, or the *Body Percussed*. For if there be a meere Yeelding, or Cession, it produceth no *Sound*.[13]

All sound involves a struggle, or, as we may prefer to say, a dance, between a force and an obstruction, however minimal it may be, and the plosive seems to dramatize this contention in the purest way.

It is not clear why this should have been extended into the term *raspberry* when the sound is produced imitatively, by the lips rather than the anus. It may involve in part the eye-rhyme provided by the adjoining of the letters *p* and *b*, which, because of the difficulty in pronouncing them, tend to be elided in words like *cupboard*.

The rapid oscillation of the lips – in practice, usually the lower lip – flapping against the protruded tongue produces a secondary or ectopic voice. The sound has the grating or buzzing tonality and pitch of a voiced sound, but the voice is in fact produced by the vibration of the external portions of the speech apparatus, not by the larynx. For this reason it is, like many of the noises of the voice, between the condition of the animate and the inert. Better, perhaps, it is driven by the second or pseudo-animate life of mechanical noise, which is at once inanimate and yet suffused with dissident, displaced will. The impersonality of the raspberry is suggested by such prankishly ventriloquial items as whoopee cushions, and the practice of blowing raspberries either in cooperation between the mouth and some other portion of the body, or even without the use of the mouth at all. The purpose of such comic eruptions is, of course, to provoke laughter, and laughter is a sort of mimic prolonging of the explosion that is its stimulus.

The sound of the fart is the sound of accident, which may be recruited to perform the essential accident of sound. It may be thought of as a blind sound, a sound doubly detached from the superintendence of the eye, because it issues both from below and from behind. As a semi-voluntary sound, which presses into awareness unbidden but may also, if only to a limited degree, be restrained and channelled, it is halfway between willed utterance and the involuntary noises of the body, the gurgles and rumblings of the intestines, the creak of flexed knees or the crack of finger-joints.

The sound of a 'closed' plosive like 'plump' or 'plop' suggests Bacon's 'entity of sound', a voiding given shape and substance, like a bubble. The baby seems to take its very name from the bubbling and burbling which is such a prominent part of its early, infant gropings with the mouth after articulate sound, like an embodiment of Ernest Jones's sober fantasy of birth from the anus. Adult language preserves this semi-liquid play with textures and quasi-forms in the very words *bubble* and *babbling*. *Burring*, the sound ascribed to the idiot or the simpleton, suggests the blurred plosive that has not formed itself fully enough to come to a focus, or for its tension to be resolved.

But the rasping sound of a raspberry can also suggest something less shaped and persistent, for example, the chaotic zoomings and writhings of a balloon as its air is suddenly released. The sound of the raspberry suggests not just a catastrophic eruption, but also the idea of tearing. If speech may be imagined as the spinning of a continuous yarn or skein, then the raspberry tears abruptly into that continuity, spreading quickly and uncontrollably (the 'rending of calico' evoked earlier). If the principal function of the plosive is to introduce discontinuity into continuity, as suggested earlier, then the raspberry that veritably 'lets rip' offers the most violent form of this severance. The raspberry is a derisive refusal of the voice as such, a refusal that nevertheless is not entirely outside voice.

But the plump, full-blown raspberry is at the extreme of a spectrum of minor explosions of the breath that punctuate speech, and are, as a result, scarcely to be rendered in writing. There is, for example, the *pah* of sharp disgust. Then there are the slightly milder reproofs of *pouf* and *piffle* – though they are mild only in English, for French has a particularly rich array of unvoiced plosives, encompassing disgust, amazement, resignation and incredulity, to name only these. At the bottom end is the resigned, minimally stopped sigh.

The brilliance of the rendering of Leopold Bloom's discreet fart, masked by the sound of a passing tram, at the end of the 'Sirens' episode of *Ulysses* lies in its suggestion of the alternation of high and low pressure in Bloom's flatulent release.

> Seabloom, greaseabloom viewed last words. Softly. *When my country takes her place among.*
>
> Prrprr.
>
> Must be the bur.
>
> Fff! Oo. Rrpr.
>
> *Nations of the earth.* No-one behind. She's passed. *Then and not till then.* Tram kran kran kran. Good oppor. Coming. Krandlkrankran. I'm sure it's the burgund. Yes. One, two. *Let my epitaph be.* Kraaaaaa. *Written. I have.*
>
> Pprrpffrrppffff.
>
> *Done.*[14]

We move from the gentle purring of 'Prrprr', through the breezy laxity of 'Fff!', and the slightly more rending 'Rrpr' to the climactically sustained thrashing hosepipe of 'Pprrpffrrppffff'. In the course of an astute discussion of the ways in which onomatopoeia, far from being the simple and immediate imitation of sounds in language, is in fact highly coded, Derek Attridge observes that the violent agitation of the sound is suggested by the resemblance of the collection of letters to a musical stave with high and low notes rapidly alternating.[15] We should remember that 'Sirens' is the musical chapter of *Ulysses*, and Joyce is mimicking an orchestral cadenza, while noting also that the piano and the forte have changed valences, since the *f* here signifies the diffused rather than the fortified form of the *p*.

Plosive *p* has a particularly close affinity with fricative *f*, the fricative functioning as a softened, blurred, moistened and bathetic form of explosion, a fizzling out or damp squib. This can again be illustrated by orthography, and in particular by the use of the *ph* combination inherited from Greek to render certain kinds of fricative, with an enfeebling effect being gained from the presence of the *p* – the onomatopoeic *phut!* is always rendered, as far as I can see, with *ph-* ,preserving Greek φ, phi, rather than *f*. The equivalent *ph-* word to *psyche* is probably *phantasy*, and the family of words that includes *phantasm* and *phenomenon*, words in which the barely obstructed escape of air between lip and tooth suggests the ethereality of the conception signified (though this effect is superfluous in the word *physical*). A contrasting example in British tabloid English is the gestural locution *phwoar!* – to signify an aggressive male appreciation of female sexual attractiveness. *Fwoar* would render the sound perfectly well, but 'phwoar' adds an extra spurt of plosive energy, making it more, well, ejaculatory. Something similar, though in a milder form, is to be found in *phew*, where the *p* seems to add an extra bit of preliminary tension to the gushing relief of the expelled air.

Much of the force of *p* and *b* in signifying the definitive is gained from the work that they do in initial and terminal positions, a force that, as we have seen, is amplified when the sound occurs both at the beginning and at the end of the word, as in *pop*, or *bomb*. But in the middle of words, *b* and *p* have a tendency to lose their interruptive sharpness and be smoothed out by neighbouring sounds The sharp adjacency of *p* and *t* at the end of *erupt* and *interrupt* is hushed to a *sh-* sound in the middle of the words *eruption* and *interruption*. A word like *occur* is a result of the softening of the initial *ob* by the influence of the *c* of *currere*. Similarly, in words like *bomb*, *comb* and *limb*, the terminal *b* has been blurred into the preceding nasal. We may perhaps suggest that there is a natural tendency in all language to drift towards such elision, so that the forming of the kind of distinctness and discontinuity characteristic of plosives requires a large input of innovative or reactionary energy. *Collapse* uses this tendency towards medial ellision to suggest the literal crumpling of tension.

The written forms of *b* and *p* are visual mirrors, and there are occasions when they seem to enact semantic opposition, too. The associations of *p* with precision make it more likely to be associated with what is small – *piddling*, *petty*, *piccolo*, *pottering*, *pizzicato*, *pica*, *nit-picking*, the *pinkie* – while the greater force exerted in the production of *b* perhaps boosts the idea of the booming, the brash, the braggart (not invariably, to be sure – think of *birdbrain* – but, as with all the examples of semantic iconicity discussed in this book, when it does, it does so because it seems to). *Beauty* seems to be a more solemn, philosophical and grown-up thing than *prettiness*. It would be hard to be *bombastic* without being *pompous* into the bargain, but the reverse seems less assured, perhaps in part because *b* seems large enough to embrace *p*, but *p* does not necessarily imply *b*. If someone were said to be *pompastic*, it would, I think strike us as a minor, more pimply form of pretension than *bombast*. In words like *bump* and *bop*, *bleep* and *blip* the relatively large and the relatively small seem combined to produce the sense of an expansive force rapidly narrowing.

Mystical writers have made much of *b*'s position as the second letter of the alphabet. For Kabbalist writers, *a* signifies the pure, unobstructed outflowing of the divine creative principle. But it is only with the letter *b* that this effusion meets its other, in the form of an obstruction overcome, a force disclosed by moving through something that it is not. *B* therefore not only signifies secondariness, it enacts the first appearance in the world of duality, and the duality of appearance itself, since the appearance of something doubles its elementary existingness. It instances the principle, central to Kabbalist mysticism, of the divine self-distancing that is necessary for creation. So, if *a* signifies the divine merely turning on or communing with itself, then *b* represents its meeting with, and self-expression through, the world of matter. Lips are to larynx as matter is to spirit, just as the closure of the consonant is to the openness of the vowel. The first word of Genesis, *bereishit*, signifying 'in the beginning', begins with a *beth*. Because *b* combines the two principles of open and occluded utterance, in its retention then release of sound, it indicates a kind of primary duality, an inaugural, elemental two-in-one. Human babies in most parts of the world discover this elemental pairing, with variations on the open, alpha-cry *ah* being succeeded by the varieties of labial stopping provided by *b* and *p* sound, as the work of the lips modifies the undirected force of the pure, open vowel *a*. This perhaps accounts for the close association of *a* with *b* and its relative *p* in many primary words – *papa* and *pap* (the breast and the first food).[16] But in fact, a plosive is a triadic rather than a binary formation; first there is the opening of the flow of utterance; then there is the stoppage; and then there is the sound which bursts through this blockage, equalizing the tension formed by openness and closure. This suggests that every apparently unprecedented first thing may in fact be a third thing, a response to a pre-existing duality. In this sense, every little bang is a recapitulation of the conundrum of the Big Bang; if there was a Big Bang, what caused it – in response to what internal pressure did the universe explode into being? What pre-existing condition of duality or tension did the beginning strive to bring to an end?

Words which employ the prefix *ob-* seem to activate a particularly effective rhyme between meaning and form, the principal signification of the Latin preposition *ob* being that which stands in front of or comes up against. In the forming of the word *obstruction*, the breath comes up against and breaks through an obstruction of its own, with similar effects being palpable in words like *obscure*, *obfuscate*, *obdurate*, *obnubilate*, and *obstreperous*. The commonest and most important of such words is *object*, which literally means that which is thrown up against one – facing the 'object', the 'subject' seems to be said to be thrown under it. Indeed, the relation between subject and object is enacted in the relation between vowel and consonant, between free and unobstructed breath: it is as though a word, any word, insofar as it is a shaped and stopped entity that modifies the lyric cry, were at once voice and a kind of obstacle, or foreign body, that voice must break through.

Conflating the voiced and unvoiced plosives, *b* and *p*, Antoine de Gébelin proposed that it is not surprising that it should designate 'the mouth, of which it is the name, or that, by extension, it should be the root for a multitude of words which designate, firstly, the face, or physiognomy; secondly, the properties of the head, roundness, length; thirdly, the operations of the mouth, speaking, eating, drinking [parler, boire, manger], etc.'[17] These associations are not nearly so strong in English, where the mouth and its operations tend to be evoked by plosives only for the purposes of discredit, as for example when a writer is told, at the beginning of Scott's *Bride of Lammermoor*, that his characters 'make too much use of the *gob-box*; they *patter* too much'.[18] Nevertheless, there may be enough susceptibility to the Gallic amuse-bouche to be able to make out in the operations of the plosive, especially in combination with the gaping O, a kind of figuration of the mouth itself. In this, the plosive seems the most representative enactment of the meeting of voice and non-voice, or soul and unensouled matter, in the voice itself. It is the form of force, a force that forces itself into form. It is appropriate that the force should be built from that which seems most formless: thin air. In it voice encompasses and assimilates the not-voice, taking to itself the impediment to voice that it itself is.

EIGHT

Tittle-tattle

This chapter considers the class of sounds known as the dentals, and, more specifically the sound, and the ideas formed upon it, of the double or geminate (twinned) t. There are languages, such as Italian, in which doubled consonants are regularly sounded, but this is not for the most part the case in English, in which the function of the doubled consonant in writing is to indicate a shortening of the preceding vowel sound. That the *Ormulum* of 1180 should have proposed and itself practised this as a systematic principle of English orthography indicates that this was already a recognizable pattern of word formation at this point. Doubled t is a kind of noise, and, we may say, a specifically 'dry' or toneless noise, a chatter or crackle, the monochrome of sound. In a popular BBC TV quiz show of the 1970s called *Face the Music*, the presenter Joseph Cooper would play a tune on a keyboard that produced no sound but a busy, bony clatter, from which contestants were supposed to recognize the tune. The emaciation of the word effected by the clustering of ts produces a particular kind of agitated inanimation.

There is a Doppler effect brought about by the contraction of phonic space consequent upon the doubling of consonants. Just as the stretching of a given quantity of sound vibrations across a longer or shorter space when an ambulance goes by produces a variation in the pitch, so the doubling of the consonant shortens, and in the process, though less conspicuously, lifts the pitch, of the preceding vowel. We might note in passing the oddity of this effect, or the usual explanation of it. For it can scarcely be the case that the double consonant actually modifies a sound; rather, the eye, in reading – or, in speaking, what we might call the phonic eye – looks ahead to the doubled consonant in order to discount in advance the possibility of a long vowel. Here is a rapid shuttle forwards and backwards, a hiccup, doubletake or interpretative *sauter pour mieux reculer* rather than any simple retroaction. Such beat-skippings were known as *syncopes*, from Greek *syn-* and *kopein*, to strike, beat or cut off, and ran together music and medicine, since a syncope was also a temporary cessation of the heart, inducing fainting or swoon. The syncope is a *lapsus linguae*, a palpitant *petit mort* of forgetfulness amid the stream of speech. The crowded pitter-patter of iterated dentals paradoxically both protests against this ablation and invites it.

So doubled *t* is a noise that furnishes some shortfall or superflux of meaningful or expressive language. Language stalls or stutters, becomes cluttered. And yet this is not an absolute white noise but, so to speak, pink noise; an inflected noise, able to embody both the noise itself and the idea of noise. Thus it is drawn back into the orbit of signification. The particular way in which it seems to exceed or fall short of full meaning is indicative as well as merely active. It means a certain kind of unmeaning, it leaves the service of signification while remaining in its pay as a kind of double agent.

The double *t* sound is implicated in many words which mean empty speech, where, as we saw in chapter Seven, the percussive vibration of the sound is imagined as that of an empty bladder, a word that is akin to words like *blither*, *blather* and *blether*, and also *bluster*, which has come to mean to puff and roar pompously, but has been related to low German *blustern*, 'to flutter or flap the wings in alarm like a frightened dove'. The medial dental of German words like *moder* and *fader* is often modified into mother and father, but *th* can also alternate with *tt*, as in the sadly obsolete word *blatter*, used for example by Matthew Parker in his rendering of Psalm 94:4, 'They prate, they speak arrogantly', as 'They blatter out: euen what they list.'[1] *Blatter* is from Latin *blaterare*, to prate or babble, and is applied also to the sounds made by dogs, frogs and camels.[2]

We have seen that part of the voice's versatility lies in its capacity to include and capitalize upon the sounds of its own detritus and demise, imitating the wheezing bagpipe, the raspberrying burst balloon, or the rattle-bag, this last the title of a poem by the fourteenth-century

Welsh poet Dafydd ap Gwilym, used by Seamus Heaney and Ted Hughes as the title of an influential poetry anthology. The rattle-bag was a bag full of stones that was shaken to drive off animals, or, on other accounts, surprisingly, to attract them. In Dafydd ap Gwilym's poem the contraption is cursed by a young man whose lass has been frightened off by the sound just as the amorous going was getting good.

> Under Christ, no sound in Christendom
> (Of a hundred foul names) was so harsh.
> A pouch at a stick's end resounding,
>
> A ringing bell of round stones and gravel [*Cloch sain o grynfain a gro*].
> A crowd of English stones making [*Crwth cerrig Seisnig yn sôn*]
> A trembling sound in a bullock's skin.
> A cage of three thousand beetles, [*Cawell teirmil o chwilod*]
> A cauldron in tumult, a black scrotum [*Callor dygyfor, du god*].
> The keeper of a meadow, as old as grass.
> Dark-skinned, pregnant with splinters.
> Whose accent is hateful to an old roebuck,
> Devil's bell, with a stake in its haunch;
> A scarred, scabby, stone-bearing gravel-womb [*Greithgrest garegddwyn grothgro*].[3]

This kind of sound is often used to signify the emptying of spirit or virtue from the voice, leaving a dry and mindless agitation, as in St Paul's warning to the Corinthians that 'Though I speak with the tongues of men and of angels, and have not charity, I am become [as] sounding brass, or a tinkling cymbal' [χαλκὸς ἠχῶν ἢ κύμβαλον ἀλαλάζον]. The 'tinkling' of the King James version is a dentalization of the more liquid ἀλαλάζον, *alalazon*, a war cry, and may have been suggested by the Latin of the Vulgate, which gives *aes sonans aut cymbalum tinniens*. But *alalazon* is closer to Latin *ululatus*, a shrieking or howling, usually in lament, but also applied by Caesar to the war-whoops of the Gaels. This has been suggested by Latin *ulula*, itself the source both of the English words *owl* and *howl*, and related to the Greek ολολύζω, a screech-owl whose cry was of ill omen.[4] This association is shared with a number of Indo-Aryan words, such as the Pali *uluka*, an owl, Panjabi *ulla*, which means both an owl and a fool, and Prakrit *ululu*, the sound of rejoicing.[5]

The point in common between the tinny rattling of the cymbal and the howling of ululation is the rapid flapping of the tongue or glottis. Perhaps the material form that mediates between them would be the bell, which can intone the solemn summons of the Lord, whether to worship or to death, but can also seem to jangle emptily, its clapper the occasion of a mere, unmelodious clanging (this being the Revised Version rendering of ἀλαλάζον). Philip Larkin evokes the call to him of poetry as a 'lifted, rough-tongued bell', which Tim Trengove-Jones has suggestively linked with Larkin's stammer, finding in it 'a compelling physical awareness of the tongue's blended awkwardness and expertise'.[6]

As with words incorporating repeated *p*, there is a large class of words that tempt or permit the tongue to toy with the challenge, as well as possibility of stuttering failure, that is posed by rapid dental iteration. The trickiness of words like *interpretative* is tamed by the simplification of American *interpretive*, though, it loses the hint of the painstaking and the meticulously-discriminated that is there in the English word. As in the repetition of *p* described in chapter Seven, iterodentality always suggests and displays tongue-twisting accomplishment, a challenging manoeuvre smoothly executed. This coheres with the accident that English is formed from the coalescence and interpenetration of two language strains, the Germanic and the Latinate. They have their well-known differences of tone, register and lexis, with Germanic languages tending to furnish words for bodily or otherwise primary qualities (swear words in English are aptly known as 'Anglo-Saxon') and Latinate words being strongly identified with learning, law, artifice and language itself, not least in the fact that, in English, as in Latinate languages, the very word for language is lingual rather than guttural. This forms a systematic contrast between the back of the mouth, embodied in the guttural or the glottal, and the front of the mouth, of which the dentals are the most pronounced form, and which represent language, so to speak, coming to light. We might almost see the speaking of English as involving the cohabitation of two mouths in the space of one, the muddy gutturals of the Caliban mouth alternating with the tight, bright, Ariel-like Tinkerbell tones of the Latinate tongue and teeth, tripping its light fantastick toe.

Sometimes these phonaesthetic values crystallize into certain kinds of name. We saw in chapter Six that the Germanic growls and gargles that cohabit with Latinate articulation announce themselves in the names of Grendel or the Gorgon. And the letter t generated another phonaesthetic personification, who is now largely forgotten, but was once celebrated and elaborated. We are fortunate in that his curriculum vitae has been constructed in very great detail by Margaret Jennings, in a book-length article that is unlikely to be superseded any time soon.[7]

The first appearance of what is known as the recording demon seems to be some time in the 1220s, in an exemplum, or moral lesson, from a sermon composed by Jacques de Vitry, a French preacher, leader of crusades and, late in his life, cardinal in Rome. The story goes like this:

> I have heard that a certain holy man, when he was in the choir, saw a devil who seemed to be struggling under the weight of a bulging sack. When he urged the devil to tell him what he was carrying, he replied 'These are the skipped syllables and words of the verses of the psalms [*sillabe et dictiones syncopate et versus psalmodie*] which these priests have stolen from God during Matins; rest assured that I am preserving them carefully to testify against them [*ad eorum accusationem*].'[8]

The story was repeated in sermons and writings, but it was not for 60 years or so that the devil acquired a name, in a section of the *Tractatus de Penitentia* by the Franciscan scholar John of Wales of around 1285, which speaks of a devil who called himself 'Titivillum' and who collected 'morsels and fragments of the psalms'.[9] John quotes two tag-lines that would come to constitute the signature tune of Titivillus for a couple of centuries thereafter: 'Fragmina verborum titiuillus colligit horum/Quibus die mille vicibus se sarcinat ille' (Titivillus gathers up their fragmented words, of which he puts in his bag a thousand a day).

The figure of Titivillus converges with that of another demonic snapper-up of unconsidered trifles. As well as picking up the errors of the preacher, Titivillus keeps a record of all the tittering, gossiping and idle talk that occurs in the congregation – principally among its female members. The most developed account of this kind of devilish recording is also to be found among the exempla of Jacques de Vitry, who tells a story of a devil who is trying to write down all the idle chatter but is unable to fit it all on the piece of parchment he is using. So he takes the parchment and attempts to stretch it with his teeth.[10] Here, the parchment offers an equivalent to the materialization of the words represented by the sack of Titivillus in other versions. In another version, the writing devil is engaged in writing down 'all the laughinges that were betwene the women atte the masse', along with 'clatoring' and iangelynge' (one wonders quite how the devil records laughing – *tittitittititti*, perhaps).[11] This writing devil becomes identified with Titivillus towards the end of the fourteenth century, in a poem that begins 'Tutivillus, the devyl of hell, / He wrytheth har names, sothe to tel/admissa extrahantes'.[12]

And the devil acquired a third role as well, one that is not reviewed in Margaret Jennings's article, since it concerns the post-medieval afterlife of Titivillus, retrained as the devil who haunts printing houses, on the lookout now not for slips of the tongue but for clumsy mishaps of the hand. Here, in the age of movable and therefore removable type, the jots and tittles, the orts and orphans, the skipped and dropped letters are literally (and I suppose litteraly) there to be gathered up, from the floor on which they may fall unremarked from the butterfingers of the compositor. In his new role, Titivillus is true (that is, untrue) to type. For one of the declensions of his own name is probably the result of a scribal error, or readerly eyeslip, in the rendering, in at least one early text, of the name of Titivillus as Tintinillus, a mistake that one could imagine being made frequently, given the easy substitutability of *u*, *v* and *n* in medieval manuscript.[13] Oddly, this is a mistake of the eye or hand that discloses an aural logic, associating the chatterings and whisperings that are the devil's object with jingling tintinnabulations, from Latin *tinnire*, ring, chink, clink, jingle, tinkle, tingle.

There may be a further modification of the itinerant tinnitant imp in an appearance of the general word 'tittifil', to mean hanger on, wastrel or vagabond, in a play of 1537 called *Thersites*, at the heart of a list of tickling worms that have taken up residence in the belly of Telemachus – for Latin *tinea* is in fact a kind of worm:

> All the courte of conscience in cockoldst yres
> Tynckers and tabberets typplers tauerners
> Tyttyfylles, tryfullers, turners and trumpers
> Tempters, traytoures, trauaylers and thumpers
> Thryftlesse, theuyshe, thycke and thereto thynne
> the maladye of this wormes cause for too blynne.[14]

Now the devil stands for, and is himself propagated by, the spirit of imperfect transmission or spontaneous mutativity. He is the parasite, the scrambler, the white noise, the tinnitus. He is both negative and positive, not just the obliterator of sense, but also at times the interpolator of spurious or ghostly material, in what have been called Satanic verses.

Indeed, the play of writing and speech seems to be closely imbricated with the play between the vowel-mouthed Germanic and the daylit consonants of Latin. When Latin entered into cohabitation with Anglo-Saxon, it was predominantly as the language of law and writing, which, so to speak, took up symbolic residence between the tongue and the teeth rather than between the palate and the glottis. Speech hung around in the back of the mouth; language, formed from the Latin *lingua*, seemed to belong to the front and to be identified with the hairsplitting differentiations of the consonants.

These alternatives are dramatized wittily and riotously in the late fifteenth-century play *Mankind*, in which Titivillus has his most developed role. The whole play may be read as a linguistic struggle played out between the alternatives of measured and melodious morality, as embodied in the words and manner of Mercy and the riotous nonsense and obscenity of the corrupting figure of Mischief and his larrikin followers, New Gyse (Guise), Nowadays and Nought. The very first words that Mischief utters are an interruption, met by Mercy's reproach: 'Ye ben culpable/To interrupte thus my talkyng delectable'.[15] Their arrival on the scene announces the descent of pious discourse into busy noise, enacted not just in their speech, but in the drubbing or 'praty scottlynge' given to the belly of Nought.[16] The face-off between corporeal English and spiritual Latin is brought to a neat focus in New Gyse's response to the vaunting, self-important polysyllables of Mercy: 'Mercy ys my name by denomynacyon/I conseyue ye haue but a lytyll fauour in my communycacyon'. 'Ey, ey!', complains New Gyse, 'Yowr body ys full of Englysch Laten' – a notion which here approximates to the Sassenach sounds (*Seisnig yn sôn*) of Daffyd ap Gwilym's rattle-bag. He mocks Mercy's prissy and churchy speech with an obscene invitation:

> I prey yow hertyly, worschyppull clerke.
> To haue this Englysch mad in Laten.
> 'I haue etun a dyschfull of curdys.
> Ande I haue schetun yowr mowth full of turdys.'
> Now opyn yowr sachell wyth Laten wordys
> Ande sey me this in clerycall manere.[17]

I have long suspected a reminiscence of New Gyse's challenge in the interjection that appears in the midst of the dialogue between the two gossipy washerwomen in James Joyce's *Finnegans Wake*: 'Latin me that, my trinity scholard, out of eure sanscreed into oure eryan'.[18] There is a nice chiasmic shimmy to be noted here. The implication behind the mockery is that Latin lacks the robustness of the native tongue, and is too primped and prettified to deal with corporeality. The roisterers insist on the explosively incontinent body against the 'louely wordys' and 'mellyfluose doctryne' of Mercy, singing a potty-mouthed burlesque of a Christmas carol and telling Mankind that 'I wolde yowr mowth and hys ars that this made/Wer maryede junctly together'.[19] And yet New Gyse clearly also sees Latin as itself a sort of excrement, which is clogging up the body and mouth of Mercy – his earlier remark that 'yowr body ys full of Englysch Laten' equating pretty clearly to 'you are full of Latin shit'. The centuries-long tide of disgust for anything to do with the Roman church among Protestants sometimes expressed itself later through a similar contempt for the empty wrangling of Latin scholasticism, as for example Peter Pett's mockery of arguments in '*barbarous* Latine' about '*quiddity, esseity, entity* and such *titivilitium*, and *to eus rationis*, that did (as I may say) destroy the *being* of *Reason*'.[20] In *Mankind*, Latinate dentality is answered by a kind of Germanic accidentality that is heard in the fizzling plosives of spitting, sputtering, spattering, splattering and, from the other end of things, shitting, squittering and piddling. Incontinent speech and simple incontinence are run together in Nought's words:

> I am doynge of my nedyngys; be ware how ye schott!
> (*Speaks to crowd*)
> Ffy, fy, fy! I haue fowll arayde my fote!
> Be wyse for schotynge wyth yowr takyllys, for Gode wott;
> My fote ys fowly ouerschett.[21]

Writing has often been seen as a kind of excremental supplement to speech, associated with materiality and mortality. As I have already suggested, Latin appears in this sense like a kind of writing in the mouth. Mischief sets up a mock trial of Mankind, with the figure of Nought acting as amanuensis. 'Nought scribit' is the suggestively laconic stage direction and, indeed, when it comes to reading the record, Mischief can make nothing of it: 'Here ys "blottybus in blottis,/Blottorum blottibus istis."/I beschrew yowr erys, a fayer hande'.[22] The mock declension makes Latin nothing more than empty, inky blather. In fact blotting and blattering are kinds of equivalent. Etienne de Bourbon wrote that the recording devil was there to take account of all those idle priests who 'truncated verses, evacuated them of their sense, skipped pronunciations [and] obliterated letters' [*truncat versus, a suo intellectu eviscerant, dictiones sincopant, litteras oblitterant*].[23] His words remind us of the origin of *obliterate* in *oblitterare*, which has the sense of a writing over, a turning of writing on itself, which reduces literature to litter.

These themes are drawn together in the figure of Titivillus himself, who is summoned to the scene about halfway through the play in order to maximise the mischief-making. Like any properly accredited devil, he announces himself in Latin: 'Ego sum dominancium dominus ande my name ys Titivillus./Ye þat haue goode hors, to yow I sey caueatis'. The figure of Titivillus had been known for two or more centuries, so would have needed no glossing. But his name has already been whispered before he arrives on the scene, when Mankind sits down to make a record of the glorious redemption of which he has been told by Mercy: 'Her wyll I sytt ande tytyll in þis papyr/The incomparable astat of my promycyon'. Hanging the paper round his neck is the sign of his redemptive entitlement, but, from the point of view of Mischief and his gang, it is no more than a tittle, a scribble, a diddle or doodle. This is then amplified when Titivillus says that 'I xall go to hys ere ande tytyll therin'.[24] Whispering, the sound that a pen or pencil makes on the page, is a kind of writing in the mouth, that is at once excessive and deficient in spirit.

Language involves the interfusion of the principles that Michel Serres has called the hard and the soft, by which he means, not just the literal contrast of different modes of material composition, but also the interrelation of the sensible and the intelligible, the actual and the virtual – or in other, more contemporary words, hardware and software.[25] The hard and the soft have, appropriately enough, two modes of meeting – a soft, in which they merge and enter into each other, and a hard, in which they seem to repel and recoil from each other. Nowhere do the hard and the soft come up against each other with such versatility as in the meetings of teeth and tongue, the least and the most elastic portions of the speech apparatus. This literal hardness and softness rhymes with the more metaphorical interfusion of the hard and the soft in the structure of all utterance – empty and mindlessly mechanical repetition or redundancy of structure on the one hand, and the unpredictable, random, corporeal accidents of speech on the other.

The meaning of the teeth is hardness and discontinuity. Where the softer portions of the mouth, the tongue, the palate, the glottis, may be said to be analogue in form, since they suggest continuously variable qualities, the teeth are digital, prestidigital even, because they seem to reduce sounds to equal quantities. The soft portions of the mouth approach and enter into the absolute ductility of the breath; they belong to the order of the continuous. The hardness of the teeth belongs to the insentience and unresponsiveness of the mineral world. Dental sounds suggest the brittle, which is hard but liable to shatter, a granite that is only a touch away from transformation into grittiness. Perhaps one grits one's teeth because they are so close to the condition of grit.

Edison used to monitor the sounds of the phonograph by biting its edge, recapitulating Beethoven's trick of amplifying sound by gripping a stick in his teeth and pressing it against a piano. This alternative route into awareness via the conduction of bone amplifies the mechanical cast of sounds, shifting the balance of the hard and the soft that is characteristic of all hearing and speech towards the hard. The geminate t can be said to decompose or atomize. At the same time, it seems to cluster and reduplicate, the effect being what we might call a compounded decomposition, or agitated aggregation, at once minced and massed.

Many of the words and sounds with which I have been preoccupied in this book demonstrate the form of apophony known as ablaut reduplication, or the changing of vowel sounds with the retention of consonants. Language abounds with such sing-song alternations, which have a special use in signifying infantile actions or utterances, or states of confused or careless variation – *chit-chat, knick-knack, mish-mash, mingle-mangle, jingle-jangle, tittle-tattle, pitter-patter, clitter-clatter, flip-flop, flim-flam, flitter-flutter, snicker-snacker, ping-pong*. Oddly, these highly structured contrasts are used to signify unstructured noise.

Ablaut reduplication is common in many languages, and with similar kinds of signification, for example in Japanese *kasa-koso*, rustle, and *gata-goto*, rattle. The enacted suggestion is that, in such utterances, language is merely idling, having been abandoned or surrendered to undirected movement. Hebrew does not seem to involve so much iterative play with dentals, but its aptness for reversible structures readily generates expressions such as *al-te-kush-kayshe-al-ha-cum-cum* – don't keep on rattling the kettle, or, as we might say in English, stop banging on. The very words used to signify this phenomenon have the idea of a kind of turning – *apophony* and *ablaut* both signify 'away from sound or voice', thus, we might say, a turning within voice away from voice's straight and narrow. The kinds of rattling vacillation often enacted by words that have geminate dentals within them are doubled in the rattling between and across words.

Ablaut reduplication is a structuring principle across many languages, since it generates the variations of vowels within consonant structures that are an essential feature of inflections – *hic*, *haec*, *hoc*. Consonants often mark and make possible these vowel-differentiations by remaining themselves invariant. Consonants make possible the principle of spacing that allows meanings to be distinguished and distributed across a field of different signifying possibilities. Expressions that enact the rapid shuttling of these alternatives collapse and cripple this spacing, creating a kind of continuous discontinuity, an unvarying variation, an agglutinated fluctuation. In them 'Vacant shuttles weave the wind', in T. S. Eliot's phrase.[26]

There are many versions of the name of the demon I have called Titivillus. He appears also as Tutivillus, Titelinus, Titulinus, Tituful-lus, Tutenillus and Tytinillus, as well as having his name generalized into the form 'titivel', meaning a gossiper or confusion-causing tittle-tattler. These variations have the effect of progressively cancelling the audible differences between the vowels, *i*, *e* and *u*, producing a hurried blur, the function of which is not exactly to make a sound, but to act as the smallest hinge of sound required to make possible the vibration of the tongue.

When consonants rapidly reverberate, they seem to embody an alternative order to that of the holiness of the breath, as carried by the vowels; in place of movement, there is pure flutter or fluctuation back and forth. As one late fifteenth-century manuscript giving advice about the reading of psalms warns 'Numquam posterior versus prius incipiatur/Quam finis anterior perfecto fine fruatur', 'Never let a new verse be begun/Until the previous one has been brought to its perfect end'.[27] In a condition of rapid reverberation, consonants seem to embody the principles of the discontinuous, the iterative and the intensive. Rapidly reiterated dentals form a kind of stationary tremolo, that, moving back and forth, stalls and thickens time, gripping it in dental detention, rather than allowing it to progress. Such consonantal forms are characteristic of the 'idle speech' that was so often condemned in medieval writings, a usage that anticipates the mechanical meaning that the term acquired in the twentieth century, to signify a disengaged engine, oscillating emptily without doing any productive work. An engine or a tongue that idles simply chugs, doodles or fiddle-faddles.

Articulated speech, speech in which vowels are given their expressive space by consonants, brings time under tension, giving it a shape and direction. Oscillating consonantal clusters, by contrast, merely mark time, making it something neutral, inert and homogenous. Dentality seems to body forth idle identicality. Articulate breath is a nothing that is a something; voiceless articulation is a something that is a nothing. It is hard to bear the thought of a time that is merely a matter of 'moment upon moment, pattering down, like the millet grains of . . . that old Greek', as Hamm puts it in Samuel Beckett's *Endgame*, so that, hearing the indeterminate dittos of the clock's tick, tick, tick, or the clicking of the indicator light we unconsciously force them to sing the song 'tick-tock', as Frank Kermode notes: 'The clock's "tick-tock" I take to be a model of what we call a plot, an organisation which humanises time by giving it a form; and the interval between "tock" and "tick" represents purely successive, disorganised time of the sort we need to humanise.'[28] This can be seen as a kind of antisyncope, a hearing-in of a difference that is not there.

This impulse is to be found in the many forms of ablaut reduplication, which tend to move from high-pitched to low-pitched, from closed to open, and from frontal to posterior, with the short *i* sound almost always being the leading sound of the reduplicate pair. Perhaps the reason that formulae like *tock-tick* or *dong-ding* feel so strange and skew-whiff is that they do not supply the combination of widening (the opening of the vowel) with completion (the conclusive lowering of the pitch) which seems to offer satisfaction, while also perhaps mimicking the reassuringly iambic lub-dub of the heart. These alternations strive to impart direction to the purposeless iteration of the indistinct, which keeps on folding time back on itself in its chattering repetitions.

Signifying Nothing

In all of these Titivillus stories there is a striking alternation between omission and preservation, deficit and superfluity. At the beginning of *Mankind*, Mischief responds indignantly to the careful moral winnowing of productive and unproductive speech, corn and chaff, offered in Mercy's opening speech

> I beseche yow hertyly, leue yowr calcacyon.
> Leue yowr chaffe, leue yowr corn, leue yowr dalyacyon.
> Yowr wytt ys lytyll, yowr hede ys mekyll, ye are full of
>   predycacyon.
> But, ser, I prey this questyon to claryfye:
> Mysse-masche, dryff-draff,
> Sume was corn ande sume was chaffe,
> My dame seyde my name was Raffe;
> Onschett yowr lokke and take an halpenye.[29]

There is play throughout with the alternatives of much and little. Mercy's principle of 'Few wordys, few ande well sett' is answered by New Gyse's 'Ser, yt ys þe new gyse ande the new jett: / Many wordys ande shortely sett. / Thys ys þe new gyse, euery dele'.[30]

Thomas Elyot's dictionary of 1538 said tersely that the word 'titivillitium' 'sygnifyeth nothynge'.[31] He might have added that the word, while not exactly full of sound and fury, certainly struts and frets sufficiently to make it an interesting oxymoron; it is a busy nothing, a nothing with much ado about it. The definition wavers between signifying 'nothing' and not signifying at all. Ultimately this is the comic conundrum that characterizes the power of the diabolic as such, as canonically defined, namely that, since the devil gets any power he has only from the permission of God, he cannot really be taken seriously. This means that everything he does is really only a pretence, a nothingness. But this nothingness is not unreal, for it can take actual and terrifying forms, not least in the mistaken but powerful belief that the devil actually has the powers to which he pretends. This is to say that the devil is never more or less than theatrical. The earliest use of the word *titivillitium* is in Plautus's comedy *Casina*, in which the character Olympio responds to the suggestion that humans must rely upon the gods, with the words 'I wouldn't buy that kind of talk for total tripe' [*Non ergo istuc verbum empsim titibilicio*].[32] The meaning of Olympio's *titibilicium* and its later form *titivilitium* must certainly depend to an extent on their chiming with similar busy, bitty words like *titillatio*, a tickling, and *titubare*, to stagger or stammer, a word that came across into English as *titubate*, which may sometimes have given it associations with *masturbate*. The word *titivate*, which seems like a blending of *titillate* and *titubate*, means to take comically extravagant care in primping or prettying oneself up. This word in fact derives from the Middle English *tid*, time, and thus has the core meaning of drawing out time in trifling or inessential adornment, though it has presumably been drawn in to the orbit of the titivillitious lexicon. John Payne Collier heard in the name of Titivillus *totus* and *vilis*, 'completely worthless', which has the virtue at least of blending totality and tittling.[33]

The story of Titivillus illustrates a striking seesaw, or, borrowing an obsolete dialect word for the same diversion, titter-totter, between losing and retention. Though one might expect Titivillus to approve and encourage the slurred psalming and idle chatter among the congregation, his role in carefully logging these instances of chitchat allies him with a principle of continence rather than the incontinence of his subjects. George Gascoigne's chapter 'Of hasty sayng of these holy houres and of ouerskypynge' in his text of 1530 *The Mirroure of Oure Lady* makes the economics of negligent enunciation quite explicit

> For lyke as clyppers or falsers of the kynges money are punysshed by deth Ryght so they that clyppe away from the money of goddes seruyce eny wordes or letters or syllables & so false yt from the trew sentence or from the trewe maner of saynge therof deserue to be greuously punysshed agenste god.[34]

Most of the accounts of Titivillus make it clear that he is himself on piece-work, required to cram his bag, or net, with a thousand such mislocutions a day – even more, in Gascoigne's account: 'I muste eche day he sayde brynge my master a thousande pokes full of faylynges & of neglygences in syllables and wordes'.[35]

Tittling is itself proliferative, since the tittler is a spreader of rumours and seeder of dissension. Ungoverned by the demands of truth or meaning, the empty language of tittle-tattle is the nothing that comes of nothing, the nothingness of language given over to the agitated idling that is the mere wagging of tongues. Condemnations of the evils of tittle-tattle tend themselves to multiply into long lists. And the more this nothingness broods and breeds on itself, the more sinister it can come to seem, precisely because of its parody of the powers of generation, its lifeless simulation of real vigour. This is why the list of the devils who torment Edgar in disguise on the heath in Shakespeare's *King Lear* includes 'Flibbertigibbet' (III.iv.118), which is associated in the definition of 'coquette' in Cotgrave's dictionary of 1611 with the titivil: 'a pratling, or proud gossip; . . . a cocket, or tatling houswife; a titifill, a flebergebit'.[36] Like Titivillus, Flibbertigibbet is an onomatopoeic rendering of the sound of unmeaning chatter that hardens, in Samuel Harsnett's *Declaration of Popish Impostures* of 1603, from which Shakespeare drew the word, into the name of a devil – though Harsnett's text is an hysterical denunciation of the hysterical practice of conjuring up devils from mere tongue-wagging.[37] The titillation or tickling with which titivilation blends is itself a somatic enactment of the principle that 'Mony a mickle maks a muckle', or that the minimal can flip easily into the maximal, tickle into torment, trickle into torrent.

Perhaps it is the word 'it' which in English epitomizes this coincidence of the contraries of maximal and minimal. 'It' is a kind of phonemic atom, its meaning centring on the dot with which it is uniquely provided in the Roman alphabet. Originally the Greek iota, from which the modern letter i derives, was adopted from Phoenician *yodh*. Early Christian manuscript took over the convention that the i was the only letter that did not rest upon the level of the line, but hovered as though weightlessly above it, which is still true of Hebrew *yodh*. Lower-case i is also the only letter, bar one, in the Roman alphabet that has a dot or tittle above it, this arising in medieval periods in order to distinguish the i from the adjacent l.

The other dotted letter, *j*, remained interchangeable with *i*. The *i* thus reduces to what an eighteenth-century book on shorthand called a 'Tittle or touch of the Pen'.[38] The iota itself shortens to the word *jot*, in a cross-language rhyme with *yodh*. It seems appropriate that, in mathematics, *i* should be the symbol of the imaginary number, the square root of -1. Algebraically, *i* is defined by a formula, $i^2 = -1$, which means that both *i* and - *i* are square roots of -1.

The *yodh* has a particularly important mystical significance in Kabbalistic tradition. Yitzchak Ginsburgh explicates the letter *yodh* as a kind of contraction of the alternatives of the all and the nothing:

> Subsequent to the initial *tzimtzum*, the contraction of G-d's Infinite light in order to make 'place' for Creation, there remained within the empty void a single, potential point or 'impression.' The secret of this point is the power of the Infinite to contain finite phenomena within Himself and express them to apparent external reality. Finite manifestation begins from a zero-dimensional point, thereafter developing into a one-dimensional line and two-dimensional surface . . . The initial point, the essential power of the yud, is the 'little that holds much.' The 'much' refers to the simple Infinity of G-d hidden within the initial point of revelation, which reflects itself as the Infinite potential of the point to develop and express itself in all the manifold finite phenomena of time and space.[39]

This notion that the least is a kind of concentrated version of the most appears in one of the earliest recorded uses of the English word *tittle*, in the rendering of Matthew 5:18 in the Wycliffe Bible of 1395, 'Forsothe Y seie to you, til heuene and erthe passe, o lettir or o titel shal not passe fro the lawe, til alle thingis be doon', which becomes in the King James Bible of 1611 'Till heauen and earth passe, one iote or one title, shall in no wise passe from the law, till all be fulfilled.'

Language never comes closer to its essence in such moments where it rocks between something and nothing. For language itself is ultimately made of nothing, or the next to nothing of the squeak and plabber of air pushed through a damp pipe. Formed in and through language as we are, the tittle-tattle of the teeth tells a tale of our own essential founding upon the principle of hardly anything at all.

NINE

Zzzz

We have seen that vocal sounds that signify nonvocal noise often do so through an effect of acceleration, in which a single sound is repeated rapidly to form an oscillation in which the individual articulations are no longer discernible, whether in growling, gurgling, muttering or jabbering. Oddly one of the commonest forms of this blurred articulation in English is the *z* or voiced sibilant – oddly, precisely because it comes about not through the adding of noise to voice, but through the voicing of the pure, sibilant noise of the breath. In fact 'buzz' is the word used in phonetics for the sound produced by the flow of air through the constricted larynx and, along with the hiss of sibilance and the pop of stops and plosives, forms the trio of basic ways in which articulate sound is produced. The voice here turns up the noise. One might think of the range of sounds centring on the *z* as a kind of double at the front of the mouth of the voicing buzz produced by bringing together the folds of the larynx. A common way of demonstrating the difference between an unvoiced and voiced consonant is to put one's finger over one's larynx and make the sound *sss* and then to feel the vibration of the larynx when one alters the sound to *zzz*. Indeed, though we feel the buzzing of *z* at the front of the mouth, most of the buzz comes from the larynx. The sound of snoring that gets represented in comics as *zzz* is often in fact produced by the rasping of the breath at the back of the nose and mouth rather than by the stridulation of the tongue at the back of the teeth. Voice, I have proposed repeatedly, seems to emerge from noise as the establishing of distinction from amid the indistinct; but *z* can be regarded as the general or indistinct noise of voice, another kind of primary prevocal plasma from which articulation must be shaped.

Buzz Buzz

Z is also a form of this blurred or indistinct utterance that allows for the imitation of nonhuman form of communication. Francis Bacon thought that z was among a class of sounds that occurred in the world as well as in human mouths:

> There is found a Similitude, betweene the *Sound* that is made by *Inanimate Bodies*, or by *Animate Bodies*, that haue no *Voice Articulate*; and diuers *Letters* of *Articulate Voices*: And commonly Men haue giuen such Names to those *Sounds*, as doe allude vnto the Articulate Letters. As *Trembling* of *Water* hath Resemblance with the *Letter L*; *Quenching* of *Hot Mettalls*, with the *Letter Z*; *Snarling* of *Dogs*, with the *Letter R*; The *Noise of Scritchowles*, with the *Letter Sh*; *Voice* of *Cats*, with the *Dypthong Eu*; *Voice* of *Cuckoes*, with the *Dypthong On*; *Sounds* of *Strings*, with the *Letter Ng*.[1]

Bacon recommended attention to such inanimate phonations for those interested in creating speaking automata: 'if a Man, (for Curiosity, or Strangenesse sake,) would make a *Puppet*, or other Dead Body, to pronounce a *Word*; Let him consider, on the one Part, the Motion of the *Instruments* of *Voice*; and on the other part the like *Sounds* made in *Inanimate Bodies*; And what Conformity there is that causeth the Similitude of *Sounds*.'[2]

But, before the development of buzzing and humming mechanical devices, the worldly sound that has most defined the voiced sibilant is that of the buzzing or sibilant humming of insects, and, in particular, flies and bees. The buzzing of flies is not only an incursion of a kind of natural noise into the voice, it is a figure for the vacancy or triviality of noise itself. What one seventeenth-century writer called 'sencelesse Buzze' is therefore speech which has no substantial import, but is just sounding.[3] Buzzing is a kind of voiced whispering – indeed, if you whisper the word 'whisper' repeatedly, then add voice, what you get may be something like 'whizzbuzzwhizzbuz'. Like whispering, buzzing is associated with the communication of rumour and innuendo, which takes place, like the communication of a disease, in the intimate congress of lips to ear, and in the expanded, impersonal space of the public – like the whisper, the buzz is both proximate and pandemic. Buzzing occurs in, at, or about the ears, and sometimes, within the brain itself, as in this imagined reproof by James II to his conniving wife, Mary of Modena: 'buzzing Beetles of the Night/Had found fresh matter for your spite,/And set to work your busie Brain . . . Strait new Chimera's fill your Brain,/The humming Beetles buz again'.[4] The half-submerged idea here may be that the source of the noise is not a full-grown insect in the ear, or in the brain, but the maggot of the fly, 'maggot' at this point having the meaning of whim or obsession. A 1605 translation of a tract in praise of silence devoted a chapter to the murmuring and detracting tongue, which it similarly compared to the buzzing of a fly or beetle:

> There is a certain little broad kind of creature, deriued or bred out of carion or foule putrifaction, which although sometimes (like the fleetest little bird) it towreth toward heauen, and with an vnpleasing buzzing, would chide (as it were) at all the other soules: yet is it so full of rotten corruption, as, after a silly flight, and a little sorie harsh singing, he returnes back to his stinking place of creation, and, as abhorring the height of heauen, seemes most proude of his noysome habitation, and loathing to feed on odoriferous things, doth feede or glut himselfe with filthinesse onelye. To such offensiue Scarabes, may I compare the detractour and murmurer, who, though they seeme like little broad birds to vulgare opinions, when (in dissembling charity) they reprooue other mens defects: yet it may plainely be discerned, how noysome they are in their owne nature, euen while they haue other mens infirmities in their mouthes.[5]

When the nonconformist Vincent Alsop reduced the arguments of his religious opponents to entomological buzzing, he was taking a similar route:

> *They scurrilously traduce all that's serious; and what they cannot do by Manly discourse, they endeavour by Buffonry: Thus these blind Beetles that rose out of filth and excrement* Buz *about the World.* And now I am sure where to find the whole Club of Atheists. Amongst those Churchmen who blaspheme the Office of the Divine Spirit as a *Noise* and Buz.[6]

Buzzing occurs both below and above the threshold of articulated speech. It is a kind of noise that is both less than speech and the sound of its surfeit. In his book on deafness and lip-reading, John Bulwer attributes to skilled lip-readers such as Nicholas Crisp the capacity to bring to bear the 'nimblenesse of his hearing eye' in circumstances where ordinary hearing was overloaded by the buzz of sound:

> for he might chance to overheare with his eye newes of the arrivall of some shippe and of some good bargaine; when others who would perhaps keepe the intelligence to themselves were not aware of it, and amid the buzzing noise of the Royall Bee-hive of our *Emporium*,where many speaking together, one articulate voyce confounds another, his eyes being vigilant upon the motions of mens mouthes, and no way distracted with that bartering noyse is there made, he might perceive a motion, which being a Merchant, he might easily turne to his owne profit; this and many other advantages might be much furthered by the nimblenesse of his hearing eye.[7]

The associations between buzzing and of empty, contemptible speech motivate Hamlet's response to the news given by the long-winded Polonius that 'The actors are come hither my lord' – 'Buzz, buzz' (II.ii.330). Eric Partridge suggests that this must have been a kind of raspberry, or farting noise made with the mouth.[8] (Indeed, the noises of the voice to which this book is devoted have a tendency to blur into each other, as though any word for an alexical noise were in some way exchangeable with any other.) Polonius is much given to droning speech, but perhaps Hamlet's dismissal is also directed partly at the actors whose proximity Polonius has announced. If it is their strutting sound and fury that are reduced to the amorphous, mumbled rhubarb of 'buzz buzz', then theatre can here be heard telling itself to buzz off.

Inestimable and even contemptible as it may seem, the letter *z* seems possessed of a capacity to lengthen and proliferate from itself, for the name of the letter was often extended into forms like *ezod*, *yzard*, *uzzard*, *izzet* and *izzart*: Johnson's *Dictionary* (1755) in fact gives *izzard* and *uzzard* as more common forms of the letter *zed*. The closeness of this word to (and rhymeability with) *buzzard* and *lizard*, makes for associations with other animals than insects. Reviewing the history of religions in his poem 'Religious Progress', Ambrose Bierce writes 'Nay, once upon a time long gone/Man worshiped Cat and Lizard:/His God he'd find in any kind/Of beast, from a to izzard'.[9] (In fact, an 'izard' is the name for a Pyrenean antelope related to the chamois and noted for its agility.) Robert Southey evokes bird sounds in his celebration of the aged Robert the Rhymer in his later years:

He sings like a lark when at morn he arises,
And when evening comes he nightingalizes,
Warbling house-notes wild from throat and gizzard,
Which reach from A to G, and from G to Izzard.[10]

Since the buzzard was held not to be trainable as the falcon was, it came to be endowed with entirely contrasting qualities; it was supposed to be deficient in vision, stupid and bumbling and irregular in flight. 'O, slow-winged turtle', says Petruchio to Katherina, as they spar in *The Taming of the Shrew*, 'shall a buzzard take thee' (II.i.208). To be 'between hawk and buzzard' could mean between good and bad, and also, because of the association between the buzzard and doziness, between sleep and waking. A seventeenth-century writer refers to a woman who 'was either a very good, or a very bad, or an indifferent, a between Hawk and Buzzard Wife'.[11] A buzzard could also mean a humming or buzzing insect, and more specifically, in the form *buzzard-clock*, a cockchafer: Tennyson's 'Northern Farmer' evokes this insect when referring to the droning of the sermon in church: 'a bummin' awaäy loike a buzzard-clock ower my 'eäd'.[12]

Buzzard is a common name for a dimwit character, and to *buzzard* somebody meant to puzzle or bewilder them.

Much heard and seldom seen

Much of the force of the buzzing noise typically rendered by the letter z, or the doubled form zz, is derived from a kind of interference of sight with sound. The letter z benefits from an unusual rhyme between its phonic and its graphic form, through the idea of the zigzag, the characteristically random-seeming movement of the fly, wasp, or other insect, that appears as futile and undirected in its movements as in the sounds it makes – in contrast perhaps with the windings of the hissing serpent, full of insidious intent. But there is another respect in which the z appears under the sign of the purposeless or the *de trop*. The most conspicuous feature of z in English spelling may in fact be its inconspicuousness. Writing in 1582, Richard Mulcaster remarked that

> [a] form that is fair to the eie in print, & cumbersom to the hand in penning, is not to passe in writing. For what but that causeth our English pen to vse z. so seldom, which we hear so often? Bussing, hussie, dissie, go roundlie to the pen with the duble ss, but verie vnredilie with the duble z, Buzzing, huzzie, dizzie. Vse hath won ss. & the pens redinesse, is the prouf to perswade it.[13]

He later observes that

> Z, is a consonant much heard amongst vs, and seldom sene. I think by reason it is not so redie to the pen as s, is, which is becom lieutenant generall to z; as gase, amase, rasur, where z, is heard, but, s, sene. It is not lightlie expressed in English, sauing in foren enfranchisments, as azur, treasur. In the same proportion is s. and as, is as strangelie vsed.[14]

As the OED observes, it is ironic that the spelling of the very words Mulcaster singles out should so rapidly have standardized on z rather than on its lieutenant *s*, and that *z* should in fact have become steadily more common in other English words. Indeed, there was a pronounced tendency in sixteenth-century English to introduce *z* between vowels in words that had previously been spelled with *s*, especially those of French origin, such as *blazon*, *brazier*, *breeze*, *buzzard*, *hazard* and *razor*.[15] However this never became universal, which makes for a certain kind of hesitation between the letters *s* and *z* in English, and it remains as true as it was in 1582 that 'so manie zeds in our tung ar herd, & so few sene'.[16] This produces the curious effect of a kind of visual amplification of what Mulcaster calls the 'zeddish' sound,[17] which appears to be more prominent and emphatic when it does appear, in words like *brazen* and *dizzy* , even though the sound denoted is in fact phonetically indistinguishable from that in words like *praise* or *lose* or *music*. Z is therefore what may be called an eye-phone, which sounds differently on the ear of the mind because of its serrated shape. When the band Slade enjoined their listeners to 'feel the noize' in the single they released in 1973, they were right to suspect that the noise would seem that much more raucous when spelled with a *z*. So we may perhaps correct Mulcaster and say that many of the zeds in our tongue are not really heard *unless* they are seen. The case is similar to that noted by Derek Attridge of the difference between hard *c* and *k*. *Klunk* seems altogether more clunkier than *clunk* because of the contrast between *c* which, in English, can be either hard (*coin*) or soft (*ceiling*), and *k*, which can only ever be hard, as though the *c* were somehow being softened or blurred by the very fact of its variability.[18] Johnson proposed that the letter-name *izzard* meant 's *hard*', that is, an indication of the sound of the letter, 'an s uttered with closer compression of the palate by the tongue, as *freeze*, *froze*'.[19] John Walker's *Pronouncing Dictionary* (1791) took issue with him on this matter, maintaining that:

> Z is the flat *s*, and bears the same relation to it as *b* does to *p*, *d* to t, hard *g* to *k* and *v* to *f*. Its common name is izzard, which Dr. Johnson explains into *s* hard; but if, however, this be the meaning, it is a gross misnomer; for the z is not the hard but the soft *s*: but as it has a less sharp, and therefore not so audible a sound, it is not impossible but it may mean, *s surd*.[20]

The shape of the z has often been associated with deformity. The Devon word *zidle-mouth* signified a crooked mouth, or an ugly person having a mouth twisted to one side.[21] The French dramatist and novelist Paul Scarron, who was badly crippled, very likely by polio, has recourse to the letter when introducing himself in the preface, 'To the Reader, Who Never Saw Me', to an English translation of his works:

> My legs and thighs made at first an obtuse, then an equal, and at last, an acute angle. My thighs and my body making another, and my head hanging down over my breast, I am a certain representative or Hieroglyphick of the Letter Z. My arms are contracted as well as my legs, and my fingers as well as my arms. In a word, I am a certain contraction or Epitome of humane misery.[22]

The Scottish fortune-hunter Sir Pertinax in Charles Macklin's *The Man of the World* (1792) explains that he 'leuked out for an ancient, weel-jointured, superannuated dowager – a consumptive, toothless, phthisicky, wealthy widow, – or a shreevelled, cadaverous piece of deformity in the shape of an izzard, or a appersiand'.[23] Alexander Geddes's satirical poem *Bardomachia* (1800) describes a poet the form of whose verse was 'liken'd to an izzard/All this stuck deep and rankled in his gizzard'.[24] Sometimes, the very look of the z in handwriting could induce a kind of mental daze equivalent to its muzzy sound. In Goldsmith's *She Stoops to Conquer*, Tony Lumpkin is given a letter to read of which he can make out little:

> TONY. (*Still gazing*.) A damn'd cramp piece of penmanship, as ever I saw in my life. I can read your print-hand very well. But here there are such handles, and shanks, and dashes, that one can scarce tell the head from the tail. *To Anthony Lumpkin, Esquire*. It's very odd, I can read the outside of my letters, where my own name is, well enough. But when I come to open it, it's all – buzz . . . A damn'd up and down hand, as if it was disguised in liquor. (*Reading*.) *Dear Sir*. Ay, that's that. Then there's an M, and a T, and an S, but

whether the next be an *izzard*, or an R, confound me, I cannot tell.[25]

The fact that *s* and, in initial position, *x*, do perfectly well to signify so many voiced sibilants in English can also suggest that there is something arbitrary or superfluous about the letter *z*, a sense that lies behind Kent's insult when he is sparring with Oswald in *King Lear* (II.ii.64): 'Thou whoreson zed! thou unnecessary letter!' According to Nick Davis, Kent attacks Oswald for being an inauthentic, unnecessary being who is himself made up of little more of letters (he is, in fact, as Davis notes, the medium of much of the postal activity in the play): 'In Kent's summary view . . . "z" – like Oswald – has no right to exist, and in context becomes a means of bringing to a focus for thought the superfluous or excessive nature of "letters" in general: Oswald is the sort of thing that arises when 'letters' are trusted.'[26] Davis points out that the name 'Oswald' combines *z* with *O*, and is therefore a kind of zero.[27] The word *zero* first appears in print in 1604, around the year that *King Lear* is composed. Although *zero* does not in fact appear anywhere in Shakespeare's work, the word *cipher*, which derives, as *zero* does, from the Arabic *çifr*, empty, void, itself a translation of the Sanskrit *sunya*, empty, appears frequently. Davis might also have noted the something-or-nothing slide between voiced and unvoiced in the *s* of Oswald's name.

An orthographic accident gives the English *z* a layer of strangeness or unfamiliarity, which is perhaps another sign of its uncertainty or superfluity. The tailed *z* had by 1300 become difficult to distinguish in manuscript from the ȝ (yogh) character that was used to represent the sound *y*, which encouraged Scottish printers to substitute *z* for ȝ, perhaps when they were running low of supplies of the latter. Its legacy is the spelling of names like Dalzell (pronounced 'Deeyell'), Mackenzie (originally pronounced 'MacKenyee') and Menzies ('Mengies').

Benjamin Franklin made play with the uncertain condition of the letter Z in a private spoof he wrote in his exasperation at the campaign waged by Ralph Izard, with whom he had previously had bitter disagreements, to have him dismissed as ambassador to France and replaced by himself. His 'Petition of the Letter Z, commonly called Ezzard, Zed, or Izard', written some time after 12 February 1779, was enclosed in a letter of 24 Jan 1786 from Franklin to his sister, Jane Mecom, with instructions that she was not to make it public. It is written as a parody of an entry in *Tatler*, edited by Richard Steele under the pseudonym 'Isaac Bickerstaff', which had ceased publication in 1711. The Petition urges

> That your Petitioner is of as high Extraction, and has as good an Estate as any other letter of the Alphabet.
>
> That there is therefore no reason why he should be treated as he is with Disrespect and Indignity.
>
> That he is not only plac'd at the Tail of the Alphabet, when he had as much right as any other to be at the Head; but is, by the Injustice of his Enemies totally excluded from the Word WISE, and his place injuriously filled by a little, hissing, crooked, serpentine, venomous letter called S, when it must be evident to your Worship, and to all the World, that Double U, I, S, E do not spell or sound *Wize* but *Wice*.[28]

Franklin's assumed editor concludes that

> Mr. Bickerstaff having examined the Allegations of the above Petition, judges and determines that Z be admonished to be content with his Station, forbear Reflections upon his Brother Letters, & remember his own small Usefulness, and the little Occasion there is for him in the Republick of Letters, since S, whom he so despises, can so well serve instead of him.[29]

Richard Mulcaster's sense of the cumbersomeness of the letter for the hand survives at least into the nineteenth century. In *Adam Bede*, George Eliot describes the difficulties of the pupils in Bartle Massey's night-school:

> He was a little more severe than usual on Jacob Storey's Z's, of which poor Jacob had written a pageful, all with their tops

> turned the wrong way, with a puzzled sense that they were not right 'somehow.' But he observed in apology, that it was a letter you never wanted hardly, and he thought it had only been there 'to finish off th'alphabet, like, though ampusand (&) would ha' done as well, for what he could see.'[30]

It is indeed the case that some early alphabets included the ampersand as their last letter, while some dictionary makers omitted words beginning with z. Mulcaster's *Elementarie* itself lists only three entries: *zelous*, *zeale* and *zealousnesse*.

An important influence on thinking about the status of z in English is the fact that it also had a very insecure place in Latin. Since its appearance in W. M. Lindsay's influential *The Latin Language* (1894), the story is still sometimes repeated that Latin originally had inherited a z-character from Etruscan, but that the letter was banned from Latin in 312 BC by the Roman censor Appius Claudius Caecus.[31] Martianus Capella, whose *De Nuptiis Philologiae et Mercurii* is the only source for this story, remarks that 'Claudius Appius really detested the letter z, because, when it was uttered, the teeth looked like those of a death's head' ('vero idcirco Appius Claudius detestatur, quod dentes mortui, dum exprimitur, imitatur').[32] The story has been described as 'very stupid', though the suggestion that 'its basis is evidently an older story of Claudius's conceit that the letter resembled the jagged teeth of a skull' does not help make it seem much more sensible (the teeth of skulls are more exposed to view than those in living heads, but they are not necessarily any more jagged).[33] The more usual explanation for the vanishing of z from the Roman alphabet is that the voiced s sound it represented had undergone rhotacism – that is, it shifted its value to that of r, making it, as Rex Wallace puts it, 'a "dead" letter'.[34] So rare were the appearances of z in early Latin, however, that it has seriously been doubted that it ever in fact formed part of Latin at this stage.[35] It is not disputed, however that, following the Roman conquest of Greece in the first century BC, the z was introduced, or readmitted, to allow for the representation of Greek words. Quintilian was among those who applauded this development. He found Latin 'harsher in its actual sounds, because we lack the two most pleasing of the Greek letters, one vowel and one consonant [*upsilon* and *zeta*], the sweetest sounds in their language'.[36] Where Claudius Appius saw in the *zeta* the skull beneath the skin, Quintilian thought that, when this letter appeared, 'the language at once seems to brighten up and smile [the smile is not literal however in Quintilian's Latin – 'hilarior protinus renidet oratio'], as in words like *zephyrus* and *zopyrus*. If these words are written in our letters, they produce only a dull barbarous sound.'[37]

Muzzy

An important part of the indistinct idea-cluster convened in the z is that of indistinctness, or clusteredness itself. We have seen that, in his *Principles of Psychology* (1890), William James evoked the perceptual experience of the baby in terms of a 'great blooming, buzzing confusion'.[38] Confusion is frequently implied by words incorporating the letter z. One could be forgiven for assuming that the word *mizzle*, which seems to have begun to be used more frequently by British weather forecasters in the last couple of decades, is a blending of *mist* and *drizzle*, though in fact it has had an independent meteorological existence for at least as long as *drizzle* itself. However, another early meaning of the word *mizzle* is in fact to confuse, muddle, or intoxicate: in his *Anatomy of Abuses* of 1583 the enthusiastic Puritan Phillip Stubbes speaks of idle women with 'their heades pretely mizzeled with wine'.[39] The muzzy or muddled condition with which z is most frequently called into association is that of intoxication, no doubt in part because of the voicing of sibilants that is characteristic of slurred drunken speech. *Boose* has moved steadily over time towards *booze*; and the z or zz also do their bibulous work in words like *buzz*, to drink or 'empty a bottle of wine in carousing'; *stozzle*, to drink, and *stozzled*, drunk; to *bezzle*, meaning to tope or booze; and the Worcestershire dialect word *wazzle*, drink, perhaps a festive slurring of *wassail*.[40] The Lincolnshire *geezer* means a state of inebriety, and the very last entry in Wright's *Dialect Dictionary* is *zwodder*, a Devon word meaning a drowsy or stupefied state of mind, which may derive from Middle Dutch *zwadderen*, to sag or stagger drunkenly.[41] Noting the prominence of the z in the song which evokes 'those lazy, hazy, crazy days of summer', John Michell demonstrates its role 'in conjuring up the muzzy, fuzzy atmosphere of a hot summer's day, when bees are buzzing, one's eyes are glazed and the mind feels dizzy, dazy, fazed, bemused, woozy and drowsy. From the heads of dozing, snoozing (perhaps boozed) cartoon characters issue the letters zzzzzzz.'[42] We may observe that a salient feature of the work of the *z* is to signify or enact slowing, as in the word *ooze* or in the pronunciation of the word *greasy* as 'greazy', which seems to add significantly to the clogged sensation evoked by the word.

In 1808, W. Allen and W. H. Pepys noted 'that buzz in the ears which is noticed in breathing nitrous oxide'.[43] Deriving perhaps from the auditory effects of increased blood pressure, the word *buzz* became a general term for the fuzzy kind of arousal characteristic of many drugs. *Zap*, prison slang for amyl nitrite, conjoins intoxication and electrification.[44] In fact, the involvement of the sound of *z* in many names for drugs and their effects neatly sums up one of the most striking ambivalences of the sound, namely that between the sedative and the stimulant – as hinted at in the fact that *zeds* is slang for downers, or depressant drugs, and that *zen* is a slang term both for LSD and MDMA (ecstasy).[45] Excitement and loss of focus are also conjoined in the drinking game Fizzbuzz (or sometimes Bizz Buzz). A group of drinkers counts round the table, substituting 'fizz' for multiples of five and 'buzz' for multiples of seven – thus one, two, three, four, fizz, six, buzz, and so on. As the numbers get larger and larger, introducing the possibility of 'fizzbuzz' (multiples of five and seven, like 35 and 70), mistakes get easier to make, which will require the one in error to drink a forfeit, thus increasing their propensity for further boozed bungles. Here, then, the *z* is not just the indicator but also the amplifier of error.

Intoxication is easily associated with mingling or entanglement, and there is a tendency for English words which signify this kind of confusedness to incorporate the suggestive form of medial *-zz-*. *Crizzled* means crumpled or twisted up, like frosted leaves, but referred more specifically in the seventeenth century to the roughened or crazed surface of stone or glass. *Twizzled* means twisted or entangled. To *dozzle* means to daze or stupefy. *Frazzling* and *frazzled* derive from *fasel* or *fazle*, to ravel or entangle. *Frizzled* means tightly curled. *Fuzzled* is a seventeenth-century alternative for fuddled, muddled or drunk, like *sozzled*, originally a dialect word meaning mixed in a sloppy or careless manner. The primary meaning of *grizzled* is grey, in parallel with French *gris*, *grisaille*, but, when used of hair, it often also implies matted, knotted or tangled. It is this which gives us the name Grizzly Bear, translating the Latin *Ursus horribilis*, literally with skin or fur standing up. *Hazzling* is the light or superficial drying of a surface. *Araucaria araucana* is the monkey-puzzle tree, so named because its tough, spiky leaves make it a tricky problem even for a monkey to climb. A *shemozzle*, perhaps from Yiddish *shlimazl*, misfortune, is a muddle, row or rumpus. To *mozzle* (an inversion of Yiddish *mazl*, good luck) is Australian slang for to jinx, hinder or interrupt, and is consonant with *whizzle*, used in the eighteenth century to mean to obtain slyly or by stealth, and the transformation of *swindle* into *swizzle*. *Razzle* is a nineteenth-century American coinage, expressing the idea of bewilderment, bustle or intoxicated jolliness. A *swizzle stick* is used to stir a drink into a state of froth. To *muzzle* could mean to render dazed or muzzy, or to put into a tizzy.

The -zz- flourishes in dialect words. *Crozzled* means curled up. To *bazzle* is to rush about in a hurried or laborious manner . An *azzald* or *azzard* is a peevish or wayward child, or a silly, insignificant person. To *blizz* or *bluzz* means to blind or blindfold, *bluzz-boggart* being another name for blind-man's buff. Sometimes, the oscillating force of zz passes across to other medial letters, like *-gg-*; to *zaggle* or *ziggle* means to confuse, by contrary statements.[46] For what z-forms have in common, whether signalling sound or shape, is the idea of rapid and unpredictable oscillation or deviations of course. If they have the taint of trickery, perversity or craziness about them, they also embody a kind of zest or effervescence. The crooked or diagonal line is to be found in the medieval world principally in the bend sinister of the heraldic shield, that descends from right to left and indicates illegitimacy. It is the crooked or diagonal stripe which seems to express most of all the pathology of the surface. The crazy, zigzag form is a structure of interruptions, which both fixes and dizzies the eye.

Perhaps because of its suggestions of slurring, the presence of z in a word can often signify a slide down the scale from formality to familiarity. Nowhere is this clearer than in the shortening of expressions like 'God's blood', 'God's wounds', 'God's Hooks', 'God's (eye)lids' and 'God's heart' into oaths like *Zblood*, *Zounds*, *Gadzooks*, *Zlid* and the West Country *Zart*. The conversion of the medial voiced *s* of *Jesus* to *z* suffices to degrade parable into parroting. A particularly telling example of mocking distortion is the Suffolk dialect word *jiziwit*, a modification of *Jesuit*, which means 'an insinuating but deceitful person; an empty talker; idle gossip'; as a verb it means to trifle or act in a trifling way.[47] The friendly fuzziness of the *z* is apparent in matey transformations like that of Gary to Gazzer and Barry to Bazzer, and the affectionately unfussy contraction of Australia to Oz.

Not surprisingly, *z* also appears frequently in words signifying madness or eccentricity, like *crazy* or *zany*. The latter word is a rendering in English of the soft Venetian or Lombardic pronunciation of the name Gianni, signifying a not very intelligent rustic, which became the generic name for the clownish servant characters in the *commedia dell'arte*. Close to this is the nineteenth-century slang word *zoty*, meaning a fool or buffoon.[48]

All That Jazz

Buzzing has gradually moved from the pole of discredit or mockery to that of pleasurable approbation – as in the buzz of excitement, or of intoxication. It is first recorded in a general sense to denote enjoyable excitement in 1942, though it had been associated with the excited murmur of crowds well before that.[49] *Buzz* has strong associations with *jazz*, an early record of which is provided by Lafcadio Hearn, who said in 1912 that 'the Creoles of New Orleans use the word "Jazz," taken from the negro patois and signifying "to excite," to designate a music of a syncopated and rudimentary type.'[50] The excited thrill associated with hearing good swing was also termed 'buzz' in a 1937 headline, MICH SWINGSTERS GET NORVAL BUZZ (referring to the marimba player Kenneth Norval), in the music magazine *Down Beat*.[51]

There are very few words the origin of which has been the source of more speculation and disagreement than *jazz*. Among the many suggestions made are that it derives from the name of a musician, such as the late nineteenth-century Mississippi drummer Chas Washington, or Chas Alexander of Alexander's Ragtime Band of 1910, or that, given the importance of New Orleans in the history of jazz, it is a corruption of the French verb *jaser*, to discourse emptily, or the gliding dance-step the *chassé*.[52] The most plausible account to date is that the word was heard in a crap game by Spike Slattery, a West Coast reporter, around 1913, as an invocation of good luck while the dice were being rolled – 'Come on, the old jazz.' It was then transferred by sports reporters to baseball, where, according to Ernest Hopkins, writing in the *San Francisco Bulletin* on 5 April 1913, it meant 'life, vigor, energy, effervescence of spirit, joy, pep, magnetism, verve, virility, ebulliency, courage, happiness – oh, what's the use? – JAZZ. Nothing else can express it.'[53] Edward 'Scoop' Gleeson, writing about the word a couple of weeks earlier, glossed it as 'that "old life," the "gin-i-ker," the "pep," otherwise known as the enthusiasalum'.[54] The most plausible suggestion for the source of the word is in *jism* or *jizm*, a nineteenth-century American word which means vim or vitality. P. T. Barnum uses it in the sense of alcoholic zing, writing that 'When liquor of good quality costs from four to fifteen dollars a gallon, and an imitation can be had that tastes just as good, and has just as much "jizm" in it . . . somebody will surely make and sell that imitation.'[55] The word seems to have been applied, as it still usually is nowadays, to the irregularly spurting expression of vitality in semen. No doubt the force of the word is assisted by its recall of *spasm* and *orgasm*, especially in the alternative form of the word *jasm*. A character in a popular American novel of 1863 explains *jasm* as '"a sort of word, I guess, that made itself . . . It's a good one, though – jasm is. If you'll take thunder and lightning, and a steamboat and a buzz-saw, and mix 'em up, and put 'em into a woman, that's jasm".'[56] The word lurks in the vicinity of the strange climax of Lewis Carroll's *The Hunting of the Snark*, in which the Baker suddenly vanishes:

> Erect and sublime, for one moment of time,
> In the next, that wild figure they saw
> (As if stung by a spasm) plunge into a chasm,
> While they waited and listened in awe.[57]

Jazz is not only generative of folk-etymologies but suggests other words, like *razzmatazz* and *pizzazz*, the latter of which seems to have made its first appearance in *Harper's Bazaar* in 1937, and split off into many other forms like *bezaz*, *bezazz*, *bizzazz*, *pazzazz* and *pezazz*, to signify an indeterminate quality of dynamism. The most likely, or perhaps simply the most concordant suggestion is that *jazz* just means jerky, unpredictably generative movement. As such it can be regarded as to a degree self-designating, describing the very semantic and phonological zig-zags undergone by the word, its sound and its explicators, as well as the kind of music that it names.

The presence of z in *jazz* has no doubt reinforced and been itself reinforced by its presence in many words that signify the modern, especially in contexts that suggest the dynamism of modernity (Ernest Hopkins's 1913 article in praise of jazz is subtitled 'A Futurist Word Which Has Just Joined the Language'.) The go-ahead American Professor of English who galvanizes and appalls sleepy British academics in David Lodge's academic novels *Changing Places* (1975) and *Small World* (1984) is aptly named Morris Zapp. One of the reasons that the idea of the modern has developed a strong affinity to the z-sound, one must suppose, is because of its associations with mechanical instruments and functions. In a word like *zip*, or the even brisker *zipper*, the associations with muzzy indistinctness are cancelled, making the z signify sudden and decisive movements. Similar words like *zing* and *zoom* suggest a distinctly modern kind of energetic efficiency. In the Second World War *buzz-bomb* the two ideas of the swift and the mysterious are rather frighteningly conjoined.

The influence of the word *jazz* seems to have helped condition a strong preference for the letter z in other areas of popular music, whether in the glamrock evocations of the extraterrestrial in David Bowie's Ziggy Stardust, or in the faux-naif flaunting of no-nonsense phoneticism in hip-hop names: Swizz Beatz, Botany Boyz, Jay-Z, Outlawz, Sticky Fingaz, YoungBloodZ, Z-Ro and, of course, the ubiquitous Niggaz.

Zedlands

Yet the zippy modern associations of the letter z are in contrast with other semantic fields with which it intersects. Both in Latin and in English, z tended to be introduced into words of foreign origin, which means that it seems to carry a charge of the exotic and even the magical. Samuel Johnson wrote that 'Z begins no word originally English.'[58] The letter *zeta*, from which the English word *zed* derives, was introduced, or, possibly, as we have seen, reimported, into the Roman alphabet to allow for the pronunciation of Greek words having the sound *dz*, and in English the z also has a strong association with ideas of specifically Middle Eastern magic and mysticism, and especially Arabic, perhaps in part because of the large number of learned words which entered English from Arabic in the late medieval period. Examples of imported words in English which help give a learned cast to the letter are astronomical terms like *zenith*, *azimuth* and *azure* (from Arabic *al-lazward*). This list might also have included *nazir*, had the Arabic *naẓīr*, opposite to, over against, not unpredictably hardened into *nadir*. To this may be joined chemical terms like *azote*, and imported words like *muezzin* and *ziggurat*, from Assyrian *ziqquratu*, eminence or high place. *Gazebo* seems not to have an Oriental source, though the fact that most assume it does is a sign of the Orientalizing glow of z-words.

The exoticism of the learned combines with suggestions of magic and enchantment in many other Arabic words, no doubt reinforced from the eighteenth century onwards by the popularity of the *Arabian Nights*, which includes characters like Abanazar, Abu-al-Muzzaffar, Dunyazad, Camar-al-Zaman, Marzawan, Moozuffer, Zubayda, Zummurrud and, most memorably, Shahrazad. *Shazam*, a made-up word signifying the accomplishment of some spell or magical operation, seems, if we credit the OED, to have been committed to print only in 1940, fittingly enough in a comic called *Whiz!* A word like *pizzazz* seems to be a blending of the semantic fields of the Oriental-magical and the modern. *Wizard* surprisingly does not belong to this family, but the passage from *wise* to *wizard* may still have been influenced by the occultizing force of the z. The many Hebrew and Middle Eastern names with z also account for some of the exotic cast of the sound: *Zebedee*, *Zachariah*, *Nebuchadnezzar*, *Zohar*, *Zoroaster* and *Beelzebub*. This last-named is the one in which the sound of the *z* functions most directly, since it is often interpreted as meaning 'lord of the flies' or even, 'the buzzing lord', fly being rendered in Hebrew, with admirable onomatopoeic exactness, as *zvuv*. Like the narcotic humming of the *m* in the lexicon of the numinous considered earlier, the *z* seems accordingly also to hint at trance and the ecstasy of the indistinct.

Charlotte Dacre's *Zofloya, or The Moor* (1806), is one of a number of Gothic novels in which Oriental villains or demons are given names beginning with *z*. Up until the end of the eighteenth century, the letter had tended to indicate Semitic (Jewish or Muslim) characters. While acknowledging the presence of *z* as an indicator of villainy in some earlier Gothic texts, such as Dr. John Moore's *Zeluco* (1786) and the character of Zampari in Ann Radcliffe's *The Italian*, Kim Ian Michasiw observes in a 'Note on Names' appended to her edition of Charlotte Dacre's *Zofloya* that Dacre's 'devotion to the letter *z*' is a 'significant innovation'.[59] Dacre's Zofloya is not only a Moor, his outward appearance conceals the fact that he is in fact Satan. At the climax of the novel, he reveals himself in his true colours, standing with Victoria, the girl he has led into corruption, at the brink of an abyss, in a scene buzzing with *z*s: 'Terror and despair seized the soul of Victoria; she shrieked, and would have fallen from the dizzying height, had not his hand, who appeared Zofloya no longer, seized her with a grasp of iron by the neck!'[60]

According to Michasiw, Charlotte Dacre's use of the letter *z* 'inflamed the onomastic imagination' of the young Percy Bysshe Shelley, spurring him to his haphazard effusion *Zastrozzi: A Romance* (1810), written as a seventeen-year-old at Eton.[61] Zastrozzi is a villainous atheist who nevertheless believes in enough of Christianity to plot to drive his half-brother Verezzi to suicide in order to secure the eternal damnation of his soul. The *z*s which throng the text – as well as Zastrozzi there are the victims of his revenge Verezzi and Julia, Marchesa di Strobazzo and a character who makes a late appearance named Ferdinand Zeilnitz – seem like graphic scorings in the body of the text of the spasmodic movements of mind and body that harass it. Zastrozzi himself seems to be an embodiment of lightning, all daggers, rocks and impetuous volts. 'He knew not what to believe – what phantom it could be that, in the shape of Zastrozzi, blasted his eye-balls.'[62] He seems always to be glimpsed against the background of craggy rocks and jagged chasms, or in the ozone-thick of thunderstorms:

> [A] flash of vivid lightning disclosed to her view the towering form of Zastrozzi.
>
> His gigantic figure was again involved in pitchy darkness, as the momentary lightning receded. A peal of crashing thunder again madly rattled over the zenith, and a scintillating flash announced Zastrozzi's approach, as he stood before Matilda.[63]

The text, with its almost unintelligible plot, is little more than an alternation between scenes of serene tranquillity and sudden accesses of emotional frenzy and paroxysms of contending emotions, as expressed especially in the persons of the tormenting villain Zastrozzi and the woman he draws into his plot, Matilda. Their turbulent feelings are repeatedly figured by the fulguration that forks from their eyes: 'his eyes darted revengeful glances'; 'The feelings of his soul flashed from his eyes'; 'Her tumultous soul, agitated by contending emotions, flashed from her eyes'; 'ardent and voluptuous fire darted from her eyes'; 'The exultation of her inmost soul flashed in expressive glances from her scintillating eyes'; 'The dark fire which flashed from her eye, more than told the feelings of her soul.' When Verezzi at last is in Matilda's power, he cries '"May the lightning of heaven consume me, if I adore thee not to distraction!"', at which 'Matilda's eyes flashed fiercest triumph.'[64] Not only does Matilda seem to generate lightning from her eyes, there is one point in the text where one has to read very carefully to be sure that she has not in fact been struck by it:

> The lurid sky was tinged with a yellowish lustre – the forest-tops rustled in the rising tempest – big drops fell – a flash of lightning, and, instantly after, a peal of bursting thunder, struck with sudden terror the bosom of Matilda. She, however,

> immediately overcame it, and regarding the battling element with indifference, continued her discourse with Zastrozzi.[65]

The obsessiveness of these lightning flashes throughout Shelley's text are in a sense a searing into it of his own impatience with the plot details that a reader might ordinarily expect, to provide a stabilizing background and occasion for these moments of sensational *éclat*. But the young Shelley has no interest in the apparatus of plot or motivation, and his tempestuous imagination always prefers, like the lightning, to take the shortest route to the ground, slashing diagonally through the flimsy fabric of his plot in his efforts to charge, or discharge the tension.

The exotic or esoteric z passes across into pantomime and circus. A *Zoyara* became the name for 'an effeminate young man, a lady-gentleman, a "Molly"', following the prominence in the early 1860s of a circus-rider bearing this name 'who affected the airs and dress of a girl so well that it was the town-question in New York for some time as to what the sex of the "phenomenon" really was'.[66] The final entry, on *Zoyara* itself, in Barrère's and Leland's *Dictionary of Slang, Jargon and Cant*, records a speculation from Leland himself about the letter z in circus names:

> The London *Globe* having inquired why the stage names of female acrobats and circus-riders so generally begin with Z, a correspondent (C. G. Leland) remarked that they are, as in *Zazel*, *Zaniel*, *Zoes*, derived from Hebrew or Yiddish words meaning devil or goblin.[67]

The foreignness of z may borrow from the idea that the letter indicates indistinctness or clumsiness of articulation, especially in the case of French and the German. There is a particular force in the fact that *zee* is often substituted by French speakers for *the*, and for other words beginning with voiced *th*, since these English words are the most common kind of demonstrative word, the function of which is precisely to indicate precise or specific position – *this*, *that*, *then*, *there* – thus perhaps imparting a certain extra fuzziness to the sliding retreat of the tongue in z.

Z hints not just at the exotic condition of the outsider, but also of the interior exotic of the unsophisticated rustic or bumpkin. In this, it has the same ambivalence we have noted with respect to *m*, which conveys the formless humming both of the mystic and the simpleton. Perhaps this alternation is another version of the shuttling between the brisk and the sluggish, between zipping and oozing, that are to be found associated with *z*. The noisiness of the *z* is often thought of as a kind of veiling or obscuring of what would otherwise be clearly distinct utterance: the music critic Virgil Thomson uses the word *buzz* to describe a slight imperfection in the voice of singer Jarmila Novotna: 'She sang at all times handsomely, though her voice has a veil on it, a slight buzz that prevents it from being the movingly beautiful thing it would be if she could give it a clearer and more ringing sound.'[68] Rural accents, which are similarly looked down on by metropolitan, educated speakers of English as an imperfect form of properly articulate speech, are often associated with a noisy preponderance of *z*s. When Edgar adopts the speech and manner of a West Country yokel to escort the blinded Gloucester in *King Lear*, his imposture is signalled in the text by the substitution of *z* for *s* and the buzzing voiced fricative *v* for *f*: 'And 'ch'ud ha' been zwaggered out of my life, 'twould not ha' been zo long as 'tis by a vortnight' (IV.vi.239–41). A broadside ballad of 1684 similarly uses copious *z*s to evoke the visit of a Devonshire man to Parliament:

Chil tell thee, *Tom*, the strangest story,
Because thou art an honest *Tory*;
  'Tis News beyond expressions:
Zich zights are no where to be zeen
In any Lond, (*God zave the Queen*)
  But at our Quarter-Zessions.[69]

Later in the ballad,the author follows up the sonic hint to make some play with the mindless buzzing of the House of Commons:

No Ants do vaster lead or drive,
Or Bees buz to or fro' the Hive

I marl they were not dizzy;
And zure the Nations great Avairs
Lay heavily upon their Cares,
They look'd zo wise and busie.[70]

In the ballad 'Plain Truth and Blind Ignorance' collected in Percy's *Reliques*, which is cast in the form of a dialogue between the Truth of Protestantism and the Ignorance that clings to Popish pleasures and superstititions, Ignorance speaks in West Country dialect:

And then to zee the rood-loft
Zo bravely zet with zaints: –
But now to zee them wandring
My heart with zorrow vaints[71]

Indeed, so defining was this sound that the West Country came to be known as 'Zedland', 'Izzardland' or even, more preciously, the realm of the 'Unnecessarians'.[72] Z came to prominence also for the internal exotic of dialect poetry, especially in rendering rural and West Country dialect, as seen in particular in the writing of William Barnes. In a letter to the *Athenaeum* of November 1878, Thomas Hardy worried about 'the grotesque element' involved in trying to convey the precise accent of a rural speaker in fiction, but nevertheless, in the preface to a selection of Barnes's poems in 1908, Hardy hoped that the volume would open the eyes and ears of 'persons to whom the Wessex R and Z are uncouth misfortunes:[73]

'Tis merry ov a zummer's day,
Where vo'k be out a-meäken haÿ;
Where men an' women, in a string,
Do ted or turn the grass, an' zing,
Wi' cheemen vaïces, merry zongs,
A-tosssen o' their sheenen prongs
Wi eärms a-zwangen left an' right.[74]

Despite the fact that Italian is so abundantly provided with the letter z, Italian writers seem to have shared the dim view of the letter and its sound taken by English writers. In his search for a vernacular tongue suitable for literature, Dante rules out the Tuscans and the Genoese on account of the prevalence of z in their speech:

> if any one thinks that what we assert of the Tuscans may not be asserted of the Genoese, let him just keep it in mind that if, through forgetfulness, the Genoese were to lose the letter z, they would either have to be completely silent or provide themselves with some altogether new language in its place; for z makes up the greatest part of their speech, and this letter cannot be pronounced without great harshness.[75]

More than 300 years later, Carlo Moscheni was still complaining about the prominence of z, with the accompanying erosion of the letter t, in the Tuscan dialect:

> in the Italian Tongue it is much sweeter and stronger to say *Oratione*, *Affectione*, than *Orazione*, *Affezzione*.Where 'tis plain that Z renders the pronounciation harsh and difficult, and changes the *Tuscan* Tongue into Doctor *Gratian*. The communication of foreign Languages with the *Tuscan*, has rather corrupted than enrich'd it, as many believe, introducing a greater Esteem for the Letter Z, which is the Symbol of Death; than for the Letter T which presages Life.[76]

In the insulting American comic figure of the Zip Coon, there is a combination of metropolitan zing and rural doziness. The Zip Coon was one of the two principal black stereotypes in antebellum America, along with Jim Crow. Where Jim Crow was lazy, dim and rural, the Zip Coon was a metropolitan black who had got ambitions beyond his station. J. Stanley Lemons describes him as

> a preposterous, citified dandy. In the minstrel shows he was easily recognized in his bright, loud, exaggerated clothes: swallow-tail coat with wide lapels, gaudy shirts, striped pants, spats, and top hat. He was a high-stepping

> strutter with a mismatched vocabulary. He put on airs, acted elegant, but was betrayed by his pompous speech filled with malapropisms.[77]

But the deprecatory associations of the *z* with marginal groups held to be ignorant or unintelligible in speech could also be exploited for purposes of concealment, as in the carnival canting language known as 'Z-Latin'. Along with other forms of cryptolect, Z-Latin works by the regular insertion of nonsense sounds and syllables into English words in order to disguise their meanings from outsiders. Don B. Wilmeth offers the following account, itself somewhat over-elaborated, of the procedure for constructing Z-Latin:

> 1. Separate any word on the basis of its natural syllables, and then divide it on the basis of its vowels. The consonant or consonants preceding the vowel are modified by adding a long 'e' to them. The vowel is replaced by the short 'a' sound, and the consonants following the vowel have a 'z' sound prefixed to them. For example, the monosyllabic word 'fin' becomes 'fee-a-zin.'[78]

Assuming that Wilmeth means, not that the vowel is replaced by a short *a* sound, but that a short *a* is inserted, this amounts to inserting the sound 'iaz' between consonants and vowels. The result is a busy tongue-jam of thrumming, vaguely Slavic-sounding dactyls – my name, for example, would become 'Stiazeviazen Kiazonniazor'.

Schizo-

Signifying the gash of the blade (the Mark of Zorro), the searing slash of the lightning bolt, or the crevasse that suddenly gapes during earthquake or avalanche, the graphic form of the *z* also has associations with violence, especially that of sudden revelation, or the catastrophic giving way of one state of things to another.[79] *Zayin*, the word for the Hebrew character that corresponds to English *z*, means weapon, or sword. Its shape has been interpreted as a picturing of a sword piercing the flesh of an animal, which evolved eventually into the Greek *zeta* and English z. Robert M. Hoffstein's kabbalistic reading of what he calls the 'English alphabet' sees the letter z inheriting much of the martial force of the *zayin*:

> The Z is related to the Hebrew letter zayin: sword, arrow, especially the sound of the weapon cleaving through the air. Thus we have the onomatopoeic *zing*, *zizz*, *zip* and *zoom* and the words *zest*, *zeal* and *zenith* echoing the force behind the arrow or the strength that wields the sword. Thus the sign of *Zeus*, the god of the elements of thunder and rain, is the thunderbolt. And so the word *zoo*, denoting animal or animation, incarnated desire and strength. Likewise a *wizard* is able to wield the wand, which like the sword, symbolizes his will.[80]

The electrical associations of the lightning bolt are redoubled for modern ears by the electrical associations of buzzing, the graphic form of the z being the convulsive mode of the steady hum suddenly discharging as the shock. Roland Barthes puts the contrast between the unvoiced s and the voiced z at the heart of his analysis of 'Sarrasine', Balzac's story of infatuation and sexual wounding. The Z that provides the initial letter of the name of La Zambinella, the castrato singer with whom Sarrasine catastrophically falls in love, is 'the letter of mutilation: phonetically, Z stings like a chastising lash, an avenging insect; graphically, cast slantwise by the hand across the blank regularity of the page, amid the curves of the alphabet, like an oblique and illicit blade, it cuts, slashes, or, as we say in French, *zebras*'.[81] Barthes's reflections on the alternate form of the s and z, which are in 'a relation of graphological inversion: the same letter seen from the other side of the mirror', find in the idea of castration their stabilizing ground.[82] Barthes switches between the phonic and graphic, to observe that something is missing from the name of Sarrasine:

> *SarraSine*: contemporary French onomastics would lead us to expect *SarraZine*: on its way to the subject's patronymic, the Z has encountered some pitfall . . . by this orthographical

> error committed in the middle of his name, in the center of his body, Sarrasine receives the Zambinellian Z in its true sense – the wound of deficiency.[83]

But there is a shiver even in the midst of the grounding idea of castration.The z encodes the sound of the castrating blade, but it is itself ablated in the muting of voice that gives us *SarraSine* where we should expect *SarraZine*, castration here itself seemingly castrated. Foothold has become pitfall. Finally, the z comes to encode, not the absolute apparition of the wound, the presence of absence, but the gap between presence and absence, of sexuality, of voice, the very slash between the *s* and the *z*: 'hence the slash (/) confronting the S of SarraSine and the Z of Zambinella has a panic function: it is the slash of censure,. the surface of the mirror, the wall of hallucination, the verge of antithesis, the abstraction of limit, the obliquity of the signifier, the index of the paradigm, hence of meaning'.[84]

Barthes notes in passing that Balzac has a z in the middle of his own name, and reminds us that he wrote another story in which the Z is singled out for special attention. 'Z. Marcas' concerns a mysterious law writer whose life of political success and decline into ruined anonymity is unfolded through his narration to his fellow lodgers. His initial letter stands for 'Zephirin', and Balzac's narrator articulates at the beginning of the story the foreboding that the letter encodes:

> Do you not make out in the construction of that letter Z an adverse influence? Does it not emblazon the aleatory and fantastic zigzag of a tormented life? What wind has blown on this letter that, in whatever language has given it entry, begins scarcely fifty words?[85]

Later in the story, the two students who are Marcas's neighbours anticipate the story of rise and fall they will later hear in their play with the enigmatic initial:

> Like the boys we were, we repeated a hundred times or more, and with all kinds of comments, mocking or melancholy,

> this name that gave itself up to our play. Juste would sometimes fire off the Z like a rocket shooting up, then, after having pronounced the first syllable with force, mimed its fall by the dumb brevity of the second.[86]

Both the Balzac and the Barthes texts seem to be recalled in Debra Daley's 1996 novel *The Strange Letter* Z. One of its central characters, Alexis Serafin, is a linguist fascinated by the life of Zeugen, a linguist based on Edmund Sapir. Following an episode of infant meningitis, he is subject to seizures triggered by the look and sound of the letter Z, during which he writes linguistic papers in a state of inspired trance:

> he became overwhelmingly aware of the book lying on the tea-table beside his armchair. Zeugen – which led, like a flame racing along a fuse, to: *NarZiss*. Zed. Zayin. A weapon. Zeus. Lightning bolts, attributes of. Z. Sometimes disguised as a double S. Stormtrooper. Night of the long knives. Zayin. A weapon. Alien letter of the Roman alphabet. Terminal letter. Death letter. Suicide note. Pull the trigger. Zeugen found floating in green water. ZZZ. Sleep . . . A photic Z appeared on the wall, shimmering. Pulsating. Projected from an incandescent source behind his eyes. A physiological vibration coincided with the visual flicker, as at the back of his throat his glottis opened and closed voicing the letter Z. Suddenly his body jerked as the zigzag of light thrust at him. It lanced through his eyes, igniting a fierce, cranial storm. It struck at the architecture of his brain. Structures reeled, collapsed, and were swallowed up by fissures in the earth.[87]

Later in the book, which focuses on a moment of violence effected by Alex in z-abounding Mexico, Alexis has a reverie in which his schizophrenic I is conflated with the historical trajectory of the letter Z, at once straight as an arrow, and branching deviously through time:

> Alex drove his pen over the page, his thoughts too urgent to type. I will not be secondary. I desire to be the first person. I. I. I. The Old Phoenician sign of Z, which has always been my one and true fetish, the key to gratification. It opens a door to the past where the chain of creativity remains unbroken. A long time ago I generated electromagnetism. Then around 3,000 BC, the eschatologically minded Egyptians drew an arrow and aimed it at my future. It tore through time, accruing identity. About 1,500 BC, the Semites in Syria and Palestine modified the arrow, calling it zayin, a weapon, before relaunching it. Engraved with the name of Zeus, it lodged in an empty space, the sixth space, in the Greek alphabets, in the green alphabet of the Dorian Islands and the dark-blue alphabet of the west coast of Asia Minor, in the Phrygian and Lycian and Lydian alphabets where the letter transformed itself into zeta, but it remained a weapon. The letter zoomed on, ripped out of the Greek alphabet by pragmatic Romans who attached it to the end of theirs in order to show that it was strange.[88]

Zeroing In

As we have noted, many of the associations that have built up around the z-sound centre on the unnecessariness or negligibility of the letter and the noise it makes. It is not surprising that the sound that is itself conceived, like many other noises of the voice, as much ado about nothing, should be implicated in the naming of nothingness, as in the word *zero*, and less well-shod words like *zip*, *zippo* or *zilch*. But, like many of the forms of vocal noise, straddling the boundary between the signifcation of noise and the noise of signifying, the empty, place-holding zero-z is also ramifying and multiplicative. This is evidenced well in the fortunes of that pluripotent nineteenth-century nonentity, the quizzical word *quoz*, as evoked by Charles MacKay in 1852:

> Many years ago the favourite phrase (for, though but a monosyllable, it was a phrase in itself) was QUOZ. This odd

> word took the fancy of the multitude in an extraordinary degree, and very soon acquired an almost boundless meaning. When vulgar wit wished to mark its incredulity and raise a laugh at the same time, there was no resource so sure as this popular piece of slang. When a man was asked a favour which he did not choose to grant, he marked his sense of the suitor's unparalleled presumption by exclaiming *Quoz!* When a mischievous urchin wished to annoy a passenger, and create mirth for his comrades, he looked him in the face, and cried out *Quoz!* and the exclamation never failed in its object. When a disputant was desirous of throwing a doubt upon the veracity of his opponent, and getting summarily rid of an argument which he could not overturn, he uttered the word *Quoz*, with a contemptuous curl of his lip and an impatient shrug of his shoulders. The universal monosyllable conveyed all his meaning, and not only told his opponent that he lied, but that he erred egregiously if he thought that any one was such a nincompoop as to believe him. Every alehouse resounded with *Quoz*; every street-corner was noisy with it, and every wall for miles around was chalked with it.[89]

The affinity of the *z* with zero, or the next-to-nothingness of pure, meaningless sound, makes it even more apt than other noises of the voice to express the very alternation between noise and meaning that is the essence of language. F. M. Hallgren and H. Weiss recorded in 1946 that 'Students at the Graduate School of Business Administration at Harvard University use a specialized vocabulary known as 'buzz words' to describe the key to any particular course or situation.'[90] It was perhaps not until the 1960s or '70s that the word 'buzz-word' itself became a buzz-word. Becoming a buzz-word means emerging out of the hum of mere verbiage, but then, as the word becomes more and more part of the conventional landscape, merging back into the condition of buzz. Here buzzing, like the sound that has preoccupied me throughout this chapter, is on both sides of the signal-noise dichotomy; making a buzz makes temporarily audible as such the buzzing condition to which all articulate language tends.

The condition of the letter z as a persistent presence-within-absence and absence-within-presence is comically dramatized in Mark Dunn's novel *Ella Minnow Pea* (2002), described in its subtitle as *A Progressively Lipogrammatic Epistolary Fable*. The novel is set in the autonomous island-nation of Nollopton, established off the coast of South Carolina in honour of Nevin Nollop, the author of the pangram sentence (that is, a sentence containing all the letters of the alphabet) *The quick brown fox jumps over the lazy dog*. One day, the z falls out from the sentence which is inscribed on the cenotaph in the capital city beneath the statue of Nollop, and this is taken by the Nollopian authorities as a decree from beyond the grave that the use of the letter z should be prohibited. As the day for the official excision of the letter approaches, Ella laments its loss in a last buzzing binge: 'Dazed or zombified citizens who recognize hazardous organizations of zealots in their hazy midst too late – too late to size down. Immobilized we iz. Minimalized, Paralyzed, Zip. Zap. zzzzzzzzz.'[91] Ella's cousin Tassie rebels against the prohibition, seeing it as the unjust muting of thought and free expression. Z-words mark out a ghostly army of words that are present and absent: 'Perhaps they will eventually disappear altogether, and the accompanying halts and stammers as well: those troublesome, maddening pauses that at present invade and punctuate through caesura all manner of discourse.'[92] And yet, of course, if it is no longer seen, the letter is still insistently to be heard, for 'the bees speak the offending letter as their wont. They sing it into the hills, our ears ringing with its scissoresonance.'[93] Progressively, all the letters of the sentence drop, and are correspondingly forbidden to the citizens of Nollop, except L, M, N, O and P: 'No mo Nollop pomp! . . . No mo Nollop! . . . O Noooooooooo!' Finally Ella herself rescues the language with an alternative pangram that restores the alphabet: 'Pack my box with five dozen liquor jugs.'[94]

Z occupies the place of the Greek Omega at the end of the alphabet, but has none of its consummating powers. John Phillips's *Christian's ABC* (1629) identified the final letter Z with salvation ('Q. Rehearse the Letter Z? A. ZEalous godly men, the iudgement being ended shal immediatly goe with Christ into heauen'[95]) but the association noted above of z with ampersand suggests that, far from rounding off the sequence of letters with a satisfying finality, making A to Z the equivalent of Alpha to Omega, the unnecessary z could sometimes be seen as part of a bathetic dribbling away of the alphabet, and therefore be elided with the empty inconclusive 'and' of the ampersand, the name of which derives from the formula 'and, per se, and', meaning '"and" in itself'. Like the ampersand, however, with which it becomes associated by this adjacency, the z is never 'per se' or *an sich*, but seems always to be a kind of extra or afterthought, only accidentally occupying the culminating place of essential consummation.

EPILOGUE

Blottybus in Blottis

Word and World

I have been trying in this book to use readings of vocal noise to make out a phantasmatics of the voice, centred on the magical or dream topology of the mouth, as the meeting point of the self and the world. The most important point about the mouth is that it is a place of traffic and rendezvous. It is the bodily place in which the world is entertained – body and world bent and blent together. The mouth is crammed with world; the world brims with oration. 'Give it mouth', says Magwitch to the young Pip when he is demanding to know his name at the beginning of *Great Expectations*: not just give it to your mouth, nor even give your mouth to it – but give it a mouth, fit it with a mouth to speak itself.[1]

The world contains words – they are things in the world along with the rest of the world's facts and phenomena. But in another sense the word contains the world, for the worldness of the world, the *the*-ness of 'the world' requires language to be signified. The world cannot 'world' itself. The world itself is, as Heidegger once curiously affirmed of animals, 'poor in world', and requires to be thought and signified as such in that space of negation and exception known as language.[2] The world can only contain itself by getting outside itself by means of the word that it itself contains. So, in a strange, knotted topology, the world contains the word, which in its turn contains it, which in its turn means that the word must be able to contain itself. ('The little boids is on the wing; ain't that absoid? The little wings is on the boid.')

The mouth is the crucible of this compounding, a commerce of image and actuality. The sounds made in and by the mouth are part of the ordinary phenomena of the world. They come about as the sounds of the world do, through actions of rubbing, blowing and obstructing, and are subject to precisely the same physical and acoustic laws as apply in the world. Yet for all that the sounds produced by the mouth are nevertheless not simply or merely worldly, precisely because they are articulated in systems of relation and contrast that make them into the things we call words. The mouth is the space in which these two orders, one physical, or, in Michel Serres's terms 'hard', and the other informational, or 'soft', are sutured together.[3] The mouth is in this respect a kind of pineal gland. Voice is soft, because it is glossed with intonation or intent; noise is hard, because it is accident.

Language is a kind of secret alcove in the world, a magic cave or camera obscura that alone, of all places in the world (or out of it), allows the world to come to itself. The mouth is the place of the world's abeyance, but also, for that reason, the only place in the world in which 'The World' can be, which is to say, be said, 'The World' being the articulation of the world. The mouth is the literalization of this space apart, in which the world is enabled, but also constrained, to contain what it nevertheless cannot wholly contain, being itself contained by it. The mouth is the space, in and out of the world, in which the world can be inside and outside itself. The formula for this recursive encapsulation, in which World contains Word, which in its turn contains World, might be: World [Word {world} . . .]. Or, if one started one layer further in (or out), it might similarly be: Word [World {word} . . .].

The relation between voice and noise in the mouth replicates this nesting. The mouth produces sounds, of which voice is a subcategory. But among those vocal sounds is a subcategory of what I call noises, and what Aristotle called the unensouled, sounds included in language to signify what is excessive to, and so uncontained by, language. Thus Noise [Voice {noise} . . .] and Voice [Noise {voice} . . .]. A language I do not understand, or that I perhaps do not even understand to be language, is just noise, and may as well be the babbling of a brook as of a barbarian. And yet, I will probably give that (non)language a noisy name in mine – *babble*, *barbarism*, *gibberish*, *gobbledegook*, *hocus-pocus*, *Hottentot*, *pidgin* (sometimes thought to be derived from the Chinese pronunciation of 'business'). A certain principle of linguistic autism may be discerned here. I mean by this that language, while being the very means by which it is possible to point outside itself to a world of non-linguistic objects, seems to want to swallow up those objects in its own embrace. Language seems greedy, or induces in its users the greedy fantasy, the fantasy of a greed, to provide a mimic version in sound of everything it names. It is as though the phonic dimension of language were a kind of dumbshow, pulling faces behind the back of the words being sensibly articulated. Language is reluctant to admit any outside to itself, wanting to prove that there is nothing over there that is not already in here.

I have been speaking of the mouth, as though all language existed and took place only there. But this mouth is figural as well as literal. The definite-article individual mouth is always plural, always a profile of variations. My mouth mimes the many other mouths with whom through speaking I have converse. I cannot speak except by a joining of my mouth to yours, and to that of every other speaker of what I may recognize as my language, or perhaps any language in general. Speaking is a convocation of mouths, miming and mirroring each other. How much better it is than we could ever have suspected, the word we use to describe all of this: 'orality'.

More than anything, the mouth is a place in which something compounds with nothing, the place in which nothing is able to take place, and nonbeing to come into audible being.

Linguists interested in the phonomemetics (sound symbolism) and phenomemetics (kinaesthetic symbolism) of the voice have investigated the many different ways in which the space of the mouth seems to be structured by oppositions, which are then mapped on to the world – high and low, front and back, light and dark. But they have been less attentive than they might have been to an opposition that is both more elementary and more encompassing. This is the very opposition between sound and sense that is at work in the idea of sound symbolism – the contrast between organized, meaningful sound and pure, nonsignifying noise. This is not a spatial opposition precisely, for one cannot say that any one part of the mouth is more likely to produce articulate sounds rather than noises, and the distinction between voice and noise runs through spoken language itself rather than between it and some other category of sounds. And yet there is something like a partitioning of the mouth along the lines of this opposition that finds a kind of spatial enactment in the mouth – the association between dentals and the lightness of articulation, for example, and the relative obscurity of the velar fricative, as discussed in chapters Six and Eight. So we can say that the mouth is a heterotopic space apart in which oral space itself is dynamically produced.

Though this book has concerned itself with effects of linguistic iconicity, its principal focus has not been on how or whether language mimes the various objects in the world it names. Its real concern has rather been with vocal language's self-relation. Whenever there is iconic representation, I want to have suggested, vocal language pictures, points to, or iconically enacts its own action. In something of the same way that it can be claimed that whenever I am conscious of something I must necessarily be able to be conscious of *being* conscious of it, so whenever language performs some act of signification, it performs its own performance into the bargain. Studies of the iconicity of language focus their attention on the relations between the form of the signifier and the object it signifies. My attention has been drawn to the internal event of the performance. In contrast to iconicity studies, which focus on how language performs meaning, I have tried to watch and listen the ways in which that performance is itself performed, between sound and sense, form and the formless.

I hope it has become progressively clear that this self-performing takes a particular form, one that involves the establishment of relations between positivity and negativity, or between language considered as having a physical form and force, and language as a purely abstract kind of entity. When language acts out its capacity to act out meaning, it acts out the fact that it conjures such effects, and conjures itself effecting such effects, all out of thin air (though the imaginary variation in the quality and density of the air in the mouth is part of the churning of substances that the speaking mouth mimics). Spoken language is everything and nothing, everything precisely because it is nothing, omnipotent and impotent at once.

Iconicity is often taken as a proof of the immediate relation between language and the world. My argument is meant to be a reproof to that idea. I think that iconicity occurs via a sort of traumatic, though entirely painless knot, in which language must transact with the fact of its own pure noisiness or vacancy. Far from being the manifestation of a natural affinity between language and the world, iconicity exposes the foundational and functional emptiness of language, its foundation upon nothing.

This knot is tied in voice's confrontation with noise. Noisiness performs non-language – the unensouled. Aristotle sees voice as impelled by an act of imagination. Paradoxically, as it may seem, unensouled noise, the noise of the world in the mouth, involves no such act of picturing by the soul, precisely because it is already a sound-picture of something in the world. In providing such a sound-picture, language seems to demonstrate that language can mime anything, including its opposite and adversary, noise. But at the same moment, it shows that any attempt to mime noise imports it into voice, and thereby enlarges voice's repertoire. Noise put to work in voice is no longer noise, even if it is not quite identical with voice either, meaning that noise slips the noose the lips attempt to knot around it. In noise, voice is both maximally abased – revealed as pure growling, or howling, or hissing – and superlatively exalted – capable of transfiguring even this most mindless material into meaning. Many of the examples of iconicity I have considered in this book are imagings of forms of nonsense, the peril of signification. Noise stands revealed as what it could never have been before being taken up and set forth in voice, namely non-voice, the negative of voice, that is both inside and outside voice.

Every time there is an effect of iconicity, there is a sense of fit, of rightness and snug inherence, as language is made to seem a natural thing, in concordance with the world. But at the very same moment that the world seems affirmed by language, it may also be dissolved by it, precisely through being doubled, reduced to a flimsy phonic facsimile. Although onomatopoeia and iconicity have the reputation of giving language its naturalness and authority, they are in fact the point at which language comes close to revealing that it is founded on nothing but our willingness to assume its meaningfulness. Even as word and world are intertwined, each enclosing the other, word and world are also in a relation of reciprocal repudiation. Outside language there is the nothing of the world, that whereof one may not speak, except and unless one may say that. So the word nothings or nihilates the world. But in doing this, the word reveals itself to be a nothing, by contrast with the unspeakable things-in-themselves of the world. The word and the world are nothing to each other.

The immediacy of iconicity seems to mean that nothing comes between the word and the world. But in fact what has just been said means that in the case of such iconic immediacy, something does in fact interpose itself. 'Nothing', a kind of something that is not exactly anything, and a nothingness that is a something, or not quite nothing at all, comes between the word and the world, the nothing that each must be for the other. The world is promoted into World through the mediation of the special kind of nothing, the thing that is not exactly or fully a thing, of the word. The word becomes what it is in acknowledgement of the fact that there is a world that is nothing beside it. Word and world can appear to be sutured as a consequence of this reciprocal curtailment, or negative entailment. In iconicity, word adds nothing to world, and world adds nothing to word, and yet they are still not identical. This is because nothing divides their suture. This nothing is signified by the noise that is the suture between word and world, while it also allows for the division between word and world – either as a certain wordly excess within the word, or in the noisy excessiveness of the word to the world. Iconicity is supposed to bear out the 'doctrine of signatures' – that all things fling out broad their names, that word and world are one. But this oneness requires a bridge that is also a gap, both joining word and world and holding them asunder. Noise, the nothing that yet is something, is, or 'is', this bridge. Iconicity requires noise, because noise is actually the purest form of iconicity, that is, language performing itself, performing its own performance, asking to be taken for language. All this wordplay of course elides, probably rather annoyingly, different senses of the 'nothing' that perhaps should be kept more rigorously apart – and most particularly the negativity of not being and the positivity of being nothing, in the way disclosed by Beckett's sour joke, at the expense of a not very estimable German poet, that 'it is better to write NOTHING than not to write at all.'[4] But it is precisely this elision between the positive and the negative that noise enacts.

The seeming plenitude of iconicity depends upon the fact that word and world negate or nihilate each other. Word and world render each other nothing, even as each is itself nothing in respect to the other. But because word and world each depend upon this act and fact of negation, this 'not' is also a kind of necessity, which knots them together. The knot is a not, the nothing is a knotting. And it is this knot of nothing of which we repeatedly hear tell in the noisings of the voice.

Iconicity seems like language plus (language plus body, language plus the effect of heightened presence). But it is able to supply this dividend only through the deficit of language, language reduced to the gurgling of a brook, or the burrings of a bumpkin. Many of those who have written about the topics of iconicity, sound-symbolism, phonoaesthetics and phonosemantics write as though to unfold the latent surplus of meaning contained in certain sounds, letters or groups of letters. But iconic language is in the literal sense idiotic, speaking the idiom of the blindly singular, of purely accidental and idiomatic noise. It may well be that certain clusters of sounds seem charged with certain kinds of meaningfulness – *i* seems to connote littleness, *gl-* seems to be associated with light, and *gr-* with irascibility – but the way these sounds work is by first signifying, not particular sound-qualities, but an abstract quality of noisiness as such – the sound of sound just *sounding*. This is perhaps why so many of the effects of noise do not in fact seem chaotic at all, but like highly patterned forms of oscillation, or take this form when they are mimicked in language, as often signalled in writing by the doubling or clustering of consonants in the words used to render them – *patter, titter, babble, mumble, muddle, piddle*. Sounds like *m* or *t* or *z* are not therefore surcharged with certain meanings, but something like the opposite – they have the potential to have sense-making subtracted from them, so that they jump the rails from meaningful sounds to unmeaning noise. They are possessed, not of hidden mystical potential, but the quality Giorgio Agamben calls *impotential*, the capacity to forbear or secede from the exercise of a capacity: only a being possessed of voice can keep silence.[5]

My interest has been in the way in which noises signify their nonsignificance, simultaneously signifying nothing and signifying that signification of nothing. In so doing they corroborate the assumption they also corrode, that there is a signifiable difference between signification (word) and nonsignification (world). Beginning as a local anomaly, a snag in the weave of articulate, expressive language, noisiness can expand to encompass the whole of language, such that voice can seem to amount to treating noise as though it were significant, treating the unensouled as though it had soul. And this quasi-animation, this taking-to-be, is perhaps in the end all the soul really is. There may be no such thing as soul really, but there really is that attribution of soul that soul really and truly is. The something arises through the detour through the nothing; voice arises from the assumption that there is something behind it that makes it more than mere noise. All voice is noise we assume to have been voiced.

Somebody makes a vocal sound that seems to sound like something nonlinguistic in the world; one listening seems to understand this intent. But the word does not really sound like what it is supposed to – it is a stand-in, and alibi, precisely because it is not a sound but a word, albeit one that may appear 'noisier' than those in its vicinity. Both parties agree to this approximation, which is a matching not just of word to thing, but of language as sound to language as sense, and thereby agree to treat what is transpiring as language. They agree to pretend that this curious affair of squeaks and pops and hisses is in fact infused with meaning. Only this agreement, or the assumption that such agreement will be forthcoming, makes it plausible as language, just as it is only the hunch that everyone else will agree that a ten-pound note is worth just about ten pounds more than the paper it is written on that ensures its value. I do not have ceaselessly to reaffirm my willingness to accept the meaningfulness of linguistic noises on each separate occasion because language just is this contract.

Idiocy

Iconicity occurs in the space between language and idiocy. No wonder that the idiot is figured as doing no more than making a noise ('blithering', for example), for noise is idiocy itself. The tale told by the idiot's speech is like his life, that is, completely idiomatic, without rule, rhyme or reason. The original meaning of *idiot*, as indicated by its link to words like *idiolect* and *idiosyncrasy*, with their shared origin in Greek ἰδίος, personal, distinct, peculiar, is a private, unprofessional or unlettered individual. That it did not always imply mental deficiency is indicated by John Capgrave's remark in a manuscript *Life of St Katharine* of around 1450 that '[r]yght as be twelue ydiotes, sent Austyn seyth – he meneth the apostellis, for thei not lerned were – Thurgh-ovte þe world was sowen ovr feyth'.[6]

The family of words with the prefix *idio-* sometimes blends illegitimately with words beginning *ideo-*, derived from Greek ἰδέα, kind, sort, general or ideal form, which is formed from the stem of ἰδεῖν to see. It is as though it were the office of the eye to guarantee generality and the concordance of things one with another, while the idiotic order of the ear, a hair's breadth away from this ideal order, tips over into idiopathic elementariness. The word *identity* hinges between the two, suggesting both that which stays the same, the *it* extended out into time, and also the elementary particle of the *it*, the *id*, of which that sameness may be composed, and into which it may decompose. The idiot is one who does not count because he himself cannot.

Idiocy resembles noise because both lack any structure, which is to say, neither can be compressed. For a stream of data to be compressible, it must have self-relation, or internal comparability. But idiot discourse not only has no relation to reasonable discourse, it has no relation to itself. It cannot overhear itself, the sound of its own sounding is all there is to it, because it falls on deaf, or idiot ears, its own, that have never heard anything like this before and never will again. In 1591, in the course of a discussion of who could legally make a will, Henry Swinburne defined an idiot in part as one 'who notwithstanding he bee of lawfull age, yet he is so witlesse, that hee can not number to twentie, nor can tell what age he is of'.[7] Idiocy falls short of or overshoots any system.

The dream of iconicity is of a language that would be so at one with some thing in the world that it would cease to have any relations of contrast or similarity with the rest of the language system in which it features. In iconic noise, the world seems to pierce or poke perpendicularly through the lateral weave of language, that would ordinarily, like a snowshoe, scatter its force. Noise makes a wound in the fabric of language, which that fabric can then repair, in a *trompe l'oreille* in which the sound of the sonorous wound itself makes the wound whole (or, as we sometimes say, 'sound') again.

Noise is what it is because it is immediate, and immediable: it is itself, without anticipation or the possibility of abbreviation. As soon as noise knows something of itself, that it is noise, say, and its noisiness begins to mediate itself, then it must begin to say no to the noise it is. Once the rambling tattletail of the idiot's discourse turns on or allows cognizance of itself, once it starts to resemble the sound of 'sound and fury', it will no longer be nonsense. No longer signifying nothing, in the sense of not signifying anything at all, it now signifies 'nothing'. Iconicity seems like a doubling – the perfect rhyme between mouth and world – but it must pass through this moment or dimension of purely idiot sound, that is both inside and outside language, the tale told by an idiot, signifying nothing and yet always, before it has even accomplished that gesture, or in the same breath, signifying 'nothing'.

For, far from coming first, noise, for all its idiocy, comes second. It is an aftercomer, a sophistication of sound, not its primitive source. Voice gives birth to noise, brings it out into the open. And this is perhaps why the greatest pieces of writing, where language seems so opulent with significance and intent, like Macbeth's 'Tomorrow and tomorrow and tomorrow' speech (V.v.17–28), may seem in such close intimacy with the infant stage of babble or the fool's blather, teetering on the brink of becoming mere play, mere noise:

> To-morrow, and to-morrow, and to-morrow,
> Creeps in this petty pace from day to day,
> To the last syllable of recorded time;
> And all our yesterdays have lighted fools
> The way to dusty death. Out, out, brief candle!
> Life's but a walking shadow; a poor player,

> That struts and frets his hour upon the stage,
> And then is heard no more: it is a tale
> Told by an idiot, full of sound and fury,
> Signifying nothing.

The stuttering 'strut and fret', the capering, teetering 'petty pace', turn on the language of the speech itself, tittering behind their hands at those laboriously tolling, toiling intonations of 'To-morrow and to-morrow and to-morrow', threatening to mill articulate speech down into an elementary, idiotic rattling of dentals, that add up to the asymptotic aggregation-without-outcome of 'dusty death'. To *strut* may mean to walk with exaggerated stiffness, as though one were stilted or splinted; but it could also mean to be swollen or protrude, as though with wind. Shakespeare uses it regularly both of the gait and the discourse of actors. Hamlet says (III.ii.28–34):

> O, there be players that I have seen play, and heard others praised – and that highly – not to speak it profanely, that neither having th'accent of Christians, nor the gait of Christian, pagan, nor man have so strutted and bellowed that I have thought some of Nature's journeymen had made men, and not made them well, they imitated humanity so abhominably.

Ariel's song in *The Tempest* relates gait and empty sound in the same way: Hark hark, I hear/The strain of strutting chanticleer/Cry cock a diddle dow' (I.ii.385–7). The most developed link between the sound of the actor and the materiality of his posture is to be found in *Troilus and Cressida* (I.iii.153–6), in Ulysses's evocation of the 'o'er-wrested seeming' of a bombastic actor, who is

> like a strutting player, whose conceit
> Lies in his hamstring, and doth think it rich
> To hear the wooden dialogue and sound
> 'Twixt his stretch'd footing and the scaffoldage.

In strutting, walking becomes a kind of talking and talking a kind of walking, an empty rhyme is which each is propped up from the outside, or perhaps by each other. At least one critic has seen the judgements on acting in Macbeth's speech as coiling back on itself, or its speaker. W. W. Story suggests that Shakespeare 'here makes [Macbeth] rant intentionally', to point up the contrast with the simple pathos of Macduff when he hears of the death of his wife and children.[8] When Macbeth hears of the death of his wife, 'he makes a little poem, full of alliterations and conceits . . . This speech is "full of sound and fury, signifying nothing." There is no accent from the heart in it. It is elaborate, poetic, cold-blooded.'[9] The speech shows that Macbeth 'cannot help going on like a mad poet. His language is full of alliteration, fanciful juxtaposition of words, assonance, and jingle.'[10]

Macbeth's words seem to decompose syllables to silly babble – though there is actually nothing labial in the origin of the word *syllable*, which is from Greek συλλαμβάνειν, to take, put or bring together. But in this vision of time atomized, there is no question of any kind of syllabus or synopsis. Shakespeare uses the word 'syllable' fourteen times, nearly always to signify something like the smallest possible unit, the least jot or tittle of something: Volumnia counsels Coriolanus to make a politic speech that he does not necessarily believe with 'such words that are but roted in/Your tongue, though but bastards and syllables/Of no allowance to your bosom's truth' (II.ii.55–7). In *King Lear* Kent calls Oswald 'one whom I will beat into clamorous whining if thou deni'st the least syllable of thy addition' (II.ii.22–3).

The triplet 'to-morrow and to-morrow and to-morrow' might have been suggested by an illustration in Alexander Barclay's translation of *The Ship of Fooles* showing a fool with a crow in his cap and in each hand, each with the word *cras* written above it, as explicated in the following rhyme:

> They folowe the Crowes crye to their great sorowe,
> *Cras cras cras*, to morowe we shall amende.
> And if we mende not then, then shall we the next morowe;
> Or els shortly after we shall no more offende:

Amende, mad foole, when God this grace doth sende,
He is unwise that trusteth the crowes songe
And that affirmeth that he shall live so longe.[11]

Sinners who endlessly put off the final reckoning live in the purely additive animal present of repeated sounds, unaware even that they might accidentally be speaking Latin as they utter them.

Joyce's babbling, gabbling, gossipaceous washerwoman in the 'Anna Livia Plurabelle' section of *Finnegans Wake* wrings out Macbeth's idiot speech anew, letting us know that 'every telling has a taling.'[12] Heard idiotistically, every telling of a tale is just the telling off of a finite sum, coordination without subordination, so a tailing off (tomorrow and tomorrow and tomorrow): time . . . tomorrow . . . tale . . . told . . . idiot. Macbeth's speech makes us hear ghosts of the doubled dentality of 'tale told by an idiot' in all the alternating *d* and *t* dentals in the speech, as though they were an anatomy or identikit of the word 'idiot' in advance of its being heard – 'for such a wor*d* . . . an*d* tomorrow an*d* tomorrow' . . . *d*ay to *d*ay . . . last syllable of recor*d*e*d* *t*ime . . . ligh*t*e*d* fools . . . *d*us*t*y *d*ea*t*h . . . Out, out . . . strut*s* and fre*t*s . . . hear*d* no more'. Identity is detained in dentality. In Macbeth's speech, the final conclusive tap of the tongue is lost in the airy lisp of 'th' in the middle of the word 'nothing' – though it instantly reasserts itself in the words Macbeth addresses to the messenger who appears on the scene as he speaks: 'Thou com'st to use thy tongue; thy story quickly' (V.v.29).

When I was a student and a novice literary critic, this kind of analysis was already beng tut-tutted over by more advanced literary theorists as a trivializing ultra-formalism that distracted attention from the determining force of various kinds of historical or sociological context. There is of course, always something silly and factitious in this wresting and wrangling of meaning out of sound, as though texts were always and everywhere to be shown sonically signalling their meanings as they express them. When I do it now, I recapture, with some pleasure, that strange obsessive hyperattentiveness to sound patterns, but in order to highlight the way in which this text exposes my obsession, and exposes me in it. If the solemn explication of the idiocy of Shakespeare's patternings of sonority and noise cannot itself entirely escape the condition of clownishness, the inflation of accidental airy nothings into substance, or 'o'er-wrested seeming', that has been the point of much of this book. The meanings of the noises of the voice both are and are not there.

It can be a surprise to be reminded that there is more than one infinity – and perhaps even an infinite number of infinities (all the even numbers, all the odd numbers, all the numbers above 7, all the numbers above 770, and so on). It is similarly surprising to realize that there might be more than one kind of nothing. For, just as there are many ways in which we can imagine the extension or augmentation of a numerical series, and many different kinds of unending sequences, so there are many different ways in which something can be regarded as negative or not. As I hope to have shown in the foregoing chapters, nothingness is legion. Just as language multiplies different kinds of substance, so, for precisely this reason, it also ramifies the forms that the nothing of non-sense can take, dividing and multiplying it in unanticipated arithmetic, or ringing its changes, as Mischief does in *Mankind*: 'blottybus in blottis,/ Blottorum blottibus istis'.[13] Far from signifying nothing, the voice's noisings are evidence of the Babel of tongues needed for nothing to be given voice. This ramifying negativity is made ever more substantial as it multiplies its forms.

As it does, the accidental and localized suspensions of sense, or temporary incursions of noisy nonsense, in language come to occupy more and more of language, as though it had been defamiliarized by a large-scale version of the phenomenon whereby the repetition of a word or name seems to evacuate it of all its meaning. Language thereby becomes not just phatic – making reference to its own occasion and action – but apophatic, because it displays itself as a catachrestic substitute for what it can never in fact capture or denominate. Just as an apophatic designation in 'negative theology' signifies the divine through what it is not, calling for an act of subtraction in the listener or reader, so language intimates what it is through indicating what it is not – noise. Phatic language signifies itself: apophatic language keeps itself in abeyance, signifying the groundlessness of the assumption it makes of its own existence. Language subtracts itself from itself (language cannot be reduced to any of the mere noises that are nevertheless all that it adds up to), until there is nothing left but the nothing that it is. Language exists only in the counterfactual possibility of sense being able to be made from senseless sounds and shapes. It is the self-subtracting assurance of the 'I' in David Hume's repudiation of the Cartesian cogito, who can say, of the 'I' itself, 'I am certain there is no such principle in me.'[14]

Such uncertainties about the body of language pass across into the imagination of the speaking body, which seems to be subject to the same now-you-see-it, now-you-don't oscillation. The speaking body is more than a body that speaks, or the particular parts of the body that do. The speech that the body produces itself produces a new kind of body, a speaking homunculus, in which all the positions and proportions have been distorted in and by the act of speaking. The voice-body is more than just a particular variety of body-image, or image of the body in a particular posture. It is an intersensory hallucination, experienced as much in terms of weight, pressure and friction as in terms of a picture. The body of speech is a blindly coenaesthetic body, feeling its way in the world as it hangs on its words. It is this speaking body – a changeable, composite phase-space, or anthology of forms, actual and subjunctive – that the investigations of vocal noises in this book have attempted to compose.

References

ONE: Ahem

1 William James, *The Principles of Psychology* (New York, 1890), p. 488.
2 Steven Connor, *Dumbstruck: A Cultural History of Ventriloquism* (Oxford, 2000).
3 Aristotle, *De Anima Books* II *and* III *(With Passages From Book* I*)*, ed. and trans. D. W. Hamlyn (Oxford, 1993), p. 32.
4 Ibid.
5 Ibid., p. 33.
6 Remke Kruk, 'Pseudo-Aristotle: An Arabic Version of *Problemata Physica* X', *Isis*, LXVII (1976), p. 253.
7 Afnan H. Fatani, 'The Iconic-Cognitive Role of Fricatives and Plosives', in *Outside-In – Inside-Out: Iconicity in Language and Literature*, 4, ed. Costantino Maeder, Olga Fischer and William J. Herlofsky (Amsterdam and Philadelphia, 2005), p. 176.
8 Charles S. Peirce, *Collected Papers*, ed. Charles Hartshorne and Paul Weiss, 8 vols (Cambridge, MA, 1931–58), vol. II, p. 277.
9 Connor, *Dumbstruck* (Oxford, 2000), pp. 35–43.
10 Gérard Genette, *Mimologics*, trans. Thaïs E. Morgan (Lincoln and London, 1995).
11 Samuel Taylor Coleridge, *Poetical Works*, ed. Ernest Hartley Coleridge (Oxford and New York, 1983), p. 297.
12 Plutarch, *Plutarch's Moralia, With an English Translation By Frank Cole Babbitt*, vol. III: *Sayings of Kings and Commanders. Sayings of Romans. Sayings of Spartans. The Ancient Customs of the Spartans. Sayings of Spartan Women. Bravery of Women* (London and Cambridge, MA, 1949), p. 398.

TWO: St . . . st . . . st

1 Steven Connor, *Dumbstruck: A Cultural History of Ventriloquism* (Oxford, 2000).
2 Ibid., pp. 327–37.
3 Bartholomaeus Anglicus, *Batman Uppon Bartholome his booke De proprietatibus Rerum* (London, 1582), p. 46.
4 Bartolommeo della Rocca Cocles, *A Brief and Most Pleasau[n]t Epitomye of the Whole Art of Phisiognomie*, trans. Thomas Hill (London, 1556), sig. C3v.
5 Francis Bacon, *Sylva Sylvarum: or A Naturall Historie* (London, 1627), p. 103.
6 Alexander Ross, *Arcana Microcosmi, or, The Hid Secrets of Man's Body Discovered . . .* (London, 1652), p. 250.
7 William Abbotts, *Impediments of Speech: Stammering, Stuttering, Lisping, &c., Their Causes and Cure* (London, 1879), p. 19.
8 'C. K.' [Charles Kingsley], *Hints to Stammerers, By a Minute Philosopher* (London, 1864), p. 25.
9 Ibid.
10 Ibid., pp. 26, 27.
11 Otto Fenichel, 'A Case of Stammering', *Psychoanalytic Quarterly*, xv (1946), p. 540.
12 Otto Fenichel, 'Outline of Clinical Psychoanalysis', *Psychoanalytic Quarterly*, II (1933), pp. 96, 97.
13 Isador H. Coriat, *Stammering: A Psychoanalytic Interpretation* (New York, 1927).
14 Peter Glauber, 'The Psychoanalysis of Stuttering: Some Fundamentals of Psychoanalysis Relevant to the Understanding of Stuttering', in *Stuttering: A Symposium*, ed. John Eisenson (New York, 1958), p. 80.
15 Roger Ascham, *Toxophilus the Schole of Shootinge* (London, 1545), sigs xiv–xiir.
16 Marc Shell, *Stutter* (Cambridge, MA, and London, 2005), pp. 109–12.
17 Galfridus Grammaticus, *The Promptorium Parvulorum: The First Anglo-Latin Dictionary, c. 1440 AD*, ed. A. L. Mayhew (London, 1908), p. 472.
18 Sigmund Freud, *Beyond the Pleasure Principle*, in *The Standard Edition of the Complete Psychological Works of Sigmund Freud*, vol. XVIII: *Beyond the Pleasure Principle, Group Psychology and Other Works, 1920–22*, trans. James Strachey (London, 1964), p. 64.
19 Christopher G. Goetz, Michel Bonduelle and Toby Gelfand, *Charcot: Constructing Neurology* (New York and Oxford, 1995), p. 144.
20 Edwin Lee, *On Stammering and Squinting, and On the Methods for their Removal* (London, 1841).

21 J. F. Dieffenbach, *Memoir on the Radical Cure of Stuttering, By a Surgical Operation*, trans. Joseph Travers (London, 1841), pp. 11–12.
22 Abbotts, *Impediments of Speech*, p. 27.
23 Dieffenbach, *Radical Cure of Stuttering*, p. 13.
24 Ibid., p. 14.
25 Ibid., pp. 26–7.
26 Dwight N. Hopkins and George C. L. Cummings, eds, *Cut Loose Your Stammering Tongue: Black Theology in the Slave Narratives*, 2nd edn (Louisville, KY, 2003), p. v.
27 'John Lennon Talks with Marshall McLuhan', *In the Life of . . . The Beatles* blog, 2009, online at http://lifeofthebeatles.blogspot.co.uk.
28 Lewis Carroll, *Alice's Adventures in Wonderland and Through the Looking Glass*, ed. Roger Lancelyn Green (Oxford, 1971), p. 61.
29 Augustine of Hippo, *St Augustine's Confessions: With an English Translation By William Watts*, 2 vols (London and Cambridge, MA, 1950), vol. II, p. 164.
30 Plutarch, *The Philosophie, Commonlie Called, the Morals, Written by the Learned Philosopher Plutarch of Chaeronea*, trans. Philémon Holland (London, 1603), p. 34.
31 Ibid.
32 John Good, *The Study of Medicine*, 4 vols (London, 1822), vol. I, p. 566.
33 Shell, *Stutter*, pp. 99–101.
34 Joseph Wright, ed., *The English Dialect Dictionary*, 6 vols (London, 1898–1905), vol. V, p. 795.
35 Robert Arthur, *The Mystery of the Stuttering Parrot* (New York, 1964).
36 Anthony Copley, *Wits Fittes and Fancies: Fronted and Entermedled With Presidentes of Honour and Wisdome* (London, 1595), p. 49.
37 Mladen Dolar, *A Voice and Nothing More* (Cambridge, MA, and London, 2006) p. 15.
38 Michel Serres, *Les cinq sens: philosophie des corps mêlés* I (Paris, 1985).
39 Avin Lucier, 'I Am Sitting in a Room' (1969), online at http://ubumexico.centro.org.mx.
40 James Joyce, *Finnegans Wake* (London, 1975), pp. 215–16.
41 Ibid., pp. 626–7.
42 Shell, *Stutter*, pp. 31–2.

THREE: Hiss

1 Aristotle, *De Anima Books II and III (With Passages From Book I)*, ed. and trans. D. W. Hamlyn (Oxford, 1993), p. 32.
2 Steven Connor, *Dumbstruck: A Cultural History of Ventriloquism* (Oxford, 2000), pp. 199–200.
3 Steven Connor, 'Windbags and Skinsongs' (2003), online at

www.stevenconnor.com.

4 T. S. Eliot, *Complete Poems and Plays* (London, 1969), p. 73.

5 Jane Stuart-Smith, *Sound-change in Italic* (Oxford, 2004), pp. 162–6.

6 Roman Jakobson and Linda Waugh, *The Sound Shape of Language* (Brighton, 1979), p. 84.

7 Henry Sweet, *A Handbook of Phonetics* (Oxford, 1877), sect. 99.

8 Benjamin W. Wells, 'The Ablaut in English', *Transactions of the American Philological Association*, XIII (1882), p. 65.

9 Walter Whiter, *Etymologicon Universale: or, Universal Etymological Dictionary. On a New Plan. In Which It Is Shewn, That Consonants Are Alone to be Regarded in Discovering the Affinities of words, and That the Vowels are to be Wholly Rejected* . . . 3 vols (Cambridge, 1822–5), vol. I, p. 8.

10 Ibid., p. 85.

11 Johann Gottfried Herder, *Treatise on the Origin of Language* [1772], in *Philosophical Writings*, trans. and ed. Michael N. Forster (Cambridge, 2002), pp. 71–2.

12 David Abram, *The Spell of the Sensuous: Perception and Language in a More-Than-Human World* (New York, 1996), p. 249.

13 Ibid., p. 252.

14 Ibid., p. 260.

15 Herder, *Origin of Language*, p. 90.

16 Charles de Brosses, *Traité de la formation méchanique des langues et des principes physiques de l'étymologie* (Paris, 1765), p. 181.

17 Aristotle, *De Anima*, pp. 33–4.

18 Ben Jonson, *The English Grammar* [1640], in *The Workes of Benjamin Jonson* (London, 1631–41), p. 35.

19 Ibid., p. 48.

20 Johann Buxtorf, *The Jewish Synagogue, or, An Historical Narration of the State of the Jewes at This Day Dispersed Over the Face of the Whole Earth*, trans. A. B. (London, 1657), p. 42.

21 William Austin, *Haec Homo: Wherein the Excellency of the Creation of Woman is Described, By Way of an Essay* (London, 1637), pp. 82–3.

22 Catullus (Gaius Valerius Catullus), *Catullus, Tibullus and Pervigilium Veneris*, trans. Francis Warre Cornish et al., 2nd edn (Cambridge, MA, and London, 1988), p. 160.

23 Augustine of Hippo, *St. Augustine's Confessions: With an English Translation By William Watts*, 2 vols (London and Cambridge, MA, 1950), vol. I, p. 54.

24 Jonathan Sheehan, 'Enlightenment Details: Theology, Natural History, and the Letter h', *Representations*, LXI (1998), p. 35.

25 Jakob Boehme, *Mysterium Magnum, oder Erklärung über das erste Buch Mosis* (n.p., 1730), pp. 331–2, quoted and translated Sheehan, 'Enlightnment Details', p. 37.

26 John Spanton, *The Letter H: Its Old and Modern Uses* (Ramsay, 1894), p. 8.
27 Alfred Leach, *The Letter H Past Present and Future, A Treatise: With Rules for the Silent H, Based on Modern Usage; and Notes on WH* (London, 1880), p. 33.
28 Ibid.
29 Ibid.
30 Ibid, p. 81.
31 Ibid.
32 Hon. Henry H., *Poor Letter H: Its Use and Abuse* (London, 1854), p. 4.
33 J. S. Warden, 'The Letter "H" in Humble', *Notes and Queries*, VIII/194 (1853), p. 54.
34 Anon., 'The Letter "H" in Humble', *Notes and Queries*, VIII/204 (1853), p. 298.
35 Catherine Maria Fanshawe, *Memorials* (Westminster, 1865), pp. 41–2.
36 Leach, *The Letter H*, p. 15; Geoffrey Hill, *The Aspirate: Or the Use of the Letter 'H' in English, Latin, Greek and Gaelic* (London, 1902), p. 43.
37 John Heywood, *An Hundred Epigrammes* (London, 1550), sig. C1V.
38 Roland Barthes, *S/Z*, trans. Richard Miller (New York, 1974), p. 106.
39 Richard Baxter, *The Divine Life* (London, 1664), p. 83.
40 Nicholas Evans, *The Horse Whisperer* (London, 1975); Claire Bessant, *The Cat Whisperer: The Secret of How to Talk to Your Cat* (London, 2001); John Richardson, and Leslye Sharon Cole, *The Dog Whisperer: The Essential Guide to Understanding and Raising a Happy Dog* (Sydney and London, 2001); Paul Owens and Norma Eckroate, *The Dog Whisperer: A Compassionate, Nonviolent Approach to Dog Training* (Avon, MA, and Newton Abbot, 2007); Ingrid Tarrant, *The Rabbit Whisperer* (London, 2005); Laura Pasten, *The Tarantula Whisperer: A Celebrity Vet Shares her Secrets to Communicating with Animals* (Berkeley, CA, 1999).
41 Jonathan Swift, *The Examiner and Other Pieces Written in 1710–11*, ed. Herbert Davis (Oxford, 1957), p. 9.
42 Richard Chevenix Trench, *Dictionary of Obsolete English* (London, 1959), p. 268.
43 James Mason, *The Anatomie of Sorcerie Wherein the Wicked Impietie of Charmers, Inchanters, and Such Like, Is Discovered and Confuted* (London, 1612), pp. 63–4.
44 Robert Heath, *Clarastella Together With Poems Occasional, Elegies, Epigrams, Satyrs: Epigrams* (London, 1650), p. 37.
45 James Joyce, *Finnegans Wake* (London, 1975), p. 7.
46 Homer, *The Odyssey: With an English Translation by A. T. Murray revised by George E. Dimock*, 2 vols (Cambridge, MA and London, 1995), vol. II, pp. 402–3.
47 Gerard Manley Hopkins, *The Poems of Gerard Manley Hopkins*, 4th edn, ed. W. H. Gardner and N. H. Mackenzie (London, 1970), p. 93.

FOUR: Hic

1 Lancelot Andrewes, *XCVI Sermons* (London, 1629), p. 206.
2 Thomas Blount, *Glossographia, or, A Dictionary Interpreting All Such Hard Words of Whatsoever Language Now Used in Our Refined English Tongue* (London, 1661), n.p.
3 Isaac Basier, *The Dead Mans Real Speech: A Funeral Sermon Preached on Hebr. xi. 4, Upon the 29th day of April, 1672* (London, 1673), p. 86.
4 Hieronymus Brunschwig, *The Vertuose Boke of Distyllacyon of the Waters of all Maner of Herbes* (London, 1528), sig. H2V.
5 Philip Barrough, *The Methode of Phisicke Conteyning the Causes, Signes, and Cures of Inward Diseases in Mans Body From the Head to the Foote* (London, 1583), pp. 92–3.
6 John Gaule, *Distractions, or The Holy Madnesse* (London, 1629), p. 283.
7 Anon., *The Character of a Fanatick By a Person of Quality* (London, 1675), p. 6.
8 Ralph Brownrig, *Twenty Five Sermons* (London, 1664), p. 43.
9 'John Lennon Talks with Marshall McLuhan' *In the Life of . . . The Beatles* blog, 2009. Online at http://lifeofthebeatles.blogspot.co.uk.
10 Oliver Goldsmith, *An History of the Earth, and Animated Nature*, 8 vols (London, 1774), vol. II, p. 92.
11 Francis Bacon, *Sylva Sylvarum: or A Naturall Historie in Ten Centuries* (London, 1627), pp. 184–5.
12 Ovid (Publius Ovidius Naso), *Ovid in Six Volumes*, vol. II: *The Art of Love, and Other Poems*, trans. J. H. Mozley (Cambridge, MA, and London, 1985), p. 218.
13 Sextus Propertius, *The Elegies*, ed. H. E. Butler and E. A. Barber (Oxford, 1933), p. 8.
14 William Shakespeare, *Shakespeare's Poems*, ed. Katherine Duncan-Jones and H. R. Woudhuysen (London, 2007), p. 231.
15 Laotzu, *Laotzu's Tao and Wu Wei*, 2nd edn, trans. Bhikshu Wai-Tao and Dwight Goddard (Thetford, VT, 1939), p. 56.
16 Alvin Borgquist, 'Crying', *American Journal of Psychology*, XVII (1906), pp. 150–51.
17 Ibid., pp. 175–6.
18 John Dryden, *The Dramatic Works*, ed. Montague Summers, 6 vols (New York, 1968), vol. IV, p. 147.
19 Borgquist, 'Crying', p. 177.
20 John Trusler, *The Distinction Between Words Esteemed Synonymous in the English Language*, 2 vols (London, 1794–5), vol. II, p. 44.
21 Borgquist, 'Crying', pp. 167, 178, 195–6.
22 Ibid., p. 175.
23 Rabindranath Tagore, *Gitanjali (Song Offerings)* (London, 1914), p. 89.

24 Mark Twain, *Complete Essays*, ed. Charles Neider (Garden City, NY, 1963), p. 405.
25 Walt Whitman, *Complete Poetry and Collected Prose* (New York, 1982), p. 567.
26 John Keats, *The Poems of John Keats*, ed. Jack Stillinger (London, 1978), pp. 79, 112.
27 Helkiah Crooke, *Mikrokosmographia: A Description of the Body of Man* (London, 1615), p. 66; John Evelyn, *Sylva, or, A Discourse of Forest-trees, and the Propagation of Timber in His Majesties Dominions* (London, 1670), p. 134.
28 *The Book of Margery Kempe*, ed. Sanford Brown Meech (London, 1997), p. 98.
29 Ibid., p. 83.
30 Ibid., p. 98.
31 Ishbel Ross, *Ladies of the Press: The Story of Women in Journalism by an Insider* (New York, 1973), p. 65; Phyllis Leslie Abramson, *Sob Sister Journalism* (New York, Westport, CT, and London, 1990); Joe Salzman, 'Sob Sisters: The Image of the Female Journalist in Popular Culture' (2003), online at http://ijpc.org.
32 Ferde Grofe, *Tabloid* (New York, 1934), n.p.
33 G. M. Hyde, *Newspaper Reporting and Correspondence: A Manual for Reporters, Correspondents, and Students of Newspaper Writing* (New York, 1912), p. 236.
34 Quoted Archibald Farmer, 'Bach and the Tremulant', *Musical Times*, LXXXVII/1243 (1946), p. 281.
35 Thomas Mace, *Musick's Monument, or, A Remembrancer of the Best Practical Musick, Both Divine and Civil, That Has Ever Been Known to Have Been in the World . . .* (London, 1676), p. 170.
36 Kurt Klukist, quoted in Derek Mannering, *Mario Lanza: Singing to the Gods* (Jackson, MI, 2005), p. 168.
37 Georgia Writers' Project, *Drums and Shadows: Survival Stories Among the Georgia Coastal Negroes* (Athens, GA, 1940), p. 47.
38 Anon, *Liber Samekh: Theurgia Goetia Summa Congressus Cum Daemone. (Sub Figura* DCCC *being the Ritual employed by the Beast 666 for the Attainment of the Knowledge and Conversation of his Holy Guardian Angel during the Semester of His performance of the Operation of the Sacred Magick of* ABRAMELIN THE MAGE, Point III) Online at www.sacred-texts.com.
39 Charles Baudelaire, *Oeuvres complètes* (Paris, 1975), p. 150 (my translation).
40 Borgquist, 'Crying', p. 178.
41 Charles Darwin, *The Expression of the Emotions in Man and Animals*, ed. Francis Darwin (London, 1989), p. 119.
42 William Wordsworth, *William Wordsworth*, ed. Stephen Gill

(Oxford, 1984), p. 12.
43 Bram Stoker, *The Lair of the White Worm* (London, 1911), p. 72.
44 H. R. Voth, *The Traditions of the Hopi* (Chicago, IL, 1905), p. 106.
45 William Hughes, quoted in Thomas Blount, *A Natural History* (London, 1693), pp. 349–50.
46 Lewis Carroll, *Alice's Adventures in Wonderland and Through the Looking Glass*, ed. Roger Lancelyn Green (Oxford, 1971), p. 88.
47 Plutarch, *Plutarch's Moralia, With an English Translation By Frank Cole Babbitt*, vol. III: *Sayings of Kings and Commanders. Sayings of Romans. Sayings of Spartans. The Ancient Customs of the Spartans. Sayings of Spartan Women. Bravery of Women* (London and Cambridge, MA, 1949), p. 398.
48 Leonard Lutwack, *Birds in Literature* (Gainesville, FL, 1994), p. 1.
49 T. S. Eliot, *Complete Poems and Plays* (London, 1969), p. 64.
50 Frank S. Williamson, *Purple and Gold: Poems and Lyrics* (Melbourne, 1912), p. 39.
51 Gerard Manley Hopkins, *The Poems of Gerard Manley Hopkins*, 4th edn, ed. W. H. Gardner and N. H. MacKenzie (London, 1970), p. 30.
52 Ibid.
53 Mathilde Blind, *Dramas in Miniature* (London, 1891), p. 11.
54 John Clare, *John Clare*, ed. Eric Robinson and David Powell (Oxford and New York, 1984), p. 214.
55 W. H. Auden, *Collected Poems*, ed. Edward Mendelson (New York, 1976), p. 323.
56 D. H. Lawrence, *Sketches of Etruscan Places: And Other Italian Sketches*, ed. Simonetta De Filippis (Cambridge, 1992), p. 211.
57 Ibid., pp. 211–12.
58 Ibid., p. 212.
59 Ibid.
60 Ibid., p. 216.
61 D. H. Lawrence, *Complete Poems*, ed. Vivian de Sola Pinto and F. Warren Roberts (Harmondsworth, 1977), p. 537.
62 Francis Bacon, *The Natural and Experimental History of Winds*, trans. R. G. (London, 1671), p. 41.
63 Percy Bysshe Shelley, *Poetical Works*, ed. Thomas Hutchinson (Oxford and New York, 1970), p. 435.
64 Lawrence, *Complete Poems*, 136.
65 Whitman, *Complete Poetry and Collected Prose*, 607.
66 Samuel Taylor Coleridge, *Poetical Works*, ed. Ernest Hartley Coleridge (Oxford and New York, 1983), p. 363.
67 Charlotte Brontë, *Jane Eyre*, ed. Michael Mason (Harmondsworth, 1996), p. 283.
68 Walter Savage Landor, *Poems*, ed. Geoffry Grigson (London, 1964), p. 82.
69 Steven Connor, *Dumbstruck: A Cultural History of Ventriloquism*

(Oxford, 2000), pp. 35–40.
70 Whitman, *Complete Poetry and Collected Prose*, 397.
71 Giorgio Agamben, *Homo Sacer: Sovereign Power and Bare Life*, trans. Daniel Heller-Roazen (Stanford, CA, 1998), p. 182.
72 George Gordon Byron, *Complete Poetical Works*, vol. V: *Don Juan*, ed. Jerome J. McGann (Oxford, 1986), p. 589.

FIVE: Mmmm

1 Roman Jakobson, 'Why "Mama" and "Papa"?', in *On Language*, ed. Linda Waugh and Monique Monville-Burston (Cambridge, MA and London, 1995), p. 309.
2 Jonathan Rée, *I See a Voice: A Philosophical History of Language, Deafness and the Senses* (London, 1999).
3 Robert Bruce, *Sermons Preached in the Kirk of Edinburgh* (Edinburgh, 1591), sig. M8r.
4 Walter Haddon and John Foxe, *Against Ierome Osorius Byshopp of Siluane in Portingall and Against his Slaunderous Inuectiues An Aunswere Apologeticall*, trans. James Bell (London, 1581), p. 358.
5 Karl Friedrich Althoff, 'The Primordial Alphabet and Gospel According to John' (1998), trans. Margaret Magnus. Online at www.trismegistos.com.
6 Swami Nikhilananda, ed., *The Mandukyopanishad, With Gaudapāda's Kārikā and Śankara's Commentary* (Mysore, 1936), pp. 83–4.
7 Ibid., p. 89.
8 Ibid., p. 94.
9 F. Max Müller, ed., *The Sacred Books of the East*, vol. I: *The Upanishads: Part 1*, trans. F. Max Müller (Oxford, 1879), p. 2.
10 Sigmund Freud, *Civilization and Its Discontents*, in *The Standard Edition of the Psychological Works of Sigmund Freud*, vol. XXI: *The Future of an Illusion, Civilization and Its Discontents and Other Works*, ed. James Strachey (London, 1961), p. 63.
11 Samuel Taylor Coleridge, *Poetical Works*, ed. Ernest Hartley Coleridge (Oxford and New York, 1983), p. 297.
12 Margaret Magnus, *Gods in the Word: Archetypes in the Consonants* (n.p., 2010), n.p.
13 Sigmund Freud, *Totem and Taboo*, in *The Standard Edition of the Complete Psychological Works of Sigmund Freud*, vol. XIII: *Totem and Taboo and Other Works*, trans. James Strachey et al. (London, 1978), p. 85.
14 William James, *The Principles of Psychology* (New York, 1890), p. 487.
15 Ibid., p. 488.
16 Ibid.
17 E. M. Forster, *A Passage to India*, ed. Oliver Stallybrass

(Harmondsworth, 1985), p. 144.

18 James Joyce, *Ulysses: The Corrected Text*, ed. Hans Walter Gabler (Harmondsworth, 1984), p. 529.

19 A. Peter Hayman, ed., *Sefer Yesira: Edition, Translation and Text-critical Commentary* (Tübingen, 2004), pp. 125–6.

20 Francis Mercury Van Helmont, *The Alphabet of Nature*, trans. Allison P. Coudert and Taylor Corse (Leiden and Boston, MA, 2007), p. 115.

21 Ibid., pp. 115–17.

22 Ibid., pp. 123–5.

23 Quoted in Allison P. Coudert, *The Impact of the Kabbalah in the Seventeenth Century: The Life and Thought of Francis Mercury Van Helmont* (Leiden, Boston, MA, and Köln, 1999), p. 65.

24 Van Helmont, *Alphabet of Nature*, pp. 83, 85, 87.

25 Ibid., pp. 81, 75–7.

26 Ibid., p. 19.

27 Ibid., pp. 2–3.

28 Ibid., pp. 13, 51.

29 Joyce, *Ulysses*, p. 139.

30 James Joyce, *Selected Letters*, ed. Richard Ellmann (New York, 1975), p. 246.

31 John Wallis, *Grammatica linguae anglicanae* (Oxford, 1653), pp. 122–3 (my translation).

32 Margaret Magnus, 'The Meanings of Phonetic Features' (1998), online at www.trismegistos.com.

33 Eric Partridge, *A Dictionary of the Underworld*, 3rd edn (London, 1968), pp. 456, 457, 446, 454; Albert Barrère and Charles G. Leland, *A Dictionary of Slang, Jargon and Cant*, 2 vols (Detroit, MI, 1967), vol. II, p. 76.

34 Joyce, *Ulysses*, p. 144.

35 Ibid., p. 387.

36 Ibid., p. 40.

37 Dylan Thomas, *The Poems*, ed. Daniel Jones (London, 1979), p. 77.

38 Charles Nodier, *Dictionnaire raisonné des onomatopées françaises*, ed. Jean-François Jeandillou (Geneva, 2008), p. 151 (my translation).

39 John Keats, *The Poems of John Keats*, ed. Jack Stillinger (London, 1978), p. 371.

40 Thomas Starkey, *A Dialogue Between Pole and Lupset*, ed. T. F. Mayer (London, 1989), p. 88.

41 Anon., *Mumbo Chumbo: A Tale. Written in Antient Manner. Recommended to Modern Devotees* (London, 1765), p. 5.

42 Ibid., pp. 5, 18.

43 Lewis Carroll, *Alice's Adventures in Wonderland and Through the Looking Glass*, ed. Roger Lancelyn Green (Oxford, 1971), p. 134.

44 Francis Mercury Van Helmont, *The Paradoxal Discourses of F. M. Van Helmont, Concerning the Macrocosm and Microcosm, or the Greater and Lesser World, and Their Union* (London, 1685), Part II, pp. 52–3.

45 Joseph Blagrave, *Blagraves Astrological Practice of Physick Discovering the True Way to Cure All Kinds of Diseases and Infirmities* (London, 1671), p. 134.

46 Ibid., p. 157.

47 Robert Herrick, *Poems*, ed. L. C. Martin (London, New York and Toronto, 1965), p. 90.

48 Anon, *The Character of a Quack Doctor, or, The Abusive Practices of Impudent Illiterate Pretenders to Physick Exposed* (London, 1676), pp. 4–5.

49 Charles Goodall, *Poems and Translations* (London, 1689), p. 162.

50 Thomas Shadwell, *Thomas Shadwell's 'Bury-Fair': A Critical Edition*, ed. John C. Ross (New York and London, 1995), p. 75.

51 John Donne, *The Elegies and The Songs and Sonnets*, ed. Helen Gardner (Oxford, 1965), p. 81.

52 Cornelius L. Reid, 'Pedagogic Thought: Nasal Resonance vs. Nasality' (2011), online at www.corneliuslreid.com.

53 Samuel Taylor Coleridge, *Biographia Literaria: Or Biographical Sketches of My Literary Life and Opinions. The Collected Works of Samuel Taylor Coleridge*, vols VII/1 and VII/2, ed. James Engell and W. Jackson Bate (Princeton, NJ, 1983), vol. VII/1, p. 194.

54 Charles de Brosses, *Traité de la formation méchanique des langues, et des principes physiques de l'étymologie*, 2 vols (Paris, 1765), vol. I, pp. 158–9 (my translation).

55 Antoine Court de Gébelin, *Monde primitif, analysé et comparé avec le monde moderne, consideré dans les origines françaises; ou dictionnaire étymologique de la langue françoise* (Paris, 1778), p. 650.

56 Antoine Court de Gébelin, *Monde primitif, analysé et comparé avec le monde moderne, consideré dans les origines latines; ou dictionnaire étymologique de la langue latine* (Paris, 1779), p. 1230.

57 Antoine Court de Gébelin, *Monde primitif, analysé et comparé avec le monde moderne, consideré dans les origines grecques; ou dictionnaire étymologique de la langue grecque* (Paris, 1782), p. 566.

58 Geneviève Calame-Griaule, 'La nasalité et la mort', in *Pour une anthropologie des voix*, ed. Nicole Revel and Diana Rey-Hulmann (Paris, 1993), p. 25.

59 A. W. Howitt, 'On Australian Medicine Men', *Journal of the Anthropological Institute*, XVI (1887), p. 45.

60 De Brosses, *Traité de la formation méchanique des langues*, vol. I, p. 157.

61 Ibid., p. 154.

62 Sean Malone, 'Much Ado About Humming: Glenn Gould's Imaginary Orchestra'. Posting to *f_minor*, 17 April 2001, online

at http://glenngould.org.

63 R. Murray Schafer, *The Tuning of the World* (New York, 1977), p. 99.

64 Ibid.

65 Ibid.

66 Joseph Addison, *The Spectator*, ed. Donald F. Bond, 5 vols (Oxford, 1987), vol. I, p. 41.

67 Samuel Juni, 'From the Analysis of an Obsessive Hummer: Theoretical and Clinical Implications', *Psychoanalytic Review*, LXXIV (1987), pp. 63–81; Cora L. Díaz de Chumaceiro, 'What Else Did the Obsessive Hummer Hum About: A Contribution to Samuel Juni's Case', *Psychoanalytic Review*, LXXVII (1990), pp. 219–33; Samuel Juni and Bernard Katz, 'Theoretical and Transferential Debacles in Analysis of Humming, or, Play It Again, Sam', *Psychoanalytic Review*, LXXVII (1990), pp. 235–44.

68 E. B. Tylor, quoted in D. J. Mulvaney, 'The Anthropologist as Tribal Elder', *Mankind*, VII (1970), p. 206; A. C. Haddon, *The Study of Man* (London, 1898), p. 327.

69 Andrew Lang, *Custom and Myth*, 2nd edn (London, 1893), p. 36.

70 George McCall Theal, *Kaffir Folk-lore: or A Selection From the Traditional Tales of the People Living on the Eastern Border of the Cape Colony* (London, 1882), p. 209.

71 J. G. Frazer, *The Golden Bough: A Study in Magic and Religion*, 12 vols (London, 1936), vol. XI, p. 231.

72 Frank H. Cushing, *My Adventures in Zuñi* (Palo Alto, CA, 1970), p. 82.

73 Lorimer Fison and A. W. Howitt, *Kamilaroi and Kurnai: Group-Marriage and Relationship, and Marriage By Elopement, Drawn Chiefly From the Usage of the Australian Aborigines. Also the Kurnai Tribe Their Customs in Time of Peace and War* (Melbourne, Sydney, Adelaide and Brisbane, 1880), p. 267.

74 Lang, *Custom and Myth*, 31.

75 Ibid., p. 30.

76 A.S.F. Gow, *'ΙΫΓΞ, ΡΟΜΒΟΣ, Rhombus, Turbo'*, *Journal of Hellenic Studies*, LIV (1934), p. 6.

77 Frazer, *Golden Bough*, vol. VII, p. 19.

78 Haddon, *Study of Man*, 278.

79 Frazer, *Golden Bough*, vol. XI, pp. 233 –47.

80 Howitt, 'On Australian Medicine Men', 47.

81 Baldwin Spencer and F. J. Gillen, *The Northern Tribes of Central Australia* (London, 1904), p. 343.

82 Baldwin Spencer and F. J. Gillen, *The Native Tribes of Central Australia* (London, 1899), p. 246 n.1.

83 Frazer, *Golden Bough*, vol. XI, p. 240.

84 Ibid., pp. 240–41.

85 Ibid., p. 235.
86 F. J. Gillen, 'Notes on Some Manners and Customs of the Aborigines of the McDonnell Ranges Belonging to the Arunta Tribe', *Report on the Work of the Horn Scientific Expedition to Central Australia*, Part IV: *Anthropology*, ed. Baldwin Spencer (London, 1896), pp. 180–81.
87 Ibid., p. 238.
88 René Spitz, 'The Primal Cavity: A Contribution to the Genesis of Perception', *Psychoanalytic Study of the Child*, X (1955), pp. 215–40.
89 I. J. Dunn, 'Analysis of Patients Who Meet the Problems of the First Half of Life in the Second', *Journal of Analytic Psychology*, VI (1961), p. 59.
90 Ernest Jones, 'The Madonna's Conception Through the Ear', *Essays in Applied Psychoanalysis*, 2 vols (London, 1951), vol. II, pp. 290.
91 W. G. Niederland, 'Early Auditory Experiences, Beating Fantasies, and Primal Scene', *Psychoanalytic Studies of the Child*, XIII (1958), p. 494.
92 J. Layard, 'Boar-Sacrifice', *Journal of Analytic Psychology*, I (1955), p. 19.
93 Spencer and Gillen, *Northern Tribes of Central Australia*, pp. 347, 498.
94 Alfonso M. di Nola, 'Demythification in Certain Primitive Cultures: Cultural Fact and Socioreligious Integration', trans. Robert D. Pelton, *History of Religions*, XII (1972), pp. 2–3.
95 J. Van Baal, 'The Cult of the Bull-roarer in Australia and Southern New Guinea', *Bijdragen tot der Taal-, Land- en Volkenkunde*, LVIV (1963), p. 202.
96 Haddon, *Study of Man*, p. 308.
97 Magnus, *Gods in the Word*, n.p.

SIX: Grrr

1 James Yearsley, *Throat Ailments: More Especially The Enlarged Tonsil and Elongated Uvula, in Connexion With Effects of Voice, Speech, Hearing, Deglutition, Respiration, and the Imperfect Development of Health, Strength, and Growth, in Young Persons*, 5th edn (London, 1853), p. 18.
2 Ibid., p. 20.
3 Plato, *Plato*, vol. VI: *Cratylus; Parmenides; Greater Hippias; Lesser Hippias. With An English Translation by H. N. Fowler* (London and New York, 1926), p. 145.
4 Gérard Genette, *Mimologics*, trans Thaïs E. Morgan (Lincoln, NE, and London, 1995), pp. 41, 47, 71, 124–5. References hereafter, abbreviated to *Mimologics*, parenthetically in the text.
5 Kenelm Digby, *Of Bodies and of Mans Soul to Discover the Immortality of Reasonable Souls* . . . 2 vols (London, 1669), vol. I, p, 321.

6 Michel Serres, *The Five Senses: A Philosophy of Mingled Bodies (I)*, trans. Margaret Sankey and Peter Cowley (London, 2008), p. 314.

7 John Bernard and Arthur Delbridge, *Introduction to Linguistics: An Australian Perspective* (Sydney, 1980), p. 151.

8 Linda R. Waugh, 'Against Arbitrariness: Imitation and Motivation Revived, With Consequences for Textual Meaning', *Diacritics*, XXIII (1993), p. 77.

9 Bernard Saladin D'Anglure, 'The Shaman's Share, or Inuit Sexual Communism in the Canadian Central Arctic', trans. Jane Philibert, *Anthropologica*, XXXV (1993), p. 86.

10 Samuel Taylor Coleridge, *The Table Talk and Omniana of Samuel Taylor Coleridge* (London, 1917), p. 185.

11 Claude Searsplainpockets, 'Eating the Wind: An Anthropological Linguistic Study of the Xoŋry', *Speculative Grammarian*, CLI (2006). Online at http://specgram.com.

12 Samuel Beckett, *Molloy, Malone Dies, The Unnamable* (London, 1973), p. 17.

13 Roman Jakobson, 'Why "Mama" and "Papa"?' in *On Language*, ed. Linda Waugh and Monique Monville-Burston (Cambridge, MA, and London, 1995), p. 309.

14 Luke Thurston, 'Outselves: Beckett, Bion and Beyond', *Journal of Modern Literature*, XXXII (2009), p. 133.

15 Sylvia Plath, *Collected Poems*, ed. Ted Hughes (London, 1981), p. 223.

16 Ibid., pp. 223–4.

17 Steven Connor, *Dumbstruck: A Cultural History of Ventriloquism* (Oxford, 2000), p. 180.

18 Derek Attridge, *Peculiar Language: Literature as Difference From the Renaissance to James Joyce* (London, 1988), p. 141.

19 Lancelot Addison, *West Barbary, or, A short narrative of the revolutions of the kingdoms of Fez and Morocco with an account of the present customs, sacred, civil, and domestick* (Oxford, 1671), p. 75.

20 Annick de Souzenelle, *La Lettre chemin de vie: Le symbolisme des lettres hébraiques* (Paris, 1993), p. 93 (my translation).

21 Ibid., p. 96.

22 Yitzchak Ginsburgh, *The Hebrew Letters: Channels of Creative Consciousness*, ed. Avraham Arieh Trugman and Moshe Yaakov Wisnefsky (Cedarhurst, NY, 1992), p. 122.

23 Ibid.

24 Amos Yong, '*Ruach*, the Primordial Chaos and the Breath of Life: Emergence Theory and the Creation Narratives in Pneumatological Perspective', in *The Work of the Spirit: Pneumatology and Pentecostalism*, ed. Michael Welker (Grand Rapids, MI, and Cambridge, 2006), p. 191 n.8.

25 Ginsburgh, *Hebrew Letters*, 122–3.
26 Lawrence Kushner, *The Book of Letters: A Mystical Alef-bait* (New York, 1975), pp. 27–8.
27 Ibid., p. 28.
28 Ibid.
29 Francis Mercury Van Helmont, *The Spirit of Diseases, or, Diseases from the Spirit Laid Open in Some Observations Concerning Man and his Diseases* (London, 1694), p. 109.
30 Edward Sapir, 'A Study in Phonetic Symbolism', *Journal of Experimental Psychology*, XII (1929), pp. 225–39.
31 Vladimir Nabokov, *Lolita* (New York, 1997), p. 9.
32 Aristotle, *De Anima Books II and III (With Passages From Book I)*, ed. and trans. D. W. Hamlyn (Oxford, 1993), p. 33.
33 Will York, 'Voices from Hell', *San Francisco Bay Guardian* (July 2004). Online at www.sfbg.com.
34 Steven Connor, 'Seeing Sound: The Displaying of Marsyas' (2002). Online at www.stevenconnor.com.
35 Thalia Feldman, 'Gorgo and the Origins of Fear', *Arion*, IV (1965), p. 487.
36 Sigmund Freud, 'Medusa's Head', in *The Standard Edition of the Complete Psychological Works of Sigmund Freud*, vol. XVIII: *Beyond the Pleasure Principle, Group Psychology and Other Works*, 1920–22, trans. James Strachey (London, 1964), pp. 273–4.
37 Jane Harrison, *Prolegomena to the Study of Greek Religion* (Princeton, NJ, 1991), p. 187.
38 Ernest Weekley, *Something About Words* (London, 1935), p. 4.
39 J. Hillis Miller, 'The Critic as Host', in *The J. Hillis Miller Reader*, ed. Julian Wolfreys (Stanford, CA, 2005), p. 19.
40 Jan Baptiste Van Helmont, *Van Helmont's Works*, trans. John Chandler (London, 1664), p. 29.
41 Dwight L. Bolinger, 'Word Affinities', *American Speech*, XV (1940), pp. 70–71.
42 *Van Helmont's Works*, p. 69.
43 Janis B. Nuckolls, 'The Case for Sound Symbolism', *Annual Review of Anthropology*, XXVIII (1999), p. 238.
44 Mladen Dolar, *A Voice and Nothing More* (Cambridge, MA, and London, 2006), p. 19.
45 Jean-Paul Sartre, *Being and Nothingness: An Essay on Phenomenological Ontology*, trans. Hazel E. Barnes (London, 1984), p. 390.

SEVEN: **Pprrpffrrppffff**

1 W. R. Bion, *Learning From Experience* (London, 1962), pp. 82–3.
2 Ernest Jones, 'The Madonna's Conception Through the Ear', *Essays*

in Applied Psychoanalysis, 2 vols (London, 1951), vol. II, pp. 339–400.
3 Albert Barrère and Charles G. Leland, *A Dictionary of Slang, Jargon and Cant*, 2 vols (Detroit, MI, 1967), vol. I, p. 69.
4 James Joyce, *Ulysses: The Corrected Text*, ed. Hans Walter Gabler (Harmondsworth, 1984), p. 487.
5 Ibid., pp. 346, 415.
6 Margaret Magnus, *Gods in the Word: Archetypes in the Consonants* (n.p., 2010), n.p.
7 Joyce, *Ulysses*, p. 144.
8 Ted Hughes, *Collected Poems*, ed. Paul Keegan (London, 2003), p. 250.
9 John Palsgrave, *Lesclarcissement de la langue francoyse* (London, 1530), p. 655.
10 A. M. Binstead, *Gal's Gossip* (London, 1899), p. 144.
11 Barrère and Leland, *Dictionary of Slang, Jargon and Cant*, vol. II, pp. 170–71.
12 Francis Bacon, *Sylva Sylvarum: or A Naturall Historie In Ten Centuries* (London, 1627), pp. 122–3.
13 Ibid., p. 125.
14 Joyce, *Ulysses*, pp. 237–8.
15 Derek Attridge, *Peculiar Language: Literature as Difference From the Renaissance to James Joyce* (London, 1988), p. 142.
16 David Sacks, *The Alphabet: Unraveling the Mystery of the Alphabet From A to Z* (London, 2004), pp. 260–61.
17 Antoine Court de Gébelin, *Monde primitif, analysé et comparé avec le monde moderne, consideré dans les origines françaises; ou dictionnaire étymologique de la langue Françoise* (Paris, 1778), p. 790.
18 Walter Scott, *The Bride of Lammermoor*, ed. H. Alexander (Edinburgh and New York, 1995), p. 10.

EIGHT: Tittle-tattle

1 Matthew Parker, *The Whole Psalter Translated into English Metre . . . The First Quinquagene* (London, 1567), p. 264.
2 Charlton T. Lewis and Charles Short, *A Latin Dictionary* (Oxford, 1951), pp. 241–2.
3 Dafydd ap Gwilym, *The Poems*, trans. Richard Morgan Loomis (Binghamton, NY, 1981), pp. 232–3.
4 Lewis and Short, *Latin Dictionary*, p. 1926.
5 R. L. Turner, *A Comparative Dictionary of Indo-Aryan Languages* (London, 1962–85), p. 110.
6 Philip Larkin, *Collected Poems*, ed. Anthony Thwaite (London, 1988), p. 80; Tim Trengove-Jones, 'Larkin's Stammer', *Essays In Criticism*, LX (1990), p. 330.

7 Margaret Jennings, 'Tutivillus: The Literary Career of the Recording Demon', *Studies in Philology*, LXXIV (1977), pp. 1–95.
8 Thomas F. Crane, ed., *The Exempla or Illustrative Stories from the Sermones Vulgares of Jacques de Vitry* (London, 1890), p. 6.
9 British Library, MS Royal 10, A, IX, fol. 40vb, quoted in Jennings, 'Tutivillus', p. 16.
10 Crane, *Exempla*, 100.
11 William Caxton, *The Book of the Knight of the Tower*, ed. M. Y. Offord (London, 1971), pp. 49, 50.
12 Thomas Wright and James Orchard Halliwell, *Reliquiae Antiquae: Scraps From Ancient Manuscripts, Illustrating Chiefly Early English Literature and the English Language*, 2 vols (London, 1845), vol. I, p. 257.
13 Jennings, 'Tutivillus', 18 n.29.
14 Joannes Ravisius Textor, *A New Enterlude Called Thersytes* (London, 1562), sig. D2r.
15 Frank Knittel and Grosvenor Fattic, *A Critical Edition of the Medieval Play 'Mankind'* (Lewiston, Queenstown and Lampeter, 1995), p. 68.
16 Ibid., p. 70.
17 Ibid., p. 72.
18 James Joyce, *Finnegans Wake* (London, 1975), p. 215.
19 *Mankind*, pp. 77, 82, 84.
20 Sir Peter Pett, *The Happy Future State of England, or, A Discourse by Way of a Letter to the Late Earl of Anglesey* (London, 1688), p. 67.
21 *Mankind*, p. 111.
22 Ibid., p. 104.
23 A. Lecoy de la Marche, *Anecdotes historiques légendes et apologues tirés du receuil inédit d'Etienne de Bourbon* (Paris, 1877), p. 185.
24 *Mankind*, pp. 91, 82, 96.
25 Steven Connor, 'Michel Serres: The Hard and the Soft' (2009). Online at www.stevenconnor.com.
26 T. S. Eliot, *Complete Poems and Plays* (London, 1969), p. 38.
27 Wright and Halliwell, *Reliquiae Antiquae*, vol. I, pp. 290–91.
28 Samuel Beckett, *Complete Dramatic Works* (London, 1986), p. 126; Frank Kermode, *The Sense of an Ending: Studies in the Theory of Fiction* (Oxford and New York, 1968), p. 45.
29 *Mankind*, pp. 67–8.
30 Ibid., p. 70.
31 Sir Thomas Elyot, *The Dictionary of Syr Thomas Eliot Knyght* (London, 1538), n.p.
32 Plautus, *Plautus II: Casina. The Casket Comedy. Curculio. Epidicus. The Two Menaechmuses*, ed. and trans. Wolfgang de Melo (Cambridge, MA and London, 2011), pp. 46–7.
33 John Payne Collier, *The History of English Dramatic Poetry and Annals of*

the Stage to the Restoration, 3 vols (London, 1831), vol. II, p. 223.
34 Thomas Gascoigne, *Here After Folowith the Boke Callyd the Myrroure of Oure Lady Very Necessary for All Relygyous Persones* (London, 1530), p. xxv.
35 Ibid.
36 Randle Cotgrave, *A Dictionarie of the French and English Tongues* (London, 1611), n.p.
37 Samuel Harsnett, *A Declaration of Egregious Popish Impostures* . . . (London, 1603), p. 49.
38 Francis Tanner, *The Plainest, Easiest, and Prettiest Method of Writing Short-hand, Ever Yet Published* (London, 1712), p. 4.
39 Yitzchak Ginsburgh, *The Hebrew Letters: Channels of Creative Consciousness*, ed. Avraham Arieh Trugman and Moshe Yaakov Wisnefsky (Cedarhurst, NY, 1992), p. 154.

NINE: Zzzz

1 Francis Bacon, *Sylva Sylvarum: or A Naturall Historie In Ten Centuries* (London, 1627), p. 56.
2 Ibid.
3 S. Amy, *A Praefatory Discourse to a Late Pamphlet Entituled, A Memento for English Protestants, &c.* (London, 1681), p. 3.
4 Anon, *A New Ballad to the Tune of I'll Tell Thee, Dick* . . . (London, 1684), n.p.
5 Giacomo Affinati, *The Dumbe Diuine Speaker, or: Dumbe Speaker of Diuinity*, trans. Anthony Munday (London, 1605), p. 137.
6 Vincent Alsop, *Melius Inquirendum, or, A Sober Inquirie into the Reasonings of the Serious Inquirie Wherein the Inquirers Cavils Against the Principles, his Calumnies Against the Preachings and Practises of the Non-conformists are Examined, and Repelled* . . . (London, 1678), p. 108.
7 John Bulwer, *Philocophus, or, The Deafe and Dumbe Mans Friend* . . . (London, 1648), pp. 177–8.
8 Eric Partridge, *Shakespeare's Bawdy* (New York, 1948), p. 83.
9 Ambrose Bierce, *Collected Works*, 12 vols (New York and Washington, DC, 1909), vol. V, p. 50.
10 Robert Southey, *Poetical Works*, 10 vols (London, 1838), vol. III, p. 78.
11 John Rochester et al., *Familiar Letters*, vol. I: *Written by the Right Honourable, John, late Earl of Rochester, to the Honourable Henry Savile, esq; and Other Letters by Persons of Honour and Quality* (London, 1697), p. 180.
12 Alfred Lord Tennyson, *Poems* (London, 1972), p. 1124.
13 Richard Mulcaster, *The First Part of the Elementarie Which Entreateth Chefelie of the Right Writing of our English Tung*

(London, 1582), pp. 96–7.
14 Ibid., p. 123.
15 Christopher Upward and George Davidson, *The History of English Spelling* (Chichester, 2011), p. 170.
16 Mulcaster, *Elementarie*, p. 162.
17 Ibid., p. 132.
18 Derek Attridge, *Peculiar Language: Literature as Difference From the Renaissance to James Joyce* (London, 1988), pp. 140–41.
19 Samuel Johnson, *Johnson on the English Language: Yale Edition of the Works of Samuel Johnson*, vol. XVIII, ed. Gwin J. Kolb and Robert DeMaria Jr (New Haven, CT, and London, 2005), pp. 277, 294.
20 John Walker, *A Critical Pronouncing Dictionary and Expositor of the English Language* (London, 1791), p. 58.
21 Joseph Wright, ed., *The English Dialect Dictionary*, 6 vols (London, 1898–1905), vol. VI, p. 596.
22 Paul Scarron, *Scarron's Novels . . .*, trans. John Davies (London, 1665), sig A5r.
23 Charles Macklin, *Four Comedies: Love à la Mode, The True-Born Irishman, The School for Husbands, The Man of the World*, ed. J. O. Bartley (London, 1968), p. 234.
24 Alexander Geddes, *Bardomachia: Or, The Battle of the Bards* (London, 1800), p. 8.
25 Oliver Goldsmith, *Collected Works*, ed. Arthur Friedman, 5 vols (Oxford, 1966), vol. V, pp. 189, 190.
26 Nick Davis, *Stories of Chaos: Reason and Its Displacement in Early Modern English Narrative* (Aldershot, 1999), p. 147.
27 Ibid., pp. 147–8.
28 Benjamin Franklin, *The Papers of Benjamin Franklin*, vol. XXVIII: *November 1, 1778, Through February 28, 1779* (New Haven, CT, and London, 1990), pp. 519–20.
29 Ibid., pp. 520–21.
30 George Eliot, *Adam Bede*, ed. Carole A. Martin (Oxford, 2008), p. 214.
31 W. M. Lindsay, *The Latin Language: An Historical Account of Latin Sounds, Stems and Flexions* (Oxford, 1894), p. 6.
32 Martianus Capella, *Martianus Capella*, ed. James Willis (Leipzig, 1983), III.261, p. 69.
33 George Hempl, 'The Origin of the Latin Letters G and Z', *Transactions and Proceedings of the American Philological Association*, XXX (1899), p. 25.
34 Rex Wallace, 'The Latin Alphabet and Orthography', in *A Companion to the Latin Language*, ed. James Clackson (Chichester, 2011), p. 17.
35 Karl P. Harrington, 'Was there a Letter Z in Early Latin?' *Transactions and Proceedings of the American Philological Association*, XXIX (1898), pp. xxxiv–xxxvi.

36 Quintilian, *The Orator's Education: Books 11–12*, ed. and trans. Donald A. Russell (Cambridge, MA, and London, 2001), p. 297.
37 Ibid.
38 William James, *The Principles of Psychology* (New York, 1890), p. 488.
39 Phillip Stubbes, *Anatomy of the Abuses in England in Shakspere's Youth AD 1583: Part I*, ed. Frederick J. Furnivall (London, 1877–9), vol. I, p. 87.
40 James Orchard Halliwell, *A Dictionary of Archaic and Provincial Words*, 6th edn (London, 1904), p. 223; John S. Farmer and W. E. Henley, *Slang and Its Analogues Past and Present*, 6 vols (London, 1902), vol. VI, p. 378; Wright, *English Dialect Dictionary*, vol. I, p. 256, vol. VI, p. 409.
41 Wright, *English Dialect Dictionary*, vol. II, p. 592, vol. VI, p. 596.
42 John Michell, *Euphonics: A Poet's Dictionary of Sounds* (Windetts, Norfolk, 1988), p. 83.
43 W. Allen and W. H. Pepys, 'On the Changes Produced in Atmospheric Air, and Oxygen Gas, by Respiration', *Philosophical Transactions of the Royal Society of London*, XCVIII (1808), p. 262.
44 Angela Devlin, *Prison Patter* (Winchester, 1996) , p. 125.
45 Tom Hibbert, *Rockspeak! The Dictionary of Rock Terms* (London, 1996), p. 175; Mike Haskins, *Drugs: A User's Guide* (London, 2003), p. 286; Bruce Eisner, *Ecstasy: The MDMA Story* (Berkeley, CA, 1989), p. 1.
46 Wright, *English Dialect Dictionary*, vol. I, pp. 176, 106, 315, vol. VI, p. 595.
47 Ibid., vol. I, p. 595, vol. III, p. 369.
48 Farmer and Henley, *Slang and Its Analogues*, vol. V, p. 380.
49 Lester V. Berrey and Melvin Van den Bark, *The American Thesaurus of Slang* (New York, 1942), n.p., para. 272.
50 Quoted in H. Brook Webb, 'The Slang of Jazz', *American Speech*, XII (1937), p. 180.
51 Quoted ibid., p. 184.
52 Michael Quinion, *Port Out, Starboard Home and Other Language Myths* (London, 2005), p. 162.
53 Quoted ibid., p. 163.
54 Edward 'Scoop' Gleeson, *San Francisco Bulletin* (6 March, 1913), p. 13.
55 P. T. Barnum, *The Humbugs of the World: An Account of Humbugs, Delusions, Impositions, Quackeries, Deceits and Deceivers Generally, in All Ages* (New York, 1866), p. 160.
56 J. G. Holland, *Miss Gilbert's Career: An American Story* (New York, 1863), p. 350.
57 Lewis Carroll, *Complete* Works (London, 1939), p. 698.
58 Johnson, *Johnson on the English Language*, p. 294.
59 Charlotte Dacre, *Zofloya, or The Moor*, ed. Kim Ian Michasiw (Oxford and New York, 1997), p. 270.
60 Ibid., p. 267.
61 Ibid., p. 270.

62 Percy Bysshe Shelley, *Zastrozzi, A Romance* (London, 1810), p. 78.
63 Ibid., pp. 155–6.
64 Ibid., pp. 19, 32, 131, 142, 182, 199, 208.
65 Ibid., p. 48.
66 Alfred Barrère and Charles G. Leland, *A Dictionary of Slang, Jargon and Cant*, 2 vols (Detroit, MI, 1967), vol. II, p. 428.
67 Ibid.
68 Virgil Thomson, 'The Art of Judging Music', in *Music and Criticism: A Symposium*, ed. R. F. French (Cambridge, MA, 1948), p. 156.
69 Anon, *A New Ballad to the Tune of I'll Tell Thee, Dick . . .* (London, 1684), n.p.
70 Ibid.
71 Thomas Percy, *Reliques of Ancient English Poetry*, ed. Henry B. Wheatley, 3 vols (New York, 1966), vol. II, p. 289.
72 Farmer and Henley, *Slang and Its Analogues*, vol. VI, p. 379.
73 Thomas Hardy, *Thomas Hardy's Public Voice: The Essays, Speeches, and Miscellaneous Prose*, ed. Michael Millgate (Oxford, 2001), p. 14; William Barnes, *Select Poems*, ed. Thomas Hardy (London, 1908), p. xii.
74 William Barnes, *Poems*, ed. Bernard Jones, 2 vols (London, 1962), vol. I, p. 114.
75 Dante Alighieri, *De vulgari eloquentia libri II*, ed. Ludovicus Bertalot (Friedrichsdorf, 1917), p. 30 (my translation).
76 Carlo Moscheni, *Brutes Turn'd Criticks, or, Mankind Moraliz'd by Beasts in Sixty Satyrical Letters upon the Vices and Follies of our Age*, trans. John Savage (London, 1695), p. 146.
77 J. Stanley Lemons, 'Black Stereotypes As Reflected in Popular Culture, 1880–1920', *American Quarterly*, XXIX (1977), p. 102.
78 Don B. Wilmeth, *The Language of American Popular Entertainment: A Glossary of Argot, Slang and Terminology* (Westport, CT, and London, 1981), pp. 298–9.
79 Annick de Souzenelle, *La Lettre chemin de vie: Le symbolisme des lettres hébraiques* (Paris, 1993), p. 83.
80 Robert M. Hoffstein, *The English Alphabet: An Inquiry Into Its Mystical Construction* (New York, 1975), p. 52.
81 Roland Barthes, *S/Z*, trans. Richard Miller (New York, 1974), p. 106.
82 Ibid., p. 107.
83 Ibid., pp. 106–07.
84 Ibid., p. 107.
85 Honoré de Balzac, *Scènes de la vie Parisienne et Scènes de la vie politique. Oeuvres Complètes*, ed. Jean Ducourneau, vol. XII (Paris, 1967), p. 410 (my translation).
86 Ibid., p. 415.
87 Debra Daley, *The Strange Letter Z* (London, 1996), pp. 46–7.

88 Ibid., pp. 202–3.
89 Charles MacKay, *Memoirs of Extraordinary Popular Delusions and the Madness of Crowds*, 2 vols (London, 1852), vol. II, p. 240.
90 F. M. Hallgren and H. Weiss, '"Buzz-Words" at the "B-School"', *American Speech*, XXI (1946), p. 263.
91 Mark Dunn, *Ella Minnow Pea: A Progressively Lipogrammatic Epistolary Fable* (London, 2002), p. 14.
92 Ibid., p. 18.
93 Ibid., p. 19.
94 Ibid., pp. 193, 197.
95 John Phillips, *The Christians A.B.C., or, A Christian Alphabet* (London, 1629), p. 211.

EPILOGUE: Blottybus in Blottis

1 Charles Dickens, *Great Expectations*, ed. Charlotte Mitchell (London, 1996), p. 4.
2 Martin Heidegger, *The Fundamental Concepts of Metaphysics: World, Finitude, Solitude*, trans. William McNeill and Nicholas Walker (Bloomington, IN, 1995), p. 177.
3 Steven Connor, 'Michel Serres: The Hard and the Soft' (2009), online at www.stevenconnor.com.
4 Samuel Beckett, *Disjecta: Miscellaneous Writings and a Dramatic Fragment*, ed. Ruby Cohn (London, 1983), p. 171.
5 Giorgio Agamben, *Homo Sacer: Sovereign Power and Bare Life*, trans. Daniel Heller-Roazen (Stanford, CA, 1998), p. 182.
6 John Capgrave, *The Life of St Katharine of Alexandria*, ed. Carl Horstmann (London, 1893), p. 35.
7 Henry Swinburne, *A Brief Treatise of Testaments and Last Willes . . .* (London, 1591), pp. 39–40.
8 William Wetmore Story, *Excursions in Art and Letters* (Edinburgh and London, 1891), p. 251.
9 Ibid., pp. 252–3.
10 Ibid., p. 252.
11 Sebastian Brant, *Stultifera nauis . . . The Ship of Fooles*, trans. Jacob Locher and Alexander Barclay (London, 1570), fol. 61v.
12 James Joyce, *Finnegans Wake* (London, 1975), p. 213.
13 Frank Knittel and Grosvenor Fattic, eds, *A Critical Edition of the Medieval Play 'Mankind'* (Lewiston, Queenstown and Lampeter, 1995), p. 104.
14 David Hume, *A Treatise of Human Nature*, ed. Ernest C. Mossner (London, 1985), p. 300.

Further Reading

Abram, David, *The Spell of the Sensuous: Perception and Language in a More-Than-Human World* (New York, 1996)

Aristotle, *De Anima Books II and III (With Passages From Book I)*, ed. and trans. D. W. Hamlyn (Oxford, 1993)

Barrère, Albert, and Charles G. Leland, *A Dictionary of Slang, Jargon and Cant*, 2 vols (Detroit, MI, 1967)

Berrey, Lester V., and Melvin Van den Bark, *The American Thesaurus of Slang* (New York, 1942)

Bolinger, Dwight L., 'Word Affinities', *American Speech*, XV (1940), pp. 62–73

Borgquist, Alvin, 'Crying', *American Journal of Psychology*, XVII (1906), pp. 149–205

Brosses, Charles de, *Traité de la formation méchanique des langues et des principes physiques de l'étymologie*, 2 vols (Paris, 1765)

Connor, Steven, *Dumbstruck: A Cultural History of Ventriloquism* (Oxford, 2000)

——, 'Windbags and Skinsongs' (2003). Online at www.bbk.ac.uk

Daley, Debra, *The Strange Letter Z* (London, 1996)

Dolar, Mladen, *A Voice and Nothing More* (Cambridge, MA, and London, 2006)

Farmer, John S., and W. E. Henley, *Slang and Its Analogues Past and Present*, 6 vols (London, 1902)

Genette, Gérard, *Mimologics*, trans Thaïs E. Morgan (Lincoln, NE, and London, 1995)

Ginsburgh, Yitzchak, *The Hebrew Letters: Channels of Creative Consciousness*, ed. Avraham Arieh Trugman and Moshe Yaakov Wisnefsky (Cedarhurst, NY, 1992)

H., Hon. Henry, *Poor Letter H: Its Use and Abuse* (London, 1854)

Halliwell, James Orchard, *A Dictionary of Archaic and Provincial Words*, 6th edn (London, 1904)

Harrington, Karl P., 'Was there a Letter Z in Early Latin?' *Transactions and Proceedings of the American Philological Association*, XXIX (1898), pp. xxxiv–xxxvi

Hill, Geoffrey, *The Aspirate: Or the Use of the Letter 'H' in English, Latin, Greek and Gaelic* (London, 1902)

Hoffstein, Robert M., *The English Alphabet: An Inquiry Into Its Mystical Construction* (New York, 1975)

Jakobson, Roman, 'Why "Mama" and "Papa"?' in *On Language*, ed. Linda Waugh and Monique Monville-Burston (Cambridge, MA, and London, 1995), pp. 305–11

——, and Linda Waugh, *The Sound Shape of Language* (Brighton, 1979)

Jennings, Margaret, 'Tutivillus: The Literary Career of the Recording Demon', *Studies in Philology*, LXXIV (1977), pp. 1–95

Jones, Ernest, 'The Madonna's Conception Through the Ear', in *Essays in Applied Psychoanalysis*, 2 vols (London, 1951), vol. II, pp. 266–357

Jonson, Ben, *The English Grammar* [1640], in *The Workes of Benjamin Jonson* (London, 1631–41)

Leach, Alfred, *The Letter H Past Present and Future, A Treatise: With Rules for the Silent 'H', Based on Modern Usage; and Notes on 'WH'* (London, 1880)

Magnus, Margaret, *Gods in the Word: Archetypes in the Consonants* (n.p., 2010)

Nodier, Charles, *Dictionnaire raisonné des onomatopées françaises*, ed. Jean-François Jeandillou (Geneva, 2008)

Nuckolls, Janis B., 'The Case For Sound Symbolism', *Annual Review of Anthropology*, XXVIII (1999), pp. 225–52

Partridge, Eric, *Shakespeare's Bawdy* (New York, 1948)

——, *A Dictionary of the Underworld*, 3rd edn (London, 1968)

Quinion, Michael, *Port Out, Starboard Home and Other Language Myths* (London, 2005)

Quintilian, *The Orator's Education: Books 11–12*, ed. and trans. Donald A. Russell (Cambridge, MA, and London, 2001)

Rée, Jonathan, *I See a Voice: A Philosophical History of Language, Deafness and the Senses* (London, 1999)

Rosolato, Guy, 'La voix: entre corps et langage', *Revue française de psychanalyse*, XXVII (1974), pp. 75–94

Sacks, David, *The Alphabet: Unraveling the Mystery of the Alphabet From A to Z* (London, 2004)

Sapir, Edward, 'A Study in Phonetic Symbolism', *Journal of Experimental Psychology*, XII (1929), pp. 225–39

Searsplainpockets, Claude, 'Eating the Wind: An Anthropological Linguistic Study of the Xoŋry', *Speculative Grammarian*, CLI (2006). Online at http://specgram.com

Sheehan, Jonathan, 'Enlightenment Details: Theology, Natural History, and the Letter h', *Representations*, LXI (1998), pp. 29–56

Shell, Marc, *Stutter* (Cambridge, MA, and London, 2005)
Spanton, John, *The Letter H: Its Old and Modern Uses* (Ramsay, 1894)
Spitz, René, 'The Primal Cavity: A Contribution to the Genesis of Perception', *Psychoanalytic Study of the Child*, x (1955), pp. 215–40
Starkey, Thomas, *A Dialogue Between Pole and Lupset*, ed. T. F. Mayer (London, 1989)
Turner, R. L., *A Comparative Dictionary of Indo-Aryan Languages* (London, 1962–85)
Van Helmont, Francis Mercury, *The Alphabet of Nature*, trans. Allison P. Coudert and Taylor Corse (Leiden and Boston, MA, 2007)
Wallace, Rex, 'The Latin Alphabet and Orthography', in *A Companion to the Latin Language*, ed. James Clackson (Chichester, 2011), pp. 9–28
Wallis, John, *Grammatica linguae anglicanae* (Oxford, 1653)
Warden, J. S., 'The Letter "H" in Humble', *Notes and Queries*, VIII/194 (1853), p. 54
Waugh, Linda R., 'Against Arbitrariness: Imitation and Motivation Revived, With Consequences for Textual Meaning', *Diacritics*, XXIII (1993), pp. 71–87
Whiter, Walter, *Etymologicon Universale: or, Universal Etymological Dictionary. On a New Plan. In Which It Is Shewn, That Consonants Are Alone to be Regarded in Discovering the Affinities of Words, and That the Vowels are to be Wholly Rejected* . . . 3 vols (Cambridge, 1822–5)
Wilmeth, Don B., *The Language of American Popular Entertainment: A Glossary of Argot, Slang and Terminology* (Westport, CT, and London, 1981)
Wright, Joseph, ed., *The English Dialect Dictionary*, 6 vols (London, 1898–1905)

Acknowledgements

Earlier versions of chapters Two, Three and Eight of this book appeared in the following forms: 'Whisper Music', in *Air*, ed. John Knechtel (Cambridge, MA: MIT Press, 2010), pp. 150–75; 'Phonophobia: The Dumb Devil of Stammering', in *Resonant Bodies, Voices, Memories*, ed. Anke Bangma, Deirdre M. Donoghue, Lina Issa and Katarina Zdjelar (Rotterdam: Piet Zwart Institute, Willem de Kooning Academy, 2009), pp. 132–44; and 'Chiasmus', *Studies in Musical Theatre*, 6 (2012), pp. 8–27. I am grateful for permission to reprint this material.

Index